Growth and Development in Emerging Market Economies

Growth and Development in Emerging Market Economies

International Private Capital Flows, Financial Markets and Globalization

Edited by

HARINDER S. KOHLI

$SAGE Los Angeles • London • New Delhi • Singapore
www.sagepublications.com

First published in 2008 by

 SAGE Publications India Pvt Ltd
B 1/I-1, Mohan Cooperative Industrial Area
Mathura Road, New Delhi 110044, India
www.sagepub.in

SAGE Publications Inc
2455 Teller Road
Thousand Oaks, California 91320, USA

SAGE Publications Ltd
1 Oliver's Yard, 55 City Road
London EC1Y 1SP, United Kingdom

SAGE Publications Asia-Pacific Pte Ltd
33 Pekin Street
#02-01 Far East Square   *Compra: US$ 45.42*
Singapore 048763   *6m 2008*

Published by Vivek Mehra for SAGE Publications India Pvt Ltd, typeset in 10.5/12.5pt Charter BT by Star Compugraphics Private Limited, Delhi and printed at Chaman Enterprises, New Delhi.

Library of Congress Cataloging-in-Publication Data

Growth and development in emerging market economies: international private capital flows, financial markets and globalization/edited by Harinder S. Kohli.
        p. cm.
    Includes bibliographical references and index.
1. Capital movements—Developing countries. 2. Investments, Foreign—Developing countries. 3. Developing countries—Foreign economic relations. 4. Developing countries—Commerce.   I. Kohli, Harinder S., 1945–

HG5993.G76   332'.042091724—dc22   2008   2008002359

ISBN: 978-0-7619-3671-8 (Hb)   978-81-7829-837-5 (India-Hb)

The SAGE Team: Sugata Ghosh, Jasmeet Singh, Mathew P.J. and Trinankur Banerjee.

Contents

List of Tables

List of Figures and Boxes

Figures

Boxes

List of Abbreviations

AAOIFI	Accounting and Auditing Organization for Islamic Financial Institutions
ADRs	American Depository Receipts
AFTA	Asian Free Trade Agreement
ALADI	*Asociación Latinoamericana de Integración*
AREAER	Annual Report on Exchange Arrangements and Exchange Restrictions
ASEAN	Association of Southeast Asian Nations
BCG	Boston Consulting Group
BCIE	*Banco Centroamericano de Integración Económica*
BIS	Bank for International Settlement
BITs	Bilateral Investment Treaties
BPO	Business Process Outsourcing
BRIC	Brazil, Russia, India and China
CACM	Central American Common Market
CAF	*Corporacion Andina de Fomento*
CIMC	China International Marine Containers Group Company
CMI	Chiang Mai Initiative
CNC	China Netcom Group Corporation
CNHTC	China National Heavy Truck Group Corporation
CVRD	Companhia Vale do Rio Doce
DDA	Doha Development Program
DJIMI	Dow Jones Islamic Market Indexes
DRs	Depositary Receipts
DTTs	Double Taxation Treaties
ECBs	External Commercial Borrowings
ECLAC	Economic Commission for Latin America and the Caribbean
EEFA	Exchange Earners Foreign Currency Account
EMBI	Emerging Market Bond Index
EMCs	Emerging Market Countries

EMEs	Emerging Market Economies
EU	European Union
FCCBs	Foreign Currency Convertible Bonds
FDI	Foreign Direct Investment
FPI	Foreign Portfolio Investment
FSAF	Financial Stability Assessment Framework
FSAP	Financial Sector Assessment Program
FTAA	Free Trade Area of the Americas
FTSE	Financial Times Stock Exchange
FY	Fiscal Year
GATT	General Agreement on Tariffs and Trade
GDF	Global Development Finance
GDP	Gross Domestic Product
GDR	Global Depository Receipt
GOI	Government of India
IDB	Islamic Development Bank
IFIs	International Financial Institutions
IFS	International Financial Statistics
IIFS	Institutions offering Islamic Financial Services
IMF	International Monetary Fund
INR	Indian Rupees
IOSCO	International Organization of Securities Commission
IT	Information Technology
JVs	Joint Ventures
LAC	Latin America and Caribbean
LDCs	Least Developed Countries
M&A	Mergers and Acquisitions
MISC	Malaysia International Shipping Company
MNEs	Multinational Enterprises
MTS	Mobile Telesystems
MYR	Malaysian Ringgit
NAC	Nanjing Automobile Group Corporation
NAFTA	North American Free Trade Agreement
NGOs	Non-Governmental Organizations
n.i.e	not included elsewhere
ODA	Official Development Assistance
OECD	Organisation for Economic Co-operation and Development

OFDI	Outward Foreign Direct Investment
ONGC	Oil and Natural Gas Corporation Limited
PPPs	Public–Private Partnerships
PRC	Peoples Republic of China
PSIA	Profit Sharing Investment Accounts
RBI	Reserve Bank of India
RED	*Reporte de Economía y Desarrollo*
RMB	Renminbi
RTAs	Regional Trade Agreements
S&P	Standard and Poor's
SAIC	Shanghai Automotive Industry Corporation
SEZs	Special Economic Zones
SFC	Securities and Futures Commission
SITC	Standard International Trade Classification
SPVs	Special Purpose Vehicles
TCS	Tata Consultancy Services
TFP	Total Factor Productivity
TIC	Treasury International Capital
TNCs	Transnational Corporations
TSR	Total Shareholder Return
UAE	United Arab Emirates
UNCTAD	United Nations Conference on Trade and Development
VSNL	Videsh Sanchar Nigam Limited
WBCSD	World Business Council for Sustainable Development
WDI	World Development Indicators
WEO	World Economic Outlook
WTO	World Trade Organization

Foreword

This book is a valuable addition to the literature on prospects and challenges common to the better performing medium and low income developing countries—commonly referred to as the Emerging Market Economies (EMEs)—be they in Asia, Europe, Latin America or Africa. These countries have become concrete examples of the historic success of the international development community during the past 50 years in significantly improving the social and economic well being of a very large number of human beings throughout the world.

Private capital flows have now become the primary source of foreign capital in well-performing developing countries. Most observers expect this trend to continue. Thus, further development of EMEs and private capital flows have become much more intertwined than ever before.

The Emerging Markets Forum that commissioned the papers included in this volume is devoted to exploring common opportunities, challenges and risks, and also forging a consensus between the key decision makers in the public and private sectors on how best to sustain and build on the successes of these EMEs.

The book is unique in the sense that it comprises of chapters written by authors with world wide reputation in their respective fields as well as actual experience with high policy making around the world. As a result, its policy-analysis and proposals are grounded in reality of practical policy-making and implementation under a variety of country circumstances.

I congratulate the book's editor Harinder S. Kohli and other authors who deserve our sincere thanks for producing uniformly outstanding chapters. I know it has been a labour of love for each one of them. The end product is an excellent book that I can commend highly to all those interested in EMEs.

Gautam S. Kaji
Chairman, Advisory Board
Emerging Markets Forum

Preface

In the past decade, there has been a dramatic rise in private capital flows to Emerging Market Economies (EMEs). Until the 1990s, most private capital flows were concentrated in a few countries, mainly in Asia and Latin America. But, in the past few years, a much larger number of developing countries have become recipients of substantial private capital flows both in absolute terms and relative to their gross national product. At the same time, net capital flows from official sources—multilateral and bilateral financial institutions such as the International Monetary Fund, World Bank and regional development banks, the European Union (EU) as well as national aid agencies—have dropped significantly since 1998, except to Sub-Saharan Africa.

The Emerging Markets Forum was started in 2005 in recognition of this new reality in the development process. The Forum's basic objective is to bring together high-level government officials and corporate leaders from around the world for an informal, private and intimate dialogue on the key economic, financial and social issues facing EMEs. The Forum is focussed on some 50 EMEs mostly in Asia, Europe and Latin America (plus some countries in the Middle East and Sub-Saharan Africa), which are keen to integrate with the global economy, already have or seek to create a conducive business environment, *and* are of near-term interest to private investors, both domestic and international. The Forum seeks to promote knowledge sharing, policy guidance and private sector engagement that will facilitate achievement of their common goal of sustainable growth and development.

This volume starts with an overview chapter, and comprises nine papers presented at the 2006 Global Meeting of the Forum held in Jakarta, Indonesia, in September 2006. The theme of this meeting was International Capital Flows and Domestic Capital

Markets: Growth and Development in Emerging Markets. The papers sparked a rich and intellectually stimulating debate among the senior policy makers, business executives and leading thinkers at the meeting. The participants recommended that, given the high quality of the papers and the wide interest in the topics covered, they should be made available to a larger audience. This book is in response to this recommendation. The papers have been revised in light of the discussion at Jakarta.

I would like to thank the authors for the time and effort they have put in the preparation of the papers. In the order in which their papers appear in this book, they are: Jack Boorman; V. Sundararajan (my co-author); Heinz Hauser; Rakesh Jha; Andrew Sheng; Claudio M. Loser; Luis Miguel Castilla; Haruhiko Kuroda, Rajat Nag and Rita Nangia; and Harpaul Alberto Kohli. The authors are all renowned authorities in their respective fields and we were most fortunate to obtain their agreement to share their experience and views by preparing these papers and participating in Forum discussions.

Special thanks are due to my advisor and dear friend Bimal Jalan for inspiring this book, and to Sugata Ghosh, Jasmeet Singh and their colleagues at SAGE Publications for their help, patience and guidance throughout. I would also like to express my sincere appreciation to my colleagues at the Emerging Markets Forum, Gautam S. Kaji and P.R. Narvekar, for their support and encouragement. Finally, I owe a special debt to Yanbei Yao and, my son and professional colleague, Harpaul Alberto Kohli, for their collaborative efforts, hard work and dedication in getting this manuscript ready for publication.

Harinder S. Kohli
Chief Executive
Emerging Markets Forum

Introduction and Overview 1

Harinder S. Kohli

The papers selected for inclusion in this book were among those discussed at the Emerging Markets Forum meeting in Jakarta, Indonesia, in September 2006. The underlying premise of the meeting was that growth and development in Emerging Market Economies (EMEs) are now heavily dependent on: (*a*) international private capital flows; (*b*) development of financial markets; (*c*) the countries' ability to integrate successfully with the global economy through trade and investment; and (*d*) their ability to forge public–private partnerships (PPPs), including in infrastructure development. A particular emphasis was on contrasting and comparing experiences in Asia and Latin America. The papers included in the book cover these closely related areas.

The papers are self-contained and stand on their own. The purpose of this introduction and overview is to put these papers into an overall context, to explain how they relate to each other and to highlight the key inter-related messages that emerge from them.

In the past decade, there has been a sharp rise in private capital flows to the EMEs. Until the mid-1990s, most private capital flows were concentrated in a few countries, mainly in Asia and Latin America. In the past few years, a much larger number of developing countries in most geographic regions of the world (except in Sub-Sahara Africa) have become recipients of substantial private capital flows both in absolute terms and relative to their gross national product. At the same time, net capital flows from official sources—multilateral and bilateral financial institutions such as the International Monetary Fund (IMF), World Bank and regional development banks, the EU as well as national aid agencies—have dropped significantly since 1998 (except to Sub-Sahara Africa and parts of the Middle East). The sharp drop in net official transfers is partly due to the stagnation in new commitments, as also to the large repayments of outstanding loans to the IMF and Paris Club by many countries. As a result, in a dramatic turnaround from the situation prevailing until the early 1990s, private capital flows now dwarf official flows to developing countries.

The basic policy message is clear: private capital flows have now become the primary source of foreign capital in the well-performing developing countries, referred to here as the EMEs. Most observers agree that this trend is likely to continue.

However, the success of these countries in attracting large private flows should not obscure the fact that there are many more developing countries that still do not have access to significant private capital flows and that, even today, depend heavily on official aid to meet their external financing needs. The vast majority of such countries are the least developed countries (LDCs) mainly in Sub-Sahara Africa and South Asia, but they also include small and island economies that are particularly vulnerable to external and internal shocks.

The focus of the chapters in this volume is, however, on the EMEs. While many of the issues and policy implications of primary interest to this latter group are also of relevance to developing countries, the book does not aim to cover issues related to developing countries as a whole. Instead, its focus is on issues of particular interest to the EMEs across all regions of the world.

The Jakarta Forum discussed six related topics, each of them supported by one or more papers written by well-known authorities on the subjects: overall global financial flows and imbalances; private capital flows to EMEs; outward foreign direct investments (FDI) from emerging markets; development of financial markets, particularly in the emerging economies in Asia and Latin America; trade policies in Asia and Latin America; and PPPs in infrastructure, with particular focus on Asia. Nine of these papers are included in this book.

Context setting: Global imbalances and capital flows to EMCs

Chapter 2 by Jack Boorman is on 'Global Imbalances, Oil Revenues and Capital Flows to Emerging Market Countries'. It sets the broad context for the topics covered in the other chapters by discussing: (*a*) overall global financial flows and imbalances (including trade and fiscal imbalances and foreign exchange reserves) and other key factors that have facilitated the surge in private capital flows to EMCs during the past few years; (*b*) scenarios for the unwinding of these global imbalances; and (*c*) their implications for the continuance, or interruption, of the large private capital flows to EMCs.

In early 2007, the world economy was in the middle of an unprecedented fifth year of expansion. This expansion was fuelled, until recently, by unusually accommodative monetary policies (and resultant low interest rates) in the major developed economies, strong consumer spending and major gains in productivity (particularly in the US economy), and a sharp growth in imports from Asia. Strong global economic growth has been sustained despite the spike in the price of oil and other commodities.

The EMEs have benefited from this benign global economic environment: they have enjoyed high economic growth rates, their exports have boomed, their national balance sheets are much healthier; and countries in Asia as well as petroleum and commodities' exporters throughout have accumulated record foreign exchange reserves. These developments combined with a much better domestic policy environment in most EMCs—compared to the situation prevailing prior to the 1997 financial crisis—have significantly enhanced their creditworthiness and attraction to international private investors. As a result, EMCs have attracted massive private capital flows from Organisation for Economic Co-operation and Development (OECD) countries as well as from other emerging markets. Jack Boorman's chapter describes this benign global economic environment and its impact on capital flows to and from the EMCs.

The recent unprecedented growth in the world economy and the sharp rise of EMC exports have also resulted in the accumulation of record global imbalances, with the US becoming the major debtor nation. On the other hand, many traditional export-oriented Asian economies as well as oil exporters worldwide have accumulated massive foreign reserves; China's foreign reserves alone approached US$ 1.3 trillion in May 2007.

Until 2004, the large foreign surpluses were primarily accumulated by East Asian economies and India. Since the spike in oil prices, the situation has changed significantly. While East Asian economies continue to accumulate large additional reserves as China and Japan more than offset the disappearance of surpluses in other Asian oil importing countries like India, the surpluses generated by the oil exporting countries worldwide have risen dramatically to almost US$ 1 trillion in 2006, triple of the figure in 2002; they were equivalent to nearly half of the US total current account deficit estimated at about US$ 900 billion in 2006 (6.5 per cent of its GDP). In late 2006, China was generating foreign new exchange reserves equivalent to 10 per cent of its GDP while the surpluses in the Gulf countries approached 15 per cent of their GDP. These imbalances cannot be sustained for long without adverse impact on global trade and finance.

While the dominant view at this moment is that the global imbalances can be corrected in an orderly manner by the markets,[1] there is a risk of sudden corrections or excessive adjustments in currency values, a surge in interest rates, a sharp economic slowdown in the US and/or rising protectionism. In that case, the world economy would suffer an unexpected setback. And Asian economies as the most open and most dependent on exports to the US would be affected disproportionately. For example, opportunities to expand exports and the large private capital flows received by the EMCs in recent years under the very benign global economic environment may be reduced significantly.

The Boorman chapter discusses these issues at some length and concludes that the adjustments required are likely to be much more difficult than was the case with previous oil price shocks because of: (*a*) the sheer size of the adjustments required; (*b*) the twin deficits (fiscal and balance of payments) of the US; and (*c*) the much greater caution with which oil exporting countries are using the surge in their exports since 2005 (for example, less consumption and more accumulation of reserves; reluctance to invest in the US assets). Consequently, the chapter suggests that the risks of a 'hard landing' are not insignificant. Policy makers in EMCs and private businesses need to take these risks into account while considering prospects for future economic developments in, and private capital flows to, EMCs.

Private capital flows to EMCs: Drivers, trends and key issues

As explained earlier, private capital flows have now replaced Official Development Assistance (ODA) from multilateral and bilateral institutions as the dominant source of foreign capital to the EMEs. Accordingly, private capital flows to EMCs are the overarching theme of the Emerging Markets Forum. The Forum's background papers are aimed to be a reference document on the drivers, trends and key issues related to private capital flows to the EMCs. The paper presented in Jakarta and included in this volume follows from the Boorman paper on global imbalances and includes a fuller discussion of the three major elements of private capital flows: FDI, portfolio flows and debt flows. V. Sundararajan and Harinder S. Kohli authored the paper.

Net private flows to EMEs have grown sharply in recent years. At the same time, they have also exhibited significant volatility year to year, but with major differences between regions and between types of flows; FDIs to East Asia showed the least volatility while bank loan flows to Africa and the Middle East showed the most. In 2005, the latest year for which consistent data is available, private capital flows to EMEs reached a new high of US$ 495 billion equivalent to 4.4 per cent of the countries' GDP. Net private flows to Asia have risen steadily from US$ 121 billion (3.9 per cent of GDP) in 1999 to US$ 263 billion (4.9 per cent of GDP) in 2005. Flows to European EMCs rose from US$ 25 billion (3.2 per cent of GDP) to US$ 133 billion (6.7 per cent of GDP) during the same period; most of this increase has been since 2002. Africa has shown the most volatility; it attracted US$ 14 billion

(4.5 per cent of GDP) in 1999 before declining steadily for the next 4 years reaching a negative flow of US$ 800 million in 2003 before rebounding sharply to US$ 19 billion (3.3 per cent of GDP) in 2005. While the recent rebound in flows is partly due to better economic performance of many African countries, the main factors seem to be increased competition for oil and other natural resources and the much greater appetite for emerging market assets among international investors. Overall, while all regions have benefited from this benign environment, Eastern Europe and Asia have captured most recent growth in private capital flows.

There has also been a dramatic shift in the list of top 10 recipient countries. In 1994–95, Brazil was the largest recipient and the top 10 list included two other countries from Latin America (Argentina and Mexico). Six Asian countries were among the top 10 (China (PRC), Thailand, Hong Kong SAR, Korea, Singapore and Indonesia). By 2004–05, China (PRC), Hong Kong and Taipei China had become the top three with three other Asian countries (Korea, India and Singapore) still in the list, but Thailand, Argentina and Hungary dropped out altogether. From Latin America, only Mexico and Brazil made the list (at numbers nine and 10). These changes show that international investors can and do make rapid changes in their portfolio strategies.

There have also been significant shifts in the composition of these flows. FDIs—which traditionally have been the largest and the least volatile component—have risen steadily from US$ 191 billion in 1998 to US$ 316 billion in 2005 (63 per cent of total net flows). Equity flows have increased from US$ 46 billion to US$ 178 billion during the same period, while debt flows have gone up from US$ 35 billion to US$ 56 billion. Asia remains by far the largest recipient of FDI and portfolio flows, while in 2005 it had net outflow of bank lending. In Europe, the recent rise of total flows is explained to a large extent by large inflows of bank loans. On the other hand, in Latin America, both portfolio and debt flows have dried out since the early 1990s and in 2005, FDI accounted for most of the inflows (possibly due to the sharp rise in the price of oil and other commodities). Again, these changes demonstrate the dynamic nature of private capital flows.

Chapter 3 by V. Sundararajan and Harinder S. Kohli traces these trends in the growth, direction and volatility of private capital flows in detail, with a liberal use of charts and graphs, highlighting the developments in 2005 as net private flows to EMCs reached a new high. An important new development was the emergence and rapid growth of Islamic fixed income securities and their wider acceptance in international financial centres. It also assesses and reviews the key determinants of such flows.

The chapter then reviews the structural and financial policy responses by various countries and highlights a number of issues that need attention of policy makers at this time. The issues raised include: the consequence of potential unwinding of global imbalances on the size, structure, direction and volatility of private capital flows to EMCs; the need for emerging markets to have adequate macro-economic surveillance framework on the impact of private capital flows on domestic financial soundness; the lessons of recent developments for the strategy to further improve and broaden access to FDI flows in countries other than China; the appropriate structural reforms to develop domestic financial markets to promote more stable capital inflows and limit the impact of their volatility on domestic financial soundness; and, given the growing surpluses in the Middle East and the resultant greater demand for Islamic securities, the measures that can be taken to strengthen the financial infrastructure for issuing Islamic securities. The Forum discussions confirmed that these are complex issues and require a variety of responses depending on country circumstances. They need to be and would be explored further in follow-up papers and meetings.

Private capital flows out of EMCs, and emergence of new global players

A relatively recent phenomenon in international capital flows is the advent of large-scale investments overseas by private companies based in EMCs like China, India, Brazil, Russia, South Africa and the Persian Gulf region. This phenomenon has still not yet received the attention it deserves, perhaps because until just a few years ago the size of such outward flows was relatively small, because initially such FDIs were not global but intra-regional in nature (for example, East Asia-based companies investing in associated production networks in neighbouring countries), and because consistent data was scarce.

The Emerging Markets Forum has become one of the first to focus on this phenomenon and to provide a venue to policy makers and private business leaders to understand and debate it, grounded in analysis based on available (though still incomplete) data. So far, its discussions and background papers have focussed only on outward FDIs even though some capital surplus countries are also becoming major sources of international portfolio flows.

Outward FDI flows from EMCs totalled US$ 133 billion in 2005, equivalent to 50 per cent of total inward FDI flows of US$ 265 billion! According to the United Nations Conference on Trade and Development (UNCTAD), the share of South–South flows of FDI rose from only 16 per cent in 1995 to 36 per cent in 2003 and to 50 per cent in 2005.[2] The outward FDI stock of developing and transition economies reached US$ 1.4 trillion or 13 per cent of total global stock.

Especially for countries in Southeast Asia and resource-rich countries in Africa, FDI from other EMCs has become the dominant source of external private capital. Considering the other side of the coin, based on 2002–04 averages, at least 10 EMCs showed annual outward FDI flows exceeding US$ 1 billion: Brazil, Chile, PRC, Hong Kong SAR, India, South Korea, Malaysia, Mexico, Russia and Taipei China. Flows from China alone averaged US$ 23 billion per year. And in the case of Brazil, Korea, Malaysia, Russia and South Africa, outward FDI was 50 per cent or more of inward FDI flows.

If anything, these numbers underestimate the importance of this phenomenon today. Anecdotal data for 2006 and early 2007 suggest that outward FDI flows from EMCs have surged in the last 2 years, including to developed economies in Europe and North America. For example, Indian companies tripled their outward FDI in the first 9 months of fiscal year (FY) 2006, reaching US$ 8.6 billion during April–December 2007 and equalling India's total inward FDI in the previous year. Companies in Brazil, Saudi Arabia and South Africa have also announced major acquisitions in other EMCs as well as in developed countries. These developments have signalled the emergence of multinational companies based in EMCs as important, and in a few cases even leading, players in world markets.

The focus of the Jakarta Forum was on these two closely related aspects: first, on outward FDIs from the EMCs and second, on the parallel emergence of new global players based in emerging markets. The discussions covered the trends and key motivations behind these investments and the related issues faced by policy makers as well as the investors.

Because complete and systematic data is still not available on outward FDI from EMCs, two complementary background papers were commissioned to better understand this new phenomenon. The first is an overview chapter based on the best available statistical and anecdotal information at the global level, combined with a brief review of outward FDI from nine countries chosen on the basis of the volume of their FDI as well as their global and regional importance. Professor Heinz Hauser prepared this chapter, which also discusses the emergence of new global players from EMCs. The second chapter is a case study of outward FDI from India. It discusses developments at a country and enterprise level. It was prepared by Rakesh Jha of ICICI Bank. The two chapters strongly complement each other and between them present a fascinating story.

Chapter 4 by Heinz Hauser presents data and discusses recent developments in outward FDI from EMCs. It then summarizes the key determinants of outward FDI within the framework of the traditional FDI theory. A key finding is that the general considerations, which in the past have led firms in capital-surplus OECD countries to invest overseas, also apply to companies in EMCs. However, the recent emergence of large-scale outward FDI from EMCs shows that the time cycle within which countries change from being capital importers to major capital exporters has been shortened very considerably (for example, Brazil, Korea); and that some countries even with relatively low per capita incomes have become major sources of FDI (for example, China and India).

Hauser argues that the main drivers of South–South flows include: strong growth and maturing of domestic markets; rise in regional trade, production networks and related FDI; liberalization and privatization of infrastructure sectors; comparative advantage of emerging markets MNCs in investing in other developing countries; and the countries' desire to secure markets and sources of essential energy and other raw materials. It also discusses emergence of new global players from EMCs in industries like pharmaceuticals, shipping, steel, textiles and information technology (IT) services. The chapter concludes that these recent trends are likely to continue and perhaps gain further momentum. It raises a number of policy issues that deserve attention. While the chapter itself does not discuss it explicitly, deliberations at the Forum pointed to another important issue: whether, and to what extent, are state-owned enterprises in EMCs overpaying for assets overseas because they are not subject to the same financial and corporate discipline as publicly-listed companies in developed economies? Given the competition for energy and other natural resources, this could become a serious political issue as well.

Rakesh Jha's chapter complements Hauser's chapter by describing changes in government policies and emergence of strong domestic firms that have combined together to suddenly catapult India into the ranks of major FDI exporters even though the country itself remains a net capital importer is a low-income country and in terms of per capita income. Until the late 1990s, India's policy environment was geared towards inward-bound FDI reflecting the prevailing view that capital deficit countries like India should encourage capital inflows and discourage outflows—through investment, trade, taxation, and financial policies and regulations. These restrictive policies have undergone far-reaching, though gradual, liberalization starting in 2003. This liberalization took place just as many Indian business firms were completing internal restructuring and business activity reached new highs in response to the country's major economic reforms in the 1990s, as firms gained greater access to domestic capital and as global economic environment became more receptive. With their newly established competitiveness and greater confidence, more and more Indian firms considered outward FDI to secure strategic assets, market access, technology, skills and natural resources. And many firms aimed to become important global players in their industry through FDI overseas.

The net result was an over 11-fold increase in outward FDI between 2001 and 2006, from US$ 759 million to US$ 8.7 billion (in the first 9 months alone). Just over half of these FDI are in manufacturing and about one-third in non-financial services such as IT. Pharmaceutical, IT, steel and energy, and other resource-intensive companies are among the leading investors. While many of their acquisitions are in other EMCs (Brazil, Columbia, Russia and Malaysia), over half of Indian FDI went to Europe.

Jha discusses these trends at length, gives a detailed account of India's outward FDI by sector and destination, and summarizes the main motivations that are driving Indian companies' fast-growing appetite for investing in overseas assets. Given ICICI Bank's central role in putting together many of these deals, his chapter offers unique insights into this new and important phenomenon.

Development of financial markets

Development of financial markets is now widely accepted as essential to the long-term growth and competitiveness of EMEs. Yet, in most EMEs, financial development has not kept pace with the growth of the real sector. Given the increasingly market-driven and private sector-led economies and large domestic savings pools, faster development of the financial systems, both at the national and regional levels, is of the highest priority and also one of the major challenges faced by the EMCs.

Well-developed domestic financial systems are also important to attract greater volumes of foreign private capital flows, equity as well as debt. They allow foreign investors greater confidence in a country's economy, allow them to leverage foreign capital with domestic finance, provide more robust and multiple exit strategies, and permit opportunities to the institutional investors for equity and debt portfolio investments. From the policy makers' point of view, deep domestic financial markets increase the ability of the domestic financial system to absorb the volatility in international capital flows.

Given the importance of financial development to continued strong flows of private capital flows and keen interest of participants in comparing and contrasting the situation in Asia and Latin America, the Forum commissioned two complementary papers. The first paper is by Andrew Sheng (Chapter 6) which discusses, based on his long experience in policy making in one of Asia's leading financial centres, the importance and challenges of deepening financial markets at national and regional levels. Claudio M. Loser prepared the second paper (Chapter 7) on Latin America based on his intimate knowledge of this region and its financial systems.

The Sheng paper reviews key trends in the development of financial markets in East Asia. Despite the lessons of the Asian crisis and efforts to develop bond and equity markets, the Asian financial systems remain bank-dominated, with still fledgling bond markets, speculative stock markets and relatively small insurance, and pension and social security systems. Even though economic fundamentals and the resilience of Asian financial systems have improved, the vulnerabilities to global imbalances have also increased. It shows that financial integration is proceeding slower than trade integration, and that there remain considerable regulatory and other barriers to greater integration. The paper suggests that an even deeper problem in building markets is the mindset of policy makers who have been overly influenced by the neo-classical paradigm that has emphasized the elegance of theory at the expense of institutions and institutional management. It argues that social and economic development is not about theory, but about performance. Hence, building markets would require the management of complex social, economic and historical factors, including the pressures from globalization, technology and vested interests. It points out that building effective markets requires effective public bureaucracies where providing the property rights infrastructure, enforcing regulation and basic social services effectively for private business to thrive is a core function of social development. Finally, it examines as to what possible steps can be taken by both the private and public sectors, including the role of International Financial Institutions (IFIs), in accelerating financial market deepening and integration in Asia.

The chapter by Loser traces the recent history of economic management and performance of Latin America and puts the financial development (or lack thereof) in the region in this broader context. It documents how underdeveloped financial systems in Latin America are relative both to its stage of development and to other developing regions; the region accounts for roughly 5 per cent of global GDP, but has only about 2 per cent of global financial assets. With the exception of few countries like Chile, the financial systems are dominated by banks and savings rates are low, as is the depth of intermediation. Bank assets are less than 60 per cent of GDP compared to 135 per cent in Asia. Moreover, in many countries: (*a*) large banks are government controlled; (*b*) until recently, a rising share of bank balance sheet was absorbed by government securities; and (*c*) most remaining bank lending went for consumption and little to investment. Finally, in some countries, such as Argentina and Venezuela, deposits held by their nationals outside the country approach or even exceed the countries' broad money.

Loser traces this state of affairs to the (past) large macro-economic imbalances and the resultant hyper inflation, currency devaluations and repeated financial crises that eroded confidence in the financial systems. In the most recent years, most countries in the region have overcome such fundamental problems through much more prudent macro-economic management. But, there remain many underlying structural and institutional problems that must be tackled in order to develop more robust domestic financial markets. In the light of this and only limited regional economic cooperation and trade, it is no surprise that regional financial integration has not made much headway either.

The two chapters provide an interesting contrast for policy makers and business executives interested in comparing the two regions. As Sheng notes, there are many similarities between

Asia and Latin America: first, financial systems in both regions lag the real sector and are dominated by banks; second, a significant amount of their savings are intermediated by markets outside the regions; third, the regional financial markets have been losing market share to financial centres in the US and Europe; and finally, the US dollar is the effective currency of reference in much of their trade and investment. At the same time, three important differences stand out. First, while Asian policy makers fret that their financial systems do not match the prowess of their manufacturing sectors, the fact is that overall Asian financial systems are deeper than those in Latin America despite its GDP per capita being a multiple of that of Asia. Second, financial systems in Asia have rebounded strongly since the 1997 crisis and today appear to be much sounder than those in Latin America. And, third, the underlying tone and expectations in the two regions are qualitatively different. Asia seems much more accepting of globalization and keener on integrating with the global financial markets; hence its focus on the transformation of existing institutions and on accelerating development of regional markets. Latin America still seems much more inward-looking and uncertain about how to handle globalization. Hopefully, having finally achieved macro-economic stability and restored the health of national balance sheets in most countries—both developments are unprecedented in its recent economic history—the region is now ready to accelerate financial development and achieve higher savings and investment rates, and thus improve its overall global competitiveness.

Trade: Recent developments and prospects in Asia and Latin America

The issue of trade policies has become a central concern to policy makers and businesses operating in EMCs alike, particularly given the prolonged impasse in the Doha Round and the plethora of bilateral trade agreements in Asia and Latin America. In addition to being topical, the issue is of fundamental importance to the economic development and growth of EMEs and to private capital flows. Indeed, it is not possible to consider the economic prospects and business potential of these economies without considering their participation in global markets for goods, services and capital.

There is by now convincing evidence that the developing countries which have been most successful in sustaining growth and improving the well-being of people have also been those that have broadened their participation in global markets. The East Asian experience suggests that export-led growth and outward-oriented policies contributed significantly to the superior growth achieved by these countries. Though by no means the only factor, their trade policies have helped improve the competitiveness of their economies by raising productivity, sustaining high growth and permitting the countries to move up to higher levels of development.

Latin America has made considerable progress during the past two decades in areas such as macro-economic stability, greater openness to trade and international capital flows, as well as in the consolidation of democracy. In spite of this, the region's relative economic performance since the 1980s has been disappointing overall: economic growth has been anaemic; income distribution remains extremely uneven, and social exclusion is a common element to many Latin American countries. The region's average growth in the 1990s was lower than in the 1960s and 1970s. Most other developing regions, particularly Asia and Eastern Europe, had much higher growth rates. And most importantly, growth in Latin America was substantially below the rate needed to improve the living conditions of most of its inhabitants. While East Asia's per capita income increased seven-fold in a 40-year span, Latin America did not even succeed in doubling its per capita GDP. Many economists ascribe these sharp differences in the relative economic performance of Latin America and Asia to the differences in their savings and investment rates, improvements in productivity and resultant changes in the economic structure and competitiveness, and to their openness to and effective participation in the global economy.

Among the emerging markets, East Asian economies are the most integrated with the global markets and with each other, while Latin American economies are among the most insulated (except for Chile and Mexico). In their approach towards international trade, Asia and Latin America seem to be following very different paths. While most regional trade agreements (RTAs) in Latin America are in disarray, East Asia appears headed towards a further deepening and broadening of RTAs (with Association of Southeast Asian Nations [ASEAN] providing the launching pad) while raising its share of global trade.

The chapter by Luis Miguel Castilla presents very comprehensive and thoughtful discussion of the relative performance of Asia and Latin America: past development strategies, growth and performance. The chapter starts with a brief account of the main determinants behind the contrasting development performances of Latin America and East Asia. Having identified the importance of trade policy and export-orientation as determinants of productivity improvement, it contrasts the differing approaches Latin America and Asia have followed to international and regional trade. The debate on the co-existence of multilateralism and regionalism is also briefly covered.

The chapter makes a persuasive case that Asia's success in inte-grating with the global markets and the relative insulation of individual Latin American economies from global markets as well as from each other appears to have had an important impact on their relative economic performance. It argues that successful EMEs have been able to broaden existing and potential markets by pursuing aggressive trade liberalization agendas. However, while the global trade in goods is increasingly being driven by the dynamic trade of manufactured goods (with an increasingly larger value-added content) from East Asia, most Latin American countries continue to export mainly primary goods or natural resource-based manufactures. To a large extent, these differing trade patterns reflect relative comparative advantages and productivity differentials. Furthermore, the·persistence of trade barriers has also inhibited a larger penetration of Latin American goods in global export markets. But, the basic message is clear: overall, Latin America has been much more inward-looking than East Asia, which in turn has adversely affected the countries' ability to improve productivity, modify structure of production and enhance global competitiveness. The chapter then outlines the opportunities and challenges associated with the broadening of trade relations between Latin America and East Asia, including China.

Finally, Castilla underlines the need to accompany trade policy with an agenda for the transformation of the productive sector, to ensure that the benefits of trade do materialize. He argues that without the underpinnings of complementary measures designed to boost competitiveness, efforts to improve a country's presence in global markets could be doomed to failure. A comparison between the strategies pursued by Latin America and East Asia shows that the latter's success in effectively competing in global markets has been partly determined by improvements in infrastructure and the adoption of trade facilitation measures.

Private financing of infrastructure

The final two chapters discuss a supply-side issue of central concern to most (fast) growing emerging market countries (EMCs): how to finance the massive investment requirements in infrastructure, given the limited fiscal headroom in many countries. More and more countries are reverting back to strategies calling for increased reliance on private financing, despite the mixed results in the late 1990s and the early 2000s. The topic is of significance and immediate interest to policy makers in all EMEs. It is equally important as well to private business executives, both of companies interested in investing in EMCs (given that the availability of efficient infrastructure services is critical to the competitiveness of their operations) and of firms interested in providing infrastructure-related services and financing.

Many fast-growing EMEs suffer from major bottlenecks in infrastructure services, particularly in transport, power, water and sanitation. A common issue faced by all countries is how to overcome the existing bottlenecks and thereafter to continually upgrade and expand infrastructure to meet the needs of their fast-expanding economies, as they continue their integration with the global markets. To private companies involved in infrastructure services, the challenges faced by the countries also offer a potentially huge business opportunity.

Asia is a prime example of this challenge. During the next 10 years, Asia needs to invest between US$ 3.7 trillion and US$ 4.7 trillion in infrastructure development.[3] Except for China, these investment requirements are almost double the current investment levels. Without meeting this enormous challenge, the countries would be unable to sustain the current high growth rates for too long.

The chapter by Kuroda et al. explains why infrastructure development is central to countries' development and its increasing importance as Asian economies seek to maintain their high economic growth and promote greater regional trade and investment while continuing their integration with the global economy. It presents a thoughtful analysis of the recent history of, and issues related to, infrastructure in Asia. Except in China, in recent years, infrastructure investments have fallen compared to earlier periods and are well behind economic needs. In Indonesia, for example, infrastructure investments in the past few years fell to 2–3 per cent of GDP, compared to over 6 per cent of GDP prior to the 1997 crisis; in the Philippines, infrastructure investments were 2.8 per cent of GDP, compared to 8 per cent in 1997. Even in India, which was largely unaffected by the 1997 crisis, the investment level de-accelerated to 3.8 per cent of GDP, compared to 7.2 per cent of GDP in 1997. Obviously, the situation varies from country to country and within individual countries and between sectors. But a common major factor was the sharp shortfalls in private investments. As a result, as economic growth rates rebounded in much of Asia, infrastructure bottlenecks have emerged as a major problem.

The chapter presents a persuasive case for accelerating efforts to complement public sector resources with private sector financing and managerial skills through extensive public–private partnerships (PPPs). It goes on to discuss the evolution of private investment in infrastructure, particularly in East Asia Before 1997, many countries had attracted significant investments from international investors, particularly in telecommunications, power, ports and road transport, as also some in water supply and sanitation. But such international investments largely dried up post-1997. More recently, regional investors have entered the markets to a degree, but much more needs to be done. The chapter concludes by highlighting the key policy and institutional reforms needed in order to create a more conducive business environment for successful and sustainable PPPs as well as efforts needed to develop more bankable projects.

The second paper (Chapter 10) by Harpaul Alberto Kohli presents a comparison of key indicators of infrastructure development and services across selected countries. The basic objective is to present a broad and quick comparison across countries of the coverage, efficiency and quality of key infrastructure services during the past 30 years. Such comparative data could be of immense value to policy makers, but is currently not readily available. The comparison covers 12 countries: seven low- or middle-income EMCs (Brazil, China, India, Indonesia, Malaysia, Mexico and Turkey) and five high- or upper middle-income countries (Japan, Korea and Singapore in Asia, Chile in Latin America and Caribbean [LAC] and Germany in Europe). The first five are either at a similar stage of development or are major competitors in the global marketplace. The second set of countries can be regarded as the current 'best practice' in infrastructure services to whose level other EMCs must ultimately rise in order to become truly competitive in the global economy. Five major infrastructure sectors are covered: (a) Energy (energy overall as well as power); (b) Transport (roads, civil aviation, ports and railways); (c) Water and Sanitation; (d) Telephony; and (e) Information and Communications Technology (Internet and computers).

Four sets of indicators are provided: (a) Absolute Quantities (tonnes or kW of energy, kilometres of roads, number of passengers and so on); (b) Per Capita Consumption or Penetration (to see how far apart are the countries in meeting consumer needs); (c) Usage per unit of GDP (is infrastructure keeping up with economic growth?); and (d) Quality and Efficiency Indicators (are the consumers and the economy being well served by the service providers?). Finally, the report presents available data on private financing of infrastructure in four specific infrastructure sectors. But the data is limited and no clear trends can be derived from it, except that private flows have been very volatile both at country and sector levels.

While the purpose of this chapter is only to present data comparable across countries, two policy messages stand out. First, despite their recent progress, most low- and middle-income EMCs still have a long way to go relative to the 'best practice countries' (with the exception of China in some sectors). The countries must adopt these 'best practice standards' as the long-term goal, at least in areas like transport, power and communications that are critical to global competitiveness. Second, most countries need not only invest massively to expand infrastructure capacity, but also must very significantly improve the quality and efficiency of the services by giving much greater emphasis to better management and discipline.

The Forum meeting in Jakarta elicited a very rich discussion on the subject and confirmed that the developments in Asia as described by Kuroda et al. in Chapter 9 were largely mirrored also in other EMCs, particularly in Latin America. The discussion also revealed that the potential for PPPs varies significantly between countries and within the countries by sector. It also confirmed that the related policy and institutional reforms are complex, that political economy of the countries is often the most critical factor and that there are no ready-made solutions that can be offered. Strong and decisive leadership at the national level will be essential to meet the infrastructure challenges.

Notes

1. *World Economic Outlook (WEO)* 2006, International Monetary Fund.
2. UNCTAD World Investment Report, 2006.
3. Centennial Group estimates (March 2007).

Bibliography

International Monetary Fund (IMF). 2006. *World Economic Outlook (WEO)*. Washington, DC: IMF.
United Nations Conference on Trade and Development (UNCTAD). 2006. World Investment Report. Geneva: UNCTAD.

Global Imbalances, Oil Revenues and Capital Flows to Emerging Market Countries

2

JACK BOORMAN

Overview

The US current account deficit continues its inexorable rise; it is set to hit US$ 900 billion this year. However, the steady rise in that deficit masks a change in its composition. With the growing surpluses of oil exporting countries, mirroring the increase in oil prices, it now accounts for nearly half of the counterpart to the US deficit. This chapter raises a number of issues related to this changing profile of the global imbalances and asks what implications they may hold for the adjustment process and for global capital flows, especially to the Emerging Market Countries (EMCs).[1] On the adjustment process:

- The (probably appropriate) caution of many of the oil exporting countries in increasing spending as oil revenues rise likely to increases the burden of adjustment on the US.
- Similarly, the decreasing share of US exports in the slowly growing import basket of oil exporting countries means further pressure on the US to correct its trade imbalance.
- These macro-economic effects of the shifting profile of the US deficit towards the oil exporters may also have implications for the ease with which the US can fund both the current account deficit as well as its still-sizeable fiscal deficits.
- The investment preferences of the oil exporting countries appear to be quite different from those of the countries that

recorded the counterpart surpluses to the growing US deficit in recent years.

- In particular, US treasuries and other US assets may be less attractive as a destination for the resources generated by the oil surpluses.
- Deposits at international banks, as in earlier periods of oil exporter surpluses, as well as other investment vehicles appear relatively more attractive to these countries. With increased deposit inflows, the banks may have sought new outlets for their lending, contributing to the change in global asset allocation. This appears to have led, *inter alia*, to a rapid rise in lending to selected EMCs, including in Eastern Europe. It may also be a factor in the explosive growth of hedge funds and private equity buyouts in recent months, although data to track these connections is extremely difficult, if not impossible, to find.

All of this has coincided with a broad-based increase in the attractiveness of EMCs to foreign investors. This appears to have been driven not only by an underlying improvement in the fundamentals in many of these countries, but also by the long period of easy monetary conditions in much of the industrial world and the consequent search for yield created by such policies. The result has been:

- An increase in private capital flows to EMCs to record levels.
- A shift in the composition of capital flows, with FDI and commercial bank lending showing major gains.
- A change in the composition of FDI, with South–South flows, that is, FDI from emerging market and developing countries to other countries within those groups, sustaining foreign investment even as FDI from industrial countries has declined. This development has been coincident with a scramble to secure natural resources—energy and other commodities—needed to feed the rapid growth of countries such as India, China, Brazil and others.

These latter developments raise questions about the sustainability of these capital flows like:

- Will the recent surge in bank lending end badly as it did in previous episodes of 'recycling'?
- Will equity investors in the EMCs maintain their commitments to those markets if yields elsewhere improve or if faith in the sustainability of growth in those countries falters?
- Are there political and other risks associated with the increase in South–South FDI, at least that component driven by the scramble for natural resources?

This chapter will try to present evidence on some of the factors behind each of these changes in the global financial system and to speculate on their implications.

Introduction

A dominant factor in the international monetary and financial system over the last seven to eight years has been the almost continuous rise in the current account deficit in the balance of payments of the US. From an average of about US$ 90 billion a year throughout much of the 1990s, the deficit has increased almost every year from just over US$ 200 billion in 1998 to over US$ 800 billion in 2005 and, is estimated to love reached US$ 900 billion, or 6.5 per cent of GDP, in 2006.

As the US deficit has widened, there have been ongoing debates about the forces driving this phenomenon. Some analysts put the blame primarily on the US fiscal deficit and on the low, and recently negative, household savings rate in the country. On the former, however, the link between fiscal and current account balances is rather weak across most developed countries, including the US. In particular, while the US fiscal balance has moved from large deficits to surpluses and back over the past 15 years, the current account balance has mostly been in a declining trend (Figure 2.1).

Figure 2.1   United States: External current account balance and overall fiscal balance (% of GDP)

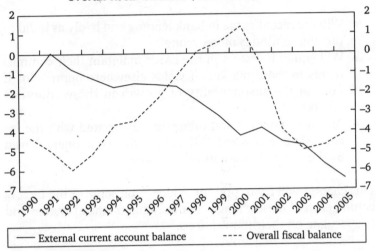

Source: IMF, 2006c.

This lack of relationship between the US budget deficit and the current account deficit is used by some to argue that global imbalances merely reflect the classic case of comparative advantage— emerging markets specialize in global manufacturing and commodity extraction while the US specializes in global capital allocation. It is argued, therefore, that in the context of rapid growth, EMCs are providing bigger and bigger savings spillovers to the rest of the world and, thus, contributing to a widening US current account deficit.

There is, no doubt, some validity to this view. However, with the US deficits as large as they are, the global economy is in uncharted territory. The sustainability of both the current account deficit and the fiscal deficit depends on the willingness of foreigners to increase substantially their holdings of US assets, including US government securities, and the willingness of the US to see greater foreign control over those assets. But how realistic is this? The ever-widening current account deficit portends exchange rate adjustments that could produce substantial capital losses on such holdings. Similarly, the recent debate over direct investment in certain industries in the US, from China and Dubai, among others, at least raises questions about the welcome that some of the needed investment may receive in the US. Thus, the apparently benign historical relationship between the current account and fiscal deficit should be of little comfort.

The increasing deficits in the US current account appear to be much more closely related to the decline in the savings–investment balance of US households (Figure 2.2). Many factors have been suggested as the cause for this decline, but one of the most important factors appears to be the impact of the housing boom, with capital gains being transformed into higher consumption (and higher imports). This then begs the question of whether monetary policy in the US has helped perpetuate the global imbalances by being too loose for too long. There is, of course, an active, but unsettled, debate on the role that monetary policy should play in countering emerging asset bubbles. A related issue in this context concerns the implications for emerging market financing of the low interest rate environment in the US (and in much of the industrial world) and the disposition of current account surpluses accumulating in the oil exporting countries.

Figure 2.2   United States: External current account balance and net household savings (% of GDP)

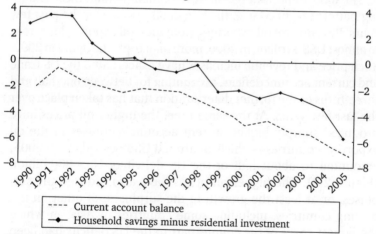

Source: IMF, 2006c.

Finally, some observers, in explaining the rise of the global imbalances, put emphasis on the 'excessive' savings rates and the insufficiency of investment or of consumer spending in other parts of the world, especially in Asia, and to structural rigidities—including inflexible labour markets—in Europe. In both cases, the lower rates of growth in those parts of the world, or the bias towards export production that may exist, aggravate the US current account deficit.

Obviously, there needs to be greater agreement on the relative importance of these forces, and the prospects going forward, if an effective multilateral policy response is to be crafted to foster an orderly adjustment to what is agreed by most observers to be an unsustainable situation. This is an issue well beyond the scope of this chapter.[2]

But there are other questions raised by these global imbalances that are also important for the workings of the international monetary and financial system that are as yet receiving less attention. In particular, the changing profile of the current account surpluses that are the counterpart to the US deficit, and the related patterns of reserve accumulation by the surplus countries, appear to be giving rise to important changes in financial flows in the global economy, including flows to the EMCs.

The most important recent development behind these changing patterns is, of course, the rise in oil prices over the past few years. Revenues of oil exporters, from their oil exports alone, rose to almost US$ 1 trillion in 2006, more than triple the figure in 2002. Such price and revenue increases have exacerbated the US trade and current account deficits, accounting for between one-half and three-fifths of the further deterioration that has taken place over the last few years. At the same time, the higher oil prices have produced sharply higher current account surpluses in the oil exporting countries—which, at around US$ 400 billion in 2005, amounted to about half of the US deficit of US$ 800 billion (Figure 2.3). The higher oil prices have also reduced the surpluses, or at least the growth in the surpluses, of other oil importing countries, including some countries in Asia, in which the largest share of the counterpart to the US deficits had been recorded in recent years and from which a large proportion of the US fiscal deficit has been financed.

Figure 2.3 External current account balance (US$ billion)

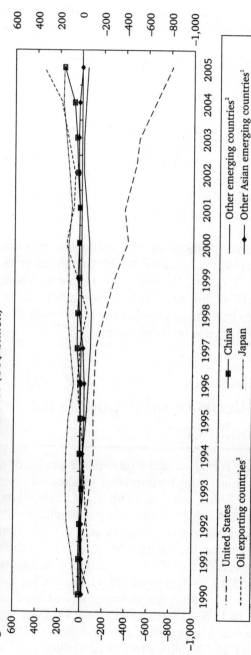

| United States | China | Other emerging countries[2] |
| Oil exporting countries[3] | Japan | Other Asian emerging countries[1] |

Source: IMF, 2006c.

Notes: [1] Other emerging Asian countries include India, Malaysia, Philippines, Thailand, Vietnam.
[2] Other emerging countries include Argentina, Bolivia, Brazil, Bulgaria, Chile, Colombia, Costa Rica, Croatia, Czech Republic, Dominican Republic, Ecuador, Egypt, El Salvador, Hungary, Jordan, Morocco, Pakistan, Panama, Paraguay, Peru, Poland, Romania, Slovak Republic, South Africa, Tunisia, Turkey, Ukraine, Uruguay.
[3] Oil exporting countries include Algeria, Angola, Azerbaijan, Bahrain, Congo, Equatorial Guinea, Gabon, Indonesia, Iran, Kazakhstan, Kuwait, Libya, Mexico, Nigeria, Oman, Qatar, Russia, Saudi Arabia, Turkmenistan, United Arab Emirates, Venezuela, Yemen.

Against this background, this chapter examines three aspects of the changing profile of the global imbalances:

- The implications of growing surpluses and the spending patterns of oil exporting countries for the global imbalances and for the burden on the US to correct its current account deficit.
- The possible impact of the investment preferences of the oil exporting countries on global capital flows, including the ease with which the US is able to finance its fiscal and current account deficits.
- How the profile of capital flows to the EMCs is being affected by these and other recent developments.

Each of these issues will be taken up in the subsequent sections of this chapter. It is important, however, to note that the examination of these issues is hindered by severe data problems. These problems will be identified and dealt with to the extent possible. But the data problems that remain temper the conclusions that can be drawn with confidence on these issues.

Some implications of the spending and investment patterns of oil exporters for the global imbalances

The large and growing surpluses of the oil exporting countries, even if they were only substituting for the earlier surpluses of some of the Asian and other EMCs, may have important implications for the prospects for global imbalances and the policy adjustments needed to address those imbalances. In particular, in the period 2001 (when oil prices began the rise that brought them to their current levels) through 2005, the US current account deficit more than doubled from US$ 390 billion to US$ 805 billion, while the surpluses of the oil exporting countries increased almost five-fold from US$ 72 billion to US$ 348 billion (Table 2.1). Over the same period, the current account surpluses of Asian countries increased from about US$ 120 billion to US$ 320 billion—more

Table 2.1 External current account balance (US$ billion)

Country	1990	1991	1992	1993	1994	1995	1996	1997	1998	1999	2000	2001	2002	2003	2004	2005
United States	-78.97	2.90	-50.08	-84.82	-121.61	-113.67	-124.90	-140.91	-214.07	-300.06	-416.01	-389.46	-475.20	-519.68	-668.08	-804.95
Japan	43.94	68.38	112.33	131.98	130.55	111.40	65.74	96.55	119.07	114.53	119.60	87.79	112.61	136.24	172.07	163.89
China	12.00	13.27	6.40	-11.90	7.66	1.62	7.24	34.44	31.64	15.67	20.52	17.41	35.42	45.87	68.66	158.62
Other emerging Asian countries[1]	-18.89	-16.96	-12.58	-15.23	-19.83	-32.06	-31.16	-18.04	17.36	30.34	20.12	16.89	26.06	29.39	23.78	-1.82
Emerging Eastern European countries[2]	-5.82	-7.57	-0.90	-12.86	4.43	-6.40	-17.78	-20.74	-17.49	-21.91	-28.30	-12.77	-18.42	-30.05	-45.54	-54.31
Other emerging countries[3]	-5.62	-2.91	-3.55	-18.40	-26.55	-43.68	-49.87	-63.82	-73.24	-45.33	-41.66	-32.40	0.24	12.44	10.56	0.13
Oil exporting countries[4]	-1.78	-77.44	-57.35	-48.83	-29.54	-0.06	28.37	9.07	-45.63	28.64	135.01	72.04	57.63	108.62	185.61	347.77

Source: IMF, 2006c.

Notes: [1] Other emerging Asian countries include India, Malaysia, Philippines, Thailand, and Vietnam.

[2] Emerging Eastern European countries include Bulgaria, Croatia, Czech Republic, Hungary, Poland, Romania, Slovak Republic, Turkey and Ukraine.

[3] Other emerging countries include Argentina, Bolivia, Brazil, Chile, Colombia, Costa Rica, Dominican Republic, Ecuador, Egypt, El Salvador, Jordan, Morocco, Pakistan, Panama, Paraguay, Peru, South Africa, Tunisia, and Uruguay.

[4] Oil exporting countries include Algeria, Angola, Azerbaijan, Bahrain, Congo, Equatorial Guinea, Gabon, Indonesia, Iran, Kazakhstan, Kuwait, Libya, Mexico, Nigeria, Oman, Qatar, Russia, Saudi Arabia, Turkmenistan, United Arab Emirates, Venezuela and Yemen.

than accounted for by the rapid increase in the surpluses of Japan and, especially, China that offset the disappearance of the surpluses of other countries in the region. Elsewhere, the EMCs in Eastern Europe saw their current account balances deteriorate rather sharply over this period, while those of countries in other parts of the world actually improved, largely reflecting the boom in commodity prices.

This pattern suggests that the US (in contrast to many other countries, notably those in Asia and Europe) has been unable to tap into the higher import demand that oil producers have generated. This is reflected in the decline in imports from the US as a share of the total imports of the oil exporting countries. Along with a more broad-based decline in the share of imports from the US in total imports for several Asian countries since 1999 (Figure 2.4), this has contributed to the continued worsening of the US current account balance. In the context of a long-term decline in the oil exporters' marginal propensity to import (Table 2.2), the declining share of imports from the US in their total imports has reduced the offset to higher oil prices in the trade balance of the US. To the extent that imports have been redirected to Europe and elsewhere, growth in those areas would be increased with positive implications for US exports. But that impact too has been limited as the overall propensity of the oil exporting countries to import has declined. The net effect then would seem to suggest a more difficult process of adjustment for the US than would otherwise be the case.

More generally, the oil exporters appear to be more cautious in judging the permanence of the recent price increases, perhaps, because of the unhappy experiences in earlier episodes wherein they expanded spending too rapidly, could not reverse that spending quickly, and suffered large fiscal and current account deficits and painful adjustment. This behaviour, in particular, is likely to further affect adversely the US current account balance and the impact could be substantial.

For example, the cumulative current account surplus of oil exporters in the Middle East and Central Asia[3] during 2003–05 was US$ 400 billion. During the same period, US$ 210 billion was saved by these countries through the accumulation of official

Figure 2.4   Imports from United States (as a share of total imports)

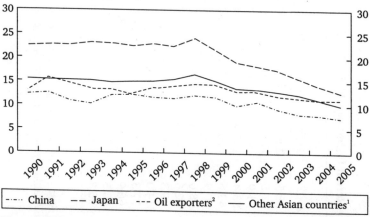

Notes: [1] Other Asian countries include India, Indonesia, Malaysia, Philippines, Thailand, and South Korea.
[2] Oil exporters include Algeria, Angola, Azerbaijan, Bahrain, Republic of Congo, Equatorial Guinea, Gabon, Indonesia, Iran, Iraq, Kazakhstan, Kuwait, Libya, Mexico, Nigeria, Oman, Qatar, Russia, Saudi Arabia, Turkmenistan, United Arab Emirates, Venezuela and Yemen.

Table 2.2   Marginal propensity to import[1]

	1973–75	*1978–81*	*2002–05*
GCC states	0.34	0.25	0.15
OPEC	0.52	0.42	0.24
Russia	1.37	1.08	0.2
Norway	–	–0.3	–0.13

Note: [1] Change in imports (net of non-oil exports) + investment income a per cent change in oil export revenues.

reserves, which reached US$ 360 billion at end-2005. An additional US$ 200 billion or more was registered in 'other asset accumulation' in the official sector[4] (Table 2.3). Similarly, the governments of oil exporting countries in the Middle East and

Table 2.3 Oil exporting countries: Current account balance and external financing[1] (US$ billion)

	2000	2001	2002	2003	2004	2005	2006 Projections
Current account balance	156.6	92.6	75.2	132.5	220.6	397.0	480.9
External financing	78.0	35.8	52.4	81.5	129.6	148.8	139.1
From official sector	5.7	−10.6	−20.7	−1.9	−9.9	−36.8	−11.9
From private sector	72.3	46.4	73.1	83.4	139.4	185.6	151.0
FDI	37.4	51.9	39.3	49.6	70.6	72.8	80.6
Portfolio equity	−0.4	−0.2	−0.1	−0.9	−4.4	2.3	−0.8
Bonds	−4.7	−0.3	−0.5	8.0	27.1	40.4	7.8
Bank loans	−2.3	−0.9	−5.6	−2.6	−2.8	−2.8	−0.9
Suppliers' credit and others	42.2	−4.1	40.0	29.3	49.0	72.9	64.3
External Asset Accumulation	234.6	128.4	127.6	214.0	350.2	545.8	620.0
By official sector, reserves	73.8	33.1	26.1	77.3	129.7	210.8	197.8
By official sector, other	44.2	22.5	8.7	66.9	105.0	124.5	202.3
By private sector, FDI	14.7	6.3	10.2	13.5	22.9	45.3	46.9
By private sector, other	102.0	66.5	82.7	56.3	92.5	165.1	173.0

Source: IMF, 2006c.

Note: [1] Oil exporting countries from the Middle East and Central Asia region including Algeria, Azerbaijan, Bahrain, Iran, Kazakhstan, Kuwait, Libya, Oman, Qatar, Saudi Arabia, Syria, Turkmenistan and the United Arab Emirates.

Central Asia saved, on an average, three-quarters of the increase in oil revenue accruing to their budgets since 2002,[5] while government spending as a share of GDP has declined.[6] As a result, the overall fiscal position of these countries changed from broad balance in 2002 to a surplus of 12 per cent of GDP in 2005 (Figure 2.5).

Figure 2.5   Oil exporting countries from the Middle East and Central Asia: Overall fiscal balance and public spendings[1] (% of GDP)

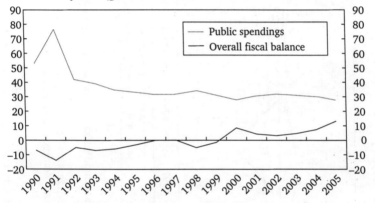

Source: IMF, 2006c.
Note: [1] Oil exporting countries from the Middle East and Central Asia including Algeria, Azerbaijan, Bahrain, Iran, Kazakhstan, Kuwait, Libya, Oman, Qatar, Saudi Arabia, Syria, Turkmenistan and the United Arab Emirates.

The corollary to the changing pattern of current account surpluses from some of the Asian countries and other non-oil exporting Emerging Market Countries (EMCs) to the oil exporters (Figure 2.6) is the changing pattern in the disposition of accumulating official international reserves (Figure 2.7).[7] This, too, could have implications for the adjustment process. Asian and other surplus countries rather reliably bought US securities, helping to finance the US current account deficit (without significant depreciation of the dollar) and the fiscal deficit

Figure 2.6 External current account balance (% of GDP)

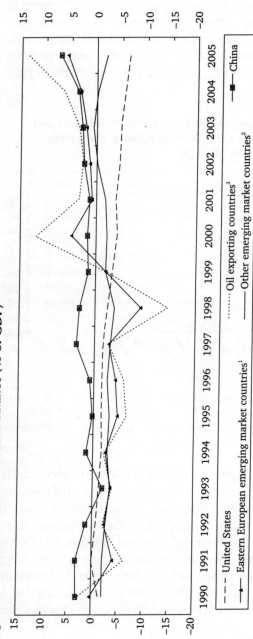

Source: IMF, 2006c.

Notes: [1] Eastern European emerging market countries include Bulgaria, Croatia, Czech Republic, Hungary, Poland, Romania, Slovak Republic, Turkey, Ukraine.

[2] Other emerging market countries include Argentina, Bolivia, Brazil, Chile, Colombia, Costa Rica, Dominican Republic, Ecuador, Egypt, El Salvador, Jordan, Morocco, Pakistan, Panama, Paraguay, Peru, South Africa, Tunisia, Uruguay.

[3] Oil exporting countries include Algeria, Angola, Azerbaijan, Bahrain, Congo, Equatorial Guinea, Gabon, Indonesia, Iran, Kazakhstan, Kuwait, Libya, Mexico, Nigeria, Oman, Qatar, Russia, Saudi Arabia, Turkmenistan, United Arab Emirates, Venezuela, Yemen.

Figure 2.7 Gross international reserves (US$ billion)

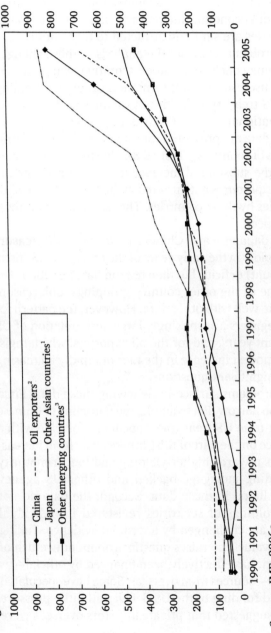

Source: IMF, 2006c.

Notes: [1] Other Asian countries include India, Angola, Malaysia, Philippines, Thailand and South Korea.
[2] Oil exporters include Algeria, Angola, Azerbaijan, Bahrain, Republic of Congo, Equatorial Guinea, Gabon, Indonesia, Iran, Iraq, Kazakhstan, Kuwait, Libya, Mexico, Nigeria, Oman, Qatar, Russia, Saudi Arabia, Turkmenistan, United Arab Emirates, Venezuela, and Yemen.
[3] Other emerging countries include Argentina, Bolivia, Brazil, Bulgaria, Chile, Colombia, Costa Rica, Croatia, Czech Republic, Dominican Republic, Ecuador, Egypt, El Salvador, Hungary, Jordan, Morocco, Pakistan, Panama, Paraguay, Peru, Poland, Romania, Slovak Republic, South Africa, Tunisia, Turkey, Ukraine, Uruguay.

(without significant increases in US interest rates). In the current environment, both economic and political, it is not clear that oil exporting countries are similarly attracted to that option.

Major data problems confront the analysis of these changing patterns, but some conclusions, albeit tentative, can be drawn. The commonly used source of information on official holdings of short-term US treasury securities by country is the so-called Treasury International Capital (TIC) data collected by the US treasury. Those data are presented for some individual countries and some groups of countries (Figure 2.8). One thing immediately evident is that the substantial increase in current account surpluses of the oil exporters is not mirrored in the accumulation of US treasury securities by those countries. That said, however, these data appear suspect.

In particular, Japanese and Chinese holdings of US treasury securities rise rapidly in the early years of the emerging US (fiscal and current account) deficits, but then remain flat after 2004. The patterns for some of the other country groupings look reasonable and correlate well with other data. However, the pattern for the UK, which registers a surprisingly large accumulation of US securities in recent years, and for the oil exporters, which registers only a very modest increase in the face of rapidly increasing surpluses, raise significant questions.

At least two problems surface in reviewing these data. First, the coverage is too narrow. For example, the flattening of Chinese holdings of short-term US treasuries appears to coincide with a shifting preference on the part of the Chinese away from increasing such holdings towards higher-yielding and longer-maturity securities, including mortgage-backed and other US agency securities not included in these data. Second, the data do not track well the holdings of securities registered in individual country data and are challenged by anecdotal evidence. Taking such data at face value also raises questions about how much of the US fiscal deficit has effectively been financed by official—as opposed to private—sources from overseas. Some have speculated that the continued funding of the US deficit with little pressure on interest rates suggested that private investors overseas were

Figure 2.8   Major foreign holders of treasury securities (holdings at the end of period, US$ billion)

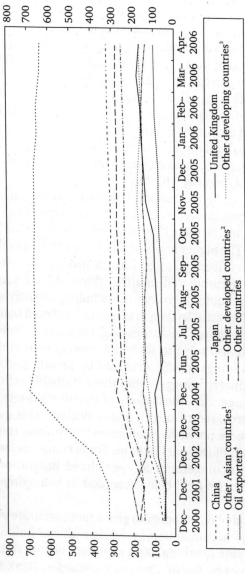

Source: Department of the Treasury, Federal Reserve Board (www.treas.gov/tic), 7/6/2006.

Notes: [1] Other Asian countries include Hong Kong, India, Korea, Singapore, Taiwan, and Thailand.
[2] Other developed countries include Belgium, Canada, France, Germany, Ireland, Israel, Italy, Luxembourg, Netherlands, Sweden, and Switzerland.
[3] Other developing countries include Bahamas, Bermuda, Brazil, Cayman Islands, Mexico, Netherlands Antilles, Panama, Poland, and Turkey.
[4] Oil exporters include Ecuador, Venezuela, Indonesia, Bahrain, Iran, Iraq, Kuwait, Oman, Qatar, Saudi Arabia, the United Arab Emirates, Algeria, Gabon, Libya and Nigeria.

stepping in as official purchases levelled off. This argument was bolstered by the high level of purchases by UK entities. However, this interpretation may have overstated the appetite of private investors overseas for acquiring US assets.

More recently, data have become available based on a new custody survey which shows the ultimate owner of securities. These custodial data show that in the 12 months through June 2005, for example, official purchases of US treasuries amounted to US\$ 339 billion. This is significantly higher than data from the TIC series, which indicated that official buying of US securities over the same period amounted to only US\$ 162 billion. The custodial data appear to explain most of the discrepancy between reported official reserve accumulations by individual countries and the accumulated monthly TIC data.

At the same time, while the custodial data show much higher levels of official accumulation of US assets, the broad total of foreign investment in US securities is roughly comparable in the two sets of data. The higher levels of official investment in the custodial data were offset by lower private investment when compared with the accumulated monthly flows. Also, foreign investment in highly liquid instruments, including treasury securities, is lower in the custodial data in favour of less liquid bonds (including mortgage-backed securities and corporate bonds). The new data would also seem to solve the mystery behind the large increase in holdings of US securities by private parties in the UK. In fact, analysts suggest that these probably reflect holdings by official agencies, most likely of the oil exporters in the Middle East, purchased through London dealers. This may be an example of a more pervasive problem in interpreting these data on the allocation of reserve holdings. Some countries have outsourced reserve management to specialized institutions, resulting in the securities held being recorded as belonging to those institutions.

In short, the custodial data appear to give a more accurate picture of US securities accumulation by foreign official holders. But they do not provide anything like a complete picture of the disposition of reserves by the oil exporting countries. Bank for

International Settlements (BIS) data help here. These data show a significant rise in oil exporters' deposits in BIS-reporting banks roughly coincident with the sharp rise in oil prices (Figure 2.9). In fact, deposits of oil exporters with BIS-reporting banks appear to be the main vehicle for the disposition of these exporters' surpluses. (That said, it should be noted that a significant, albeit still relatively minor, share of oil exporters' savings are reflected in corporate acquisitions). The large increases in deposits with BIS-reporting banks would seem to suggest a similarity between this and the earlier episodes of rapidly rising oil prices. During the earlier episodes of major increases in the price of oil, particularly in the 1970s, a large portion of the reserves of the oil exporters took the form of bank deposits that were then 'recycled' as bank lending, much of it to emerging and developing economies, especially in Latin America. This is the familiar story of the prelude to the debt crisis of the 1980s.

Figure 2.9 Gross external loans and deposits of BIS-reporting banks and oil prices

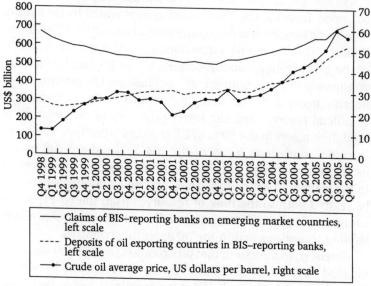

Claims of BIS–reporting banks on emerging market countries, left scale

---- Deposits of oil exporting countries in BIS–reporting banks, left scale

→ Crude oil average price, US dollars per barrel, right scale

Source: Bank for International Settlements (BIS) (2005), IMF (2005).

This time around, however, the evidence is not conclusive. On the one hand, the net liabilities (deposits minus lending) of BIS-reporting banks accruing to the oil exporting countries has increased rapidly in recent years (Figure 2.10)—indeed the increase in deposits of oil exporting countries in BIS-reporting banks accounts for more than 50 per cent of their total reserve accumulation during 2001 through 2005.[8] On the other hand, net claims (lending minus deposits) of BIS-reporting banks to the entire group of EMCs appears to remain almost flat. At the same time, however, lending by BIS-reporting banks to a selected group of EMCs, particularly in Eastern Europe, has increased sharply over the same time frame. Furthermore, it is possible that the rapid rise in net claims of BIS-reporting banks on the UK is indicative of institutions in that country being a conduit for oil exporters to secure greater exposure to EMCs.

To summarize, the US current account balance is likely to worsen further and the adjustment process made even more difficult as a result of the combined impact of the increase in oil prices and the relative decline in the propensity of oil exporters to import from the US. This is further aggravated by the caution of most oil exporters in increasing overall spending, including on imports. This, then, raises questions as to whether the financing of the US current account balance and the US fiscal deficit will continue unabated without an increase in US interest rates, notably because of the changing pattern in the accumulation of official reserves and the lower proclivity of oil exporters to hold their assets in the form of US treasury securities. The boom in equity markets in many of the EMCs, the sharp rise in real estate prices in some of those countries and the rapid increase in the activity of hedge funds and private equity firms may also be related both to the flow of resources from the oil exporting countries through the banks, as well as to direct purchases and lending by entities within the oil exporting countries.

Moreover, to the extent that oil exporters (and EMCs) are more inclined to use their reserves to purchase real assets by acquiring equity stakes through FDI, for example, it would be highly problematic for the unwinding of global imbalances if advanced

Figure 2.10   Net external loans and deposits of BIS-reporting banks (US$ billion)

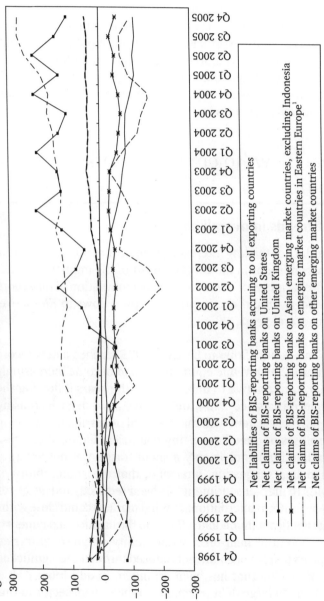

- - - - - Net liabilities of BIS-reporting banks accruing to oil exporting countries
– · – · – Net claims of BIS-reporting banks on United States
——■—— Net claims of BIS-reporting banks on United Kingdom
——*—— Net claims of BIS-reporting banks on Asian emerging market countries, excluding Indonesia
· · · · · · Net claims of BIS-reporting banks on emerging market countries in Eastern Europe[1]
———— Net claims of BIS-reporting banks on other emerging market countries

Source: Bank for International Settlements (2005).
Note: [1] Emerging market countries in Eastern Europe include Bulgaria, Croatia, Czech Republic, Hungary, Poland, Romania, Slovak Republic, Turkey, Ukraine.

economies, notably the US, were to succumb to the pressures of economic nationalism and limit access to real assets. For purposes of diversification, oil exporters and emerging market creditors will want to invest in assets other than government or corporate debt, such as 'South–North' FDI. If that is not politically feasible in the US on the scale required, oil exporters and EMCs are likely to explore other mature markets and also pursue greater 'South–South' FDI. It is to the changing world of capital flows to EMCs that this chapter now turns.

Capital flows to emerging market countries

Recent trends in overall capital flows

A by-product of the low interest rate environment and generous liquidity conditions in the US (and most of the industrial world) and, more recently, of the rapid asset accumulation of oil exporters, has been a rapid rise in private capital flows to EMCs over the past several years.

- Private capital flows to EMCs in 2005 reached a new record (Figure 2.11). While equity flows had become increasingly important relative to debt flows in the years following the Asian crisis since 2004, debt flows have been increasing rapidly, coincident with the rise in oil prices and the growing surpluses of the oil exporting countries (Figure 2.12).
- Net bond issuance is only a small fraction of net external financing, suggesting, *inter alia*, that the vulnerability of EMCs to market sentiment has been reduced, and access of many EMCs to international capital markets could close without significant immediate effects on the balance of payments. The potential near-term vulnerability of these countries appears to have been further reduced through the significant pre-financing that has been arranged. In add-ition, EMCs have made large debt payments to the official sector in the

Figure 2.11 Total capital flows to emerging market countries, 1990–2004 (US$ billion)

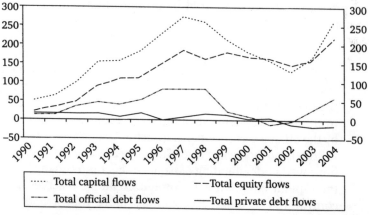

Source: World Bank (2005).

Figure 2.12 Total capital flows to emerging market countries, 1990–2004 (US$ billion)

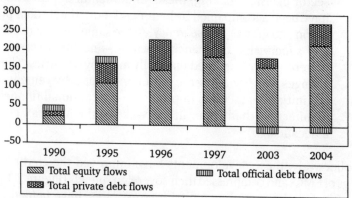

Source: World Bank (2005).

past two years, including to the IFIs and official bilateral creditors, especially the IMF and the Paris Club. This presumably implies increased access to such financing, especially from the IMF, should conditions in the global economy become less benign.

The rapid rise in capital flows to EMCs, driven, *inter alia*, by the quest for yield and the windfall gains associated with the rise in oil prices, has been supported by fundamental improvements in many of these countries. In particular:

- Since the Asian crisis, many EMCs have strengthened macroeconomic policy frameworks and improved their assessment and management of vulnerabilities. Moves towards more flexible exchange rate regimes, strengthened surveillance over financial systems, including in the context of efforts led by the official sector (Financial Sector Assessment Programs [FSAPs] and Financial Sector Stability Assessments [FSSAs]), improved understanding of balance sheet interlinkages and the rapid accumulation of foreign exchange reserves have contributed to making economies more robust and less vulnerable to crises.
- Fiscal management and overall fiscal performance have improved substantially in many EMCs (Figure 2.13).
- With the aim of improving the environment for private sector decision-making, these fundamental improvements have been accompanied by better and more timely data provision and greater transparency. At the same time, regulation and supervision of financial sectors—and the assessment thereof—have improved markedly in many countries. These changes may be among the most important achievements of the initiatives taken to improve the international financial architecture that began in the wake of the Mexican crisis a decade ago.

Collectively, these developments have improved the credit ratings of EMCs and compressed their sovereign spreads (Figure 2.14), which, together with low global interest rates, have helped reduce their debt and debt-service burdens (Figure 2.15). Capitalizing on these favourable trends, many EMCs have improved their overall debt management operations and capacity with a view to reducing exchange rate, interest rate and rollover risks.

In particular, sovereign debt as a share of GDP for a large (albeit not exhaustive) sub-group of EMCs has declined from

Figure 2.13 Emerging market countries: Overall fiscal balance and total international reserves

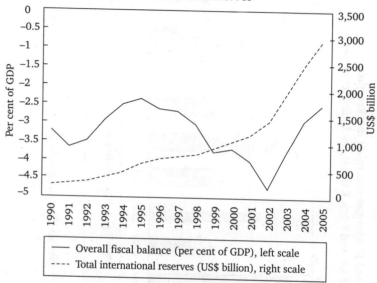

Source: IMF, 2006c.

44 per cent in 2002 to 39 per cent in 2004 (but this is still higher than the pre-Asian crisis level of 27 per cent).[9] Similarly, based largely on experiences gained from previous crises, EMCs have actively sought to reduce exposure to foreign exchange risk, notably by retiring/repaying international bonds and increasing issuance of domestic currency debt. As a result, for the sub-group of EMCs, external debt has declined to 10 per cent of GDP after peaking at 16 per cent in 1999. At the same time, the share of local-currency denominated bonds in marketable sovereign debt of EMCs in the sample increased by 9 percentage points between 1996 and 2004, to around 82 per cent. Furthermore, the maturity of EMCs' sovereign debt issues has increased in recent years. While international issuance has typically been in the form of fixed-rate medium-term bonds, the average maturity of international issuance by the EMCs in the sample has increased further to 13 years in 2005 from about 8 years in 2001.

Figure 2.14 Number of sovereign upgrades/downgrades and JP Morgan emerging market global sovereign spread 1990–2005[1,2] (by Moody's, S&P and Fitch Ratings, including changes to positive/negative outlooks)

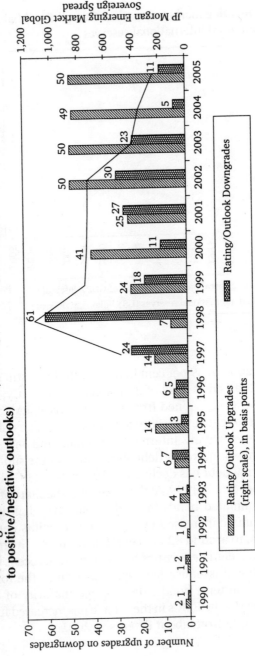

Source: Bloomberg (2006).

Notes: [1] Emerging Markets Bond Index Global (EMBIG) countries and Czech Republic, Estonia, India, Jamaica, Latvia, Lithuania, Romania, Slovakia, Slovenia.

[2] Long Term Foreign Currency.

Figure 2.15 Emerging market countries: External debt and debt services (% of GDP)

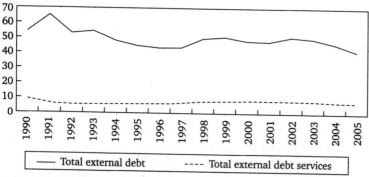

Source: IMF, 2006c.

These positive developments notwithstanding, it needs to be noted that benign external conditions may mask underlying balance sheet vulnerabilities. The recent turbulence in the equity markets, first in early-May and subsequently in June, has been a reminder on this score. The associated sell-off in EMCs appears mainly to have reflected an adjustment in the pricing of risk, not a wholesale reassessment of the fundamentals in these countries. In particular, in the first phase of the recent correction in markets, EMCs with significant investment flows and valuation gains and local markets with concentrated foreign investors' positions corrected strongly; however, in the second phase of the correction, some EMCs with better fundamentals suffered much less than those with weak fundamentals. In particular, EMCs with large current account deficits, reflecting domestic consumption-led growth, that were financed by portfolio inflows were the most seriously affected.

Clearly, some EMCs may be at risk. A number of countries in Eastern Europe, including the Baltic countries, have relatively large—and, in some cases, worsening—external imbalances that appear to be driven primarily by rapid credit growth to the private sector (a development characteristic of some of the countries in East Asia before the crisis of 1997). A few of these countries also have large fiscal deficits and have built up large short-term external debt positions, most of it in foreign currency, and large net international investment liabilities. A key question here is whether these developments have made these countries vulnerable to sudden stops in the flow of foreign capital. It is worth remembering that before the Asian crisis, some of the countries most seriously affected—like many of those currently in Eastern Europe—enjoyed good credit ratings, which then dropped sharply as foreign capital flows reversed.

Going forward, external risks—including an abrupt or unexpected rise in global interest rates, supply-side shocks to the oil markets, or a disorderly unwinding of global current account imbalances—could prove challenging. In face of such developments, the investors may increasingly differentiate among EMCs. In particular, as external financial conditions become less benign, EMCs with macro-economic imbalances and those that still rely heavily on external financing face a narrower margin for policy slippages. Similarly, EMCs that still have sizeable vulnerabilities in the fiscal position and/or public sector balance sheets are more susceptible to pressures in their external accounts and to crises more generally.

In addition, policy makers in both mature markets and in EMCs face renewed challenges. Central banks need to communicate effectively to financial markets their assessment of inflation risks and their resolve to contain inflation. Moreover, supervisors and financial institutions need to redouble their efforts to monitor and manage risk, especially counterparty risk *vis-à-vis* hedge funds, private equity firms, and those selling credit default swaps. Active debt management policies should continue as part of an overall plan to develop and strengthen local capital markets and deepen the institutional base.

Foreign direct investment in developing and emerging market countries

Notwithstanding the ever-present risks, most of the recent trends in emerging market financing are clearly welcome. They have improved the attractiveness of EMCs as an asset class, and have helped broaden the investor base towards more dedicated and longer-term investors. This is best reflected in the dramatic increase in FDI inflows to EMCs. In particular:

- FDI flows to EMCs have increased more than 10-fold from a modest US$ 20 billion in 1990 to about US$ 237 billion in 2005. This trend, however, masks the sharp decline in FDI flows to EMCs in the period following the Asian crises through 2003 and the equally dramatic rebound in 2004 and 2005.
- The increase in FDI flows to EMCs from US$ 162 billion in 2003 to US$ 237 billion in 2005 was part of the global increase in FDI to US$ 959 billion in 2005. However, the more noteworthy element in this context is that FDI (as well as capital flows more generally) between EMCs— South–South flows—are growing more rapidly than North– South FDI.
- Along with the increase in FDI, there has been a surge in external flows into the equity markets in EMCs. This has contributed to the unprecedented rise in market indices since the late 1990s (Figure 2.16).

A number of factors underpin the overall expansion of FDI, and equity flows more generally, into EMCs. These include the continued robust global economic growth and its offshoot in the commodity price boom; strong corporate profits in EMCs and the consequent reinvestment of a large proportion of those profits in the host country; the changing nature of the multinational corporation from home-country centric to what some call 'the globally integrated enterprise' (reflected, for example, in the greater willingness of multinational companies to fund research and development [R&D] in subsidiaries in the EMCs);[10] the much improved macro-economic climate in many of the EMCs; and the generally improved investment climate. These positive developments have been complemented by significant financial innovations, including structured financial instruments, such as credit default swaps and other derivatives, which have facilitated the management of risk exposure in the EMCs; the development of local financial markets that have created a synergy with FDI inflows; increased privatization and cross-border mergers and acquisitions; and the ongoing scramble for natural resources.

Figure 2.16 Selected emerging market countries: Stock market indices

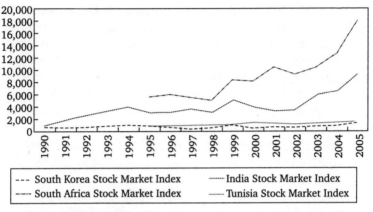

--- South Korea Stock Market Index   ······· India Stock Market Index
----- South Africa Stock Market Index   ········ Tunisia Stock Market Index

Source: Bloomberg (2006).

Notwithstanding the rapid increase in FDI flows to EMCs, there remains a significant concentration of flows to the top 10 recipient countries, which account for about 65 per cent of total FDI flows to EMCs (less than the 75 per cent of the late 1990s). While East Asia and the Pacific remain the largest regional destination for FDI, both Latin America and, even more so, the developing and emerging countries of Europe and Central Asia have seen a surge in FDI inflows, in the latter from about US$ 30 billion earlier in this decade to over US$ 75 billion in 2005. The Middle East, South Asia and Africa continue to attract only a modest share (about 15 per cent of the total), but that share has increased by over 50 per cent since 2000 and looks set to increase further.

As noted, an important feature of recent developments is the rapid increase in 'South–South' FDI flows. It is, however, important to underscore that the paucity of data and its imprecision limits the extent to which the trends, and the factors behind them, can be precisely identified. The *2006 Global Development Finance* Report does a good job in gathering information from numerous sources to try to describe recent developments in this area.[11]

- South–South FDI flows increased from US\$ 14 billion in 1995 to US\$ 47 billion in 2003, partly offsetting the decline in North–South FDI (from US\$ 130 billion in 1999 to US\$ 82 billion in 2003), and raising the share of South–South FDI in total FDI to developing countries from 16 per cent to 36 per cent over that period.[12] These flows easily dominate both syndicated bank lending and cross-border equity listings between developing countries.

- These changes are driven by many of the same factors that have led to closer integration across much of the globe in the last decade.[13] For example, the majority of developing countries—led by the EMCs—have become more open to foreign investment over the past 10 years. But these changes also reflect the increasing share of world trade that takes place between developing countries (up from 15 per cent to 26 per cent of total world trade between 1991 and 2004) and the even more rapid growth of trade between developing countries within the same region—spurred, in part, by the explosion in regional trade arrangements.[14] The evidence suggests that FDI follows, or at least runs parallel, with trade.[15]

- It is also likely that, and as the 2006 *Global Development Finance* Report notes, 'Developing country multinationals enjoy some advantages over industrial country firms when investing in developing countries because of their greater familiarity with technology and business practices suitable for developing-country markets'. In fact, the forces driving South–South FDI appear sufficiently powerful to overcome the greater impediments sometimes faced by developing country multinationals in their home country, including bureaucratic and financial constraints on outward investment.

While South–South FDI has increased rapidly in recent years, it has, like FDI more broadly, remained fairly highly concentrated among a group of countries that account for the bulk of such flows.

Moreover, it has generally been the case that South–South FDI tends to be between developing countries within the same region. More recently, however, China, India and some other developing countries are breaking this mould as the search for natural resources becomes a more and more important motivation for FDI. In 2004, for example, fully one-half of China's outward FDI was directed towards natural resource projects in Latin America. In China, and increasingly in other developing countries, these results are being driven, in part, by the increasing role played by state enterprises, or by inducements provided by export-import banks and various subsidy mechanisms, in the search for natural resources. As the search for oil and for resources in the non-oil mining sectors increases, this broadening of South–South FDI beyond the usual regional constraints is likely to continue, further increasing the competition by investors in these sectors. Moreover, countries that are significant oil and gas producers are investing heavily in other developing countries as they integrate their downstream operations such as refining, distribution and retailing.

Issues for consideration

The changed profile of capital flows, induced in part by the investment preferences of the oil exporting countries, and by their apparent caution in increasing spending in pace with the higher oil revenues, poses a number of critical questions like:

- Will the ability of the US to finance its fiscal deficit with only modest changes in interest rates and in the exchange rate of the dollar be compromised by the apparent investment preferences of oil exporters?
- Has the adjustment required to reduce the US current account deficit been made more difficult? Has this increased the possibility of a hard landing in the global economy?

The emerging pattern of capital flows in the global economy, including the substantial increase in flows through the international banks, raises the spectre of a repeat of the problems that developed in the wake of the recycling of the 1970s or the crises in East Asia following the credit boom of the mid-1990s. For sure, the fundamentals in many of the EMCs appear much stronger now than was the case during those earlier periods, but there are regions that look vulnerable, including Eastern Europe, and there are risks that may be little understood, especially from the exploding use of new and innovative financial instruments.

- Should these developments be viewed with concern?
- Are the monitoring mechanisms in place sufficient to encourage better risk analysis than was the case in earlier periods?
- Again, are there elements in these developments that could increase the possibility of a hard landing if the needed adjustments to the underlying imbalances are not made quickly and in an orderly manner?

While the increased flows of FDI to EMCs, including the rapid growth of South–South flows, are to be welcomed from many perspectives, the possible risks in these developments should not be ignored.

- Are there political/strategic risks from the increasing competition to secure natural resources? For example, will the kind of tensions and competition that was seen between the US—or the West, more generally—and the former Soviet Union, which gave rise to so much proxy conflict in Africa, arise again as the countries seeking natural resource supplies confront each other in the (oil and non-oil) resource-rich states?
- Are there risks to the initiatives of recent years to pressure developing and EMCs to improve their governance? For example, does Angola care any more about this pressure— if it ever did—when China alone has loaned the country US$ 3 billion in the two years to early 2006, and as most oil companies continue to resist calls for greater transparency in their operations in these countries?

Acknowledgement

Thanks are due to Krishna Srinivasan and Ivetta Hakobyan, both of the IMF, for their very helpful assistance with this chapter.

Notes

1. The definition of EMCs used in this chapter includes Argentina, Bolivia, Brazil, Bulgaria, Chile, China (PRC), Colombia, Costa Rica, Croatia, Czech Republic, Dominican Republic, Ecuador, Egypt, El Salvador, Hungary, India, Indonesia, Jordon, Malaysia, Mexico, Morocco, Pakistan, Panama, Paraguay, Peru, Philippines, Poland, Romania, Russia, Slovak Republic, South Africa, Thailand, Tunisia, Turkey, Ukraine, Uruguay, Venezuela and Vietnam.
2. This is the task recently charged to the IMF in the multilateral consultations that were carried out in 2006 and were reported at the IMF's Annual Meetings in Singapore in September 2006. The conclusions coming out of those discussions and the policy choices made thereafter will have important implications for the extent to which the needed adjustment in the global imbalances will be more or less orderly.
3. Oil exporters from the Middle East and Central Asia region include Algeria, Azerbaijan, Bahrain, Iran, Iraq, Kazakhstan, Kuwait, Libya, Oman, Qatar, Saudi Arabia, Syria, Turkmenistan and the United Arab Emirates (UAE). These oil exporters have witnessed particularly rapid increases in their current account balances, official reserves, and in other asset accumulation in the official sector.
4. This is a murky area, but 'other asset accumulation' is believed to include oil stabilization funds, so-called funds for future generations, and the like. Inclusion of figures for Russia and Norway would result in significant increases in these figures. Russia's gold and foreign exchange reserves total more than US$ 300 billion and there are reported to be well over US$ 100 billion additional resources in a separate reserve fund designed to provide budgetary support in the event of a downturn in oil revenues.
5. Measured as the ratio of the increase in the fiscal balance to the increase in the government's oil revenues.
6. In this context, it should be noted that policy advice from the IMF has underscored the importance of increasing spending on projects with high returns, particularly infrastructure, including with a view to help reduce global imbalances.

7. As noted, estimates of oil exporters' foreign exchange reserves do not generally give a full and fair account of the current account surpluses that are accruing. This is because, while they include accruals to formal central bank reserves, they do not include increased holdings in oil stabilization or investment funds or accounts of other official agencies or institutions.
8. The remainder has likely taken the form of greater holdings of the US treasury and agency securities, including through dealers in the UK (as noted above) and, a variety of other investments, including in regional equity markets, and debt repayments.
9. See IMF, 2006c.
10. Palmisano (IBM).
11. As data are scarce, the report calculates South-South FDI as a residual, subtracting FDI outflows from high income to developing countries from total FDI inflows to developing countries.
12. Paucity of data does not enable a further disaggregation to analyze South–South FDI flows, although the bulk of the flows appear to be to EMCs.
13. By one measure, the vast majority of developing countries—76 out of a total of 84 rated developing countries—have become more open to FDI, both inward and outward flows, in the past 10 years.
14. From 2000 to 2004, South–South trade grew at an annual rate of 17.6 per cent, faster than South–North and North–South exports (12.6 per cent and 9.7 per cent, respectively [IMF, 2006a]).
15. By way of example, while 30 per cent of all FDI in telecommunications in developing countries was south–south, more than 85 per cent of that was inter-regional.

Bibliography

Bank for International Settlements (BIS). 2005. *BIS Annual Statistics.* Basel, Switzerland: BIS.

———. 2006. Annual Report 2005–2006, June. Basel, Switzerland: BIS.

Bloomberg. 2006. http://www.bloomberg.com. Last accessed: July 2006.

International Monetary Fund (IMF). 2005. International Financial Statistics, Annual Year Book 2005. Washington, DC: IMF.

———. 2006a. 'Global Financial Stability Report (GFSR)', April 2006. Washington, DC: IMF.

———. 2006b. *Regional Economic Outlook: Middle East and Central Asia,* May 2006. Washington, DC: IMF.

International Monetary Fund (IMF). 2006c. *World Economic Outlook (WEO)*. Washington, DC: IMF.

———. 2006d. 'Who's Buying Treasuries?' *World Economic Outlook (WEO)*, 16 May. Washington, DC: IMF.

Stephen King. 2006. *Global Imbalances: Economic Myth and Political Reality: The U.S. Current Account Deficit, 16th Century Spain and 21st Century China*. Hong Kong: HSBC Global Research.

United States Department of the Treasury. 2006. Federal Reserve Board Bulletin, 6 July 2006, Washington, DC. Available at http://www.treas.gov/tic.

World Bank. 2005. *Global Development Finance*. Washington, DC: World Bank.

Private Capital Flows to Emerging Market Economies: Major Drivers, Recent Developments and Key Issues

3

V. SUNDARARAJAN AND HARINDER S. KOHLI

Introduction

The chapter presents data on developments in inward private capital flows—Foreign Direct Investment (FDI), portfolio equity, portfolio debt and bank financing—to Emerging Market Economies (EMEs) and outlines their major structural and macroeconomic determinants. It focuses mainly on portfolio flows and FDI, with only a limited coverage of bank financing. Drawing on recent developments, selected key issues in managing private capital flows are highlighted in the concluding section.

Definition of EMEs and data on capital flows

There is no single, universally accepted definition of EMEs. We have chosen a broad definition that is used by major investors and their supporting agencies such as those who construct stock indices for various categories of countries. A full list and explanation of EMEs used by us is given in Annex 1 of this chapter.

The data reported here is from a comprehensive economic and social database maintained by the Centennial Group. The underlying data in this database is, in turn, drawn primarily from the Balance of Payment Statistics reported in International Monetary Fund's *International Financial Statistics* (*IFS*), supplemented by country sources, where available, in cases where *IFS* data is incomplete. In addition, we have consulted 2006 *Global Development Finance* (*GDF*) published by the World Bank; information missing these global databases was derived from the respective central banks. The definitions used and their relationship to other commonly used data sources are briefly noted in Annex 2 of this chapter.

Background and motivation

Net inward private capital flows to EMEs have risen sharply in recent years, while exhibiting significant period-to-period volatility. Some components of capital flows have been more volatile than others. Also, capital flows into some regions have been more volatile than in others.

In 1996–97, just before the onset of the Asian financial crisis, net inward private capital flows averaged US$ 284 billion per annum. The size of these flows fell in 1998 to US$ 160 billion, due to reversals in both portfolio flows and bank lending. It rebounded significantly to US$ 254 billion (annual average) during the global equity boom in 1999–2000. It fell again in 2001–02, when the equity boom collapsed, and since then has risen sharply to an annual average in excess of US$ 400 billion in 2003–05.

Asia, which witnessed largest growth in the inflow compared to other regions, also seems to have experienced the greatest volatility. Portfolio and bank inflows show much greater volatility than FDI. Both portfolio and FDI seem concentrated in regions and countries, while significant shifts in regional shares seem to be occurring over time. The size, volatility and direction of these flows pose important challenges for policy makers, besides raising important questions for private investors as well. In addition to the challenges posed by massive capital inflows for the conduct of monetary policy, the volatility associated with these flows poses risk management challenges for both the private and public sectors. The issue of how best to mobilize stable capital flows, while ensuring resilience to unavoidable fluctuations in capital movements, is a continuing policy challenge for which country experiences are beginning to provide broad guidance.

The chapter aims to briefly summarize as best as possible the underlying forces determining the pattern of inward private capital flows to EMEs, and their components, drawing on recent official reports and academic studies on the subject, and on that basis, presents some issues for discussion and analysis.

Organization of the chapter

The chapter is organized as follows after this introductory section:

- The section on 'Trends in Private Capital Inflows' presents data on capital flows and sketches out important features of private capital flows and their components, including their growth, volatility and relative importance of different forms of capital flows.
- The section on 'Developments During 2005' highlights developments during 2005, when private capital flows to EMEs reached a new high.
- The section on 'Determinants of Portfolio Equity Flows' assesses and reviews some of the determinants of private capital inflows. In addition, it reviews recent reports and studies on developments in private capital flows, and the structural and financial policy responses by various countries.
- Finally, in the section titled 'Summary of Issues', several key issues for discussion—including the emergence and rapid growth in Islamic fixed income securities—are highlighted.
- In addition, at the end of the chapter, a series of graphs and tables present the detailed data (by types of capital flows and by five regions for the period 1990–2005) on which the report is based.

Trends in private capital inflows

The overall size and regional trends in private capital inflows— sum of FDI inflows, net inflows of portfolio debt and equity, and net bank financing, all flows as defined in Annex 1—are first reviewed, before discussing individual components of private capital flows.

During 2003–05, a cumulative US$ 1,200 billion (4 per cent of GDP) of private capital flowed into EMEs, compared to US$ 720 billion (3 per cent of GDP) during 2000–02 (Tables 3.1 and 3.2 and Figures 3.1 to 3.3). The surge in capital inflows that began in 2002 continued through 2005. Since 2001, the shift away from bank-based capital inflows towards portfolio inflows seems to have accelerated, and the share of portfolio flows in total inflows has risen sharply to 34 per cent during 2003–05 compared to 16 per cent in 2000–02. Although the growth in portfolio debt has gathered momentum due to the coming on stream of a range of structural reforms in EMEs, the growth in portfolio equity has outpaced the growth in debt. While all regions have benefited from the revival of demand for emerging markets assets, emerging Europe and Asia have captured much of the recent growth in inflows.

Historic evolution of portfolio equity, portfolio debt, FDI and bank financing by region (Americas, Asia, including Central Asia, Middle-East, Europe and Africa) since 1990 are shown in billions of dollars and as percentage of GDP in Table 3A(2)2 to Table 3A(2)6 and Figure 3.4 to Figure 3.8.

Asia continues to dominate in the amount of capital inflows—both FDI and portfolio inflows—with Europe and Latin America also showing significant revival since 2003, after several years of decline in inflows. Portfolio equity inflows in particular rose sharply in Latin America in 2005, while Europe experienced particularly sharp increases in portfolio debt since 2002. Both these regions have also shown strong recovery in FDI since 2002. Middle-East and Africa also attracted both portfolio investment and FDI, but the size and growth of the flows were quite small relative to other regions. The recent sharp upsurge in oil prices seems to have led to increased private investment in oil export countries during 2006 and 2007, but data to confirm this is not yet available.

In reviewing the historic evolution of capital flows, it is useful to focus on different sub-periods corresponding to different degrees

Table 3.1 Total private capital inflows by region, 1990–2005

Total capital inflows (US$ billion)	1990	1991	1992	1993	1994	1995	1996	1997	1998	1999	2000	2001	2002	2003	2004	2005
Africa	1.0	1.3	4.0	2.8	7.3	8.9	7.7	17.1	12.9	14.1	7.4	5.2	1.9	-0.8	11.7	19.0
Americas	32.6	39.4	49.2	89.3	94.6	39.0	90.8	105.0	94.1	86.9	75.9	55.5	40.8	37.1	51.3	69.6
Asia	18.4	32.6	47.7	91.1	101.1	118.6	142.9	99.3	11.1	121.5	146.4	155.3	130.8	168.5	257.5	263.0
Europe	-3.9	-0.7	5.7	17.6	2.8	34.7	30.7	48.8	26.8	24.9	15.3	7.9	50.7	62.7	94.1	133.2
Middle-East	-0.4	0.4	10.5	6.1	6.3	0.1	0.7	24.9	15.2	8.4	8.4	11.1	8.0	11.6	8.6	10.6
Total EMF	**47.6**	**72.9**	**117.0**	**206.9**	**212.0**	**201.2**	**272.8**	**295.2**	**160.0**	**255.7**	**253.4**	**235.2**	**232.2**	**279.2**	**423.2**	**495.4**

Total Capital Flow/GDP (%)	1990	1991	1992	1993	1994	1995	1996	1997	1998	1999	2000	2001	2002	2003	2004	2005
Africa	0.4	0.5	1.4	1.0	2.7	2.9	2.4	5.3	4.1	4.5	2.3	1.7	0.6	-0.2	2.4	3.3
Americas	3.1	3.6	4.1	6.8	6.3	2.4	5.2	5.5	4.9	5.2	4.1	3.1	2.6	2.3	2.7	3.1
Asia	1.2	2.0	2.7	4.7	4.4	4.3	4.7	3.2	0.4	3.9	4.3	4.5	3.5	4.0	5.4	4.9
Europe	-0.4	-0.1	0.6	2.0	0.3	3.7	3.1	4.9	3.0	3.2	1.8	0.9	4.9	5.0	5.9	6.7
Middle-East	-0.1	0.2	3.4	1.6	1.6	0.0	0.1	4.5	2.9	1.5	1.3	1.8	1.3	1.7	1.1	1.1
Total EMF	**1.1**	**1.7**	**2.6**	**4.3**	**4.0**	**3.3**	**4.1**	**4.3**	**2.5**	**4.0**	**3.6**	**3.3**	**3.2**	**3.4**	**4.4**	**4.4**

Sources: Centennial Group, IMF (*IFS* and *World Economic Outlook* [*WEO*]), World Bank (*World Development Indicators* [*WDI*] and *GDF*), Central Banks of India, Indonesia and Taiwan, Hong Kong Monetary Authority, Singapore Department

Table 3.2   **Index of openness to capital flows for selected countries**

	1985–90	*1991–96*	*1997–98*	*1999–2000*
Argentina	0.75	0.43	0.42	0.46
Brazil	1	1	0.88	0.85
Chile	1	1	1	0.923
Colombia	1	0.97	0.84	0.85
Ecuador	0.68	0.5	0.46	0.42
Mexico	0.92	0.84	0.83	0.84
LATIN AMERICA				
Hong Kong	0.08	0.08	0.08	0.231
India	0.92	0.92	0.92	0.92
Korea	0.85	0.85	0.81	0.77
Malaysia	0.85	0.85	0.81	0.77
Philippines	0.92	0.88	0.85	0.85
Singapore	0.23	0.23	0.35	0.42
ASIA				
Turkey	0.85	0.64	0.75	0.75
South Africa	0.86	0.89	0.84	0.84

Source: Miniane (2004).

of openness to capital flows into EMEs. Prior to 1990, only a few emerging markets were open to foreign investment. Roughly from 1991 to 1996, there was a progressive opening of equity markets by EMEs, resulting in large inflows during that period. There followed a period of crisis in 1997–98 in the aftermath of the devaluation of the Thai Baht. Finally, there is the current period (1999 onwards) of substantial opening and large capital flows into emerging markets in all regions. Table 3.2 shows the index of openness for selected countries constructed by Miniane (2004) by averaging the information on the existence (scored as 1), or absence (scored as 0) of controls in 13 categories of capital account restrictions published in IMF's Annual Report on Exchange Arrangements and Exchange Restrictions (AREAER), and also including the existence or absence of multiple exchange rate arrangements (treated as a form of capital control). While data in Table 3.2 only shows the evolution of capital controls during 1985–2000, more recent information from AREAER

Figure 3.1   Total capital flows into EMEs (US$ billion)

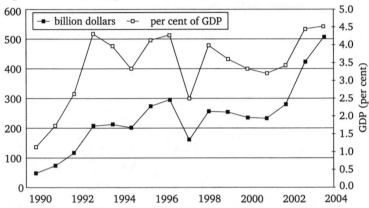

Sources: Centennial Group, International Monetary Fund's (IMF), *IFS*,
Central Banks of Taiwan, India and Indonesia, Monetary Author-
ity of Hong Kong, Singapore Department of Statistics, CEIC,
World Bank (*Global Development Finance* [*GDF*]) and United
Nations Conference on Trade and Development (UNCTAD).

**Figure 3.2   Capital flows into emerging markets, by type
(US$ billion)**

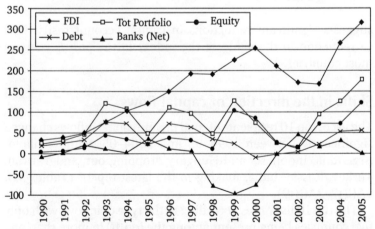

Sources: Centennial Group, IMF (*IFS* and *WEO*), World Bank (*WDI* and
GDF), Central Banks of India, Indonesia and Taiwan, Hong Kong
Monetary Authority, Singapore Department of Statistics, CEIC
and UNCTAD.

Figure 3.3 Total capital inflows as per cent GDP, by emerging market region (%)

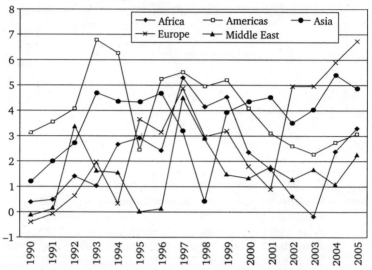

Sources: Centennial Group, IMF (*IFS* and *WEO*), World Bank (*WDI* and *GDF*), Central Banks of India, Indonesia and Taiwan, Hong Kong Monetary Authority, Singapore Department of Statistics, CEIC and UNCTAD.

suggests significant reductions in capital account restrictions (a reduction in the value of the index) in the past 5 years in most countries.

Shifts in the direction of capital flows

The list of top 10 recipients of total private capital inflows changed significantly between 1994–95 and 2004–05, with Thailand, Argentina, Indonesia and Hungary dropping out, and Taiwan, Turkey, Russia, India, making in the latest top 10 (Tables 3.3, 3A(2)7–3A(2)9).

The top 10 list varies according to the type of inflow, with only five countries being present among the top 10 in more than one category of capital inflows (Hong Kong in FDI, equity and bank financing; India in equity and bank financing; China in FDI and equity; Russia in FDI, debt and bank financing; Korea in equity and debt). As a group, European countries are among the top 10 in both debt and bank financing.

As an indicator of a reduction in the extent of concentration of capital inflows, the share of top three countries in total inflows has fallen significantly for all categories of capital flows. For example, the share of top three countries in global portfolio inflows into EMEs fell from 63 per cent in 1994–95 to 33 per cent during 2004–05. This confirms that after having been concentrated in about a dozen countries until the mid-1990s, private capital flows are now benefiting a much larger set of emerging markets as a result of policy and institutional reforms in the recipient countries and the much greater appetite among international institutional investors for investments in emerging markets (Table 3.3).

Growth, volatility and concentration of capital inflows

Table 3.4 presents long-term trends in different types of capital inflows and their relative shares. The long-term trends in the size of various types of private capital flows is illustrated at the end of this chapter in Tables 3A(2)10–3A(2)12 where inflows during various sub-periods are presented for different EME regions.

Table 3.3 Top 10 countries: Total private capital inflows

1994–95	US$ billion	2004–05	US$ billion
Brazil	33.6	China (PRC): Mainland	85.2
China (PRC): Mainland	32.5	China, P.R.: Hong Kong	48.3
Thailand	16.9	Taiwan, China	27.4
China, P.R.: Hong Kong	16.3	Turkey	23.9
Korea	15.2	Korea	23.4
Argentina	14.4	Russia	23.3
Singapore	13.1	India	23.1
Indonesia	8.5	Singapore	21.9
Mexico	7.0	Mexico	19.5
Hungary	5.8	Brazil	19.4

Sources: Centennial Group, IMF (*IFS* and *WEO*), World Bank (*WDI* and *GDF*), Central Banks of India, Indonesia and Taiwan, Hong Kong Monetary Authority, Singapore Department of Statistics, CEIC and UNCTAD.

Table 3.4 Total private capital inflows by type (US$ billion), 1990–2005

Emerging market total	1990	1991	1992	1993	1994	1995	1996	1997	1998	1999	2000	2001	2002	2003	2004	2005
FDI	32.7	38.5	49.1	75.0	102.5	120.6	149.8	192.4	190.9	225.1	254.1	210.5	170.7	167.0	265.7	315.7
Total Portfolio	23.4	31.3	46.8	120.7	107.1	45.1	110.5	96.8	46.5	127.6	74.0	25.2	15.3	94.9	125.4	177.8
Equity	4.3	6.3	14.0	45.1	34.7	22.2	38.2	32.8	11.4	104.2	85.8	27.4	11.5	72.4	72.1	122.7
Debt	19.1	24.9	32.8	75.6	72.4	22.9	72.3	64.0	35.1	24.3	−9.7	−1.6	3.9	22.6	53.3	55.7
Banks (Net)	−8.5	3.1	21.1	11.3	2.4	35.4	12.6	6.0	−77.4	−97.0	−74.6	−0.5	46.2	17.3	32.1	2.0
Total Capital Inflows	47.6	72.9	117.0	206.9	212.0	201.2	272.8	295.2	160.0	255.7	253.4	235.3	232.2	279.2	423.2	495.4

Sources: Centennial Group, IMF (*IFS* and *WEO*), World Bank (*WDI* and *GDF*), Central Banks of India, Indonesia and Taiwan, Hong Kong Monetary Authority, Singapore Department of Statistics, CEIC and UNCTAD.

FDI inflows nearly doubled during 2003–05, with Asia and Europe absorbing most of the growth in inflows. Figure 3.4 shows trend in FDI flows in different regions between 1990 and 2005.

Recent FDI growth was driven in particular by investments in oil rich countries (Russia, Kazakhstan and Azerbaijan), in EU accession countries (Czech Republic, Poland, Hungary), and in minerals resources in Latin America and Africa.

Nonetheless, Asia continued to dominate, with China alone absorbing 25 per cent of total global FDI inflows in 2005, reflecting in part increases in foreign investments in the banking sector. Growth in FDI in India was modest in 2005, returning to the level reached in 2002, with its share in global FDI flows falling slightly. Based on anecdotal evidence, India appears to have done much better in 2006.

After several years of declines in FDI inflows into Latin America, there was finally a reversal for the better in the last 2 years, in response to both policy reforms within the countries and rising

Figure 3.4   Foreign direct investment (US$ billion)

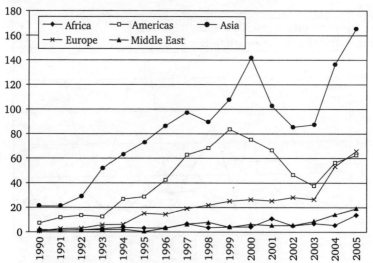

Sources: Centennial Group, IMF (*IFS* and *WEO*), World Bank (*WDI* and *GDF*), Central Banks of India, Indonesia and Taiwan, Hong Kong Monetary Authority, Singapore Department of Statistics, CEIC and UNCTAD.

international demand for commodities. Africa too witnessed a significant expansion in FDI, although from a much small base. South Africa recorded nearly five-fold increase in direct investment, mainly due to large acquisitions in the banking and mobile phone sectors. Elsewhere in Africa, investments in mineral resources, including from other emerging markets, were an important factor.

Portfolio capital inflows recovered strongly after the 1997 financial crisis to a high of US$127 billion (2 per cent of GDP) in 1999. Figure 3.5 shows portfolio flows by region between 1990 and 2005. These declined to an all-time low of US$15 billion in 2002 in the midst of the global equity price collapse. Since then they have recovered strongly to a new peak of over US$178 billion in 2005, with Asia contributing to most of the recent growth. A near tripling of equity inflows into Europe, and a return of foreign investments into the local equity markets in Latin America also played an important role (Figure 3.6). Despite the volatility

Figure 3.5 Total portfolio (US$ billion)

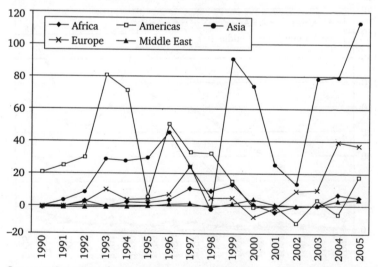

Sources: Centennial Group, IMF (*IFS* and *WEO*), World Bank (*WDI* and *GDF*), Central Banks of India, Indonesia and Taiwan, Hong Kong Monetary Authority, Singapore Department of Statistics, CEIC and UNCTAD.

of these flows, their share in total private capital flows seems to be on the rise.

Portfolio inflows as well as bank inflows (Figure 3.7) exhibit substantial volatility, with FDI flows remaining relatively stable. While the volatility of portfolio debt inflows and that of FDI declined since 2000 with increased openness of the economies, volatility in portfolio equity and bank financing has remained high. For portfolio debt, in particular, there is some evidence that widespread adoption of active debt management by issuers and financial innovations in the EME debt markets together could reduce debt market volatility—in terms of both financing volumes and risk spreads. Continued reforms of local equity markets should also lead to more resilient and less volatile portfolio equity flows in due course.

Both portfolio capital flows and FDI tend to be concentrated regionally, although some shifts in regional shares are surfacing, reflecting greater global competition for resources and broader adoption of policies to enhance access to foreign capital

Figure 3.6 Equity (US$ billion)

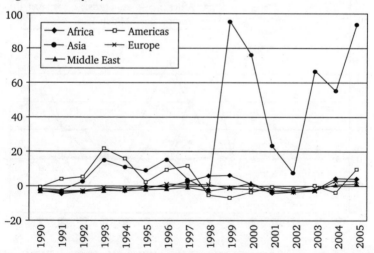

Sources: Centennial Group, IMF (*IFS* and *WEO*), World Bank (*WDI* and *GDF*), Central Banks of India, Indonesia and Taiwan, Hong Kong Monetary Authority, Singapore Department of Statistics, CEIC and UNCTAD.

(Tables 3A(2)13–3A(2)23). Subsequent to reforms undertaken in the aftermath of the 1997 crisis, a progressively larger share of portfolio capital inflows has been drawn into Asia, in part reflecting both improved macro-economic fundamentals as well as structural reforms to strengthen capital markets, with the share in Latin America falling until 2004. The share of Europe in portfolio capital has recovered particularly strongly following several years of declines. Nevertheless the dominance of China (PRC), Hong Kong (China) and Taipei China together is striing. All three economies are on the top 10 list and together accounted for 34.5 per cent of total portfolio capital flows into EMEs in 2005.

A major recent development in FDI flows is the emergence of emerging market investors as an important factor. While detailed data is still hard to find on country-to-country flows of sector-specific FDI by country, overall data—from UNCTAD, for example—suggests perhaps as much as 35–40 per cent of FDI

Figure 3.7   Debt (US$ billion)

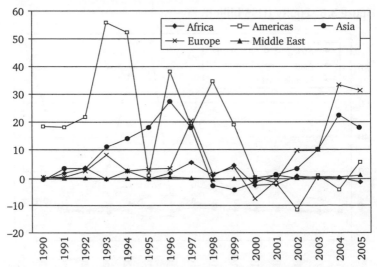

Sources: Centennial Group, IMF (*IFS* and *WEO*), World Bank (*WDI* and *GDF*), Central Banks of India, Indonesia and Taiwan, Hong Kong Monetary Authority, Singapore Department of Statistics, CEIC and UNCTAD.

may be from other emerging markets. Two other chapters in this book (Chapter 4 and Chapter 5) discuss this development in greater length.

Gross syndicated bank lending to developing countries rose by about 74 per cent in 2005, and by 64 per cent in net (of amortization) terms, according to World Bank's GDF 2006 report, with significant expansion reported in Europe and Asia. For the EMEs considered in this chapter, and using the measure of net bank financing flows (net inflows of bank financing into EMEs minus net outflows of bank financing from the EMEs, including resident outflows), net bank financing declined in 2005 after a rapid rise in 2004. The decline in 2005 was on account of large net outflows from the banking system in China (PRC), Hong Kong (China), Taipei China, Malaysia, Mexico, Czech Republic and Israel, which offset large inflows of bank financing into Europe (Russia, Hungary, Romania, Bulgaria, Croatia, Turkey, Ukraine), parts of Asia (India, Korea, Kazakhstan) and Saudi Arabia.

Figure 3.8   Banks (Net, US$ billion)

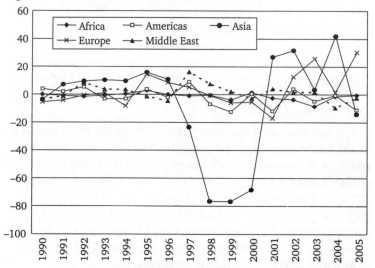

Sources: Centennial Group, IMF (*IFS* and *WEO*), World Bank (*WDI* and
GDF), Central Banks of India, Indonesia and Taiwan, Hong Kong
Monetary Authority, Singapore Department of Statistics, CEIC
and UNCTAD. Pre-1998 data does not include Hong Kong.

In sum, in the period since 1999, developments in private capital inflows show the following patterns of behaviour:

- A massive growth in volumes, particularly since 2002.
- Significant shifts in regional and country composition of private capital inflows.
- Increasing access to private capital flows among a larger number of countries, and a steady decline in the share of top recipient countries.
- Still significant concentration of capital flows in both among and within regions.
- Growing importance of portfolio capital relative to other forms of capital inflows.
- Emergence of 'south-to-south' investments as an important factor.
- Some reduction in the significant historic volatility, with the recent emergence of many structural factors that could further dampen volatility.

Developments during 2005

During 2005, our group of EMEs saw a record amount of private capital inflows totalling US$ 495 billion equivalent to 4.4 per cent of GDP. This represented an increase of US$ 72 billion, or 17 per cent over 2004.

The increase is all the more impressive in the three relatively more stable sources of private finance—FDI, portfolio equity and debt flows—while bank lending showed a sharp drop in net outflows from US$ 32 billion in 2004 to only US$ 2 billion in 2005, for the reasons mentioned earlier. Total FDI flows reached US$ 315 (an increase of US$ 50 billion or 19 per cent). Total equity portfolio flows were US$ 122.7 (increase of 98 per cent over 2004). And, portfolio debt flows reached US$ 55.7 billion (compared to US$ 53.3 billion in 2004).

Within these totals, Asia remained by far the largest recipient region with total flows of US$ 263 billion (4.9 per cent of GDP), of which FDI accounted for US$ 165 billion, portfolio equity for US$ 93 billion, and portfolio debt for US$ 18 billion. Asia's total capital inflows, however, were only 1 per cent above 2004 (US$ 257 billion) because of net outflows of bank loans totalling US$ 14 billion. Emerging Europe had the second largest capital flows totalling US$ 133 billion, which represented a 41 per cent increase over 2004 (US$ 94 billion); net flow of bank financing rose to US$ 30.3 billion compared to only US$ 1.5 billion in the previous year. EMEs in Latin America showed a healthy increase of 36 per cent and came third at US$ 70 billion. Sub-Sahara Africa attracted US$ 19 billion. The Middle-East attracted US$ 10.6 billion of external flows (in 2005, the Middle-East was major capital exporter to other regions of the world).

Determinants of portfolio equity flows

Many of the macro-economic and structural determinants that led to increased demand for EME assets since 2002—discussed in our Capital Flow Report for the 2005 meeting of the Emerging Markets Forum—continued to hold in 2005 and 2006, while some of the so-called 'push factors' are weakening. Nevertheless, the ongoing structural reforms and financial innovations in many EME capital markets have the potential to attract strategic investors, and minimize excessive capital flow volatility, while building efficient defenses against inevitable volatility that will remain. Adoption of such reforms in a broader range of countries would enhance the efficiency of the financial globalization process.

Key factors influencing the size and direction of capital inflows can be categorized as follows.

Factors affecting relative investment returns and risk–return mix

These factors include prospects for growth, expected exchange rate changes and relative yields on various instruments, taking into account corporate profitability (for equity instruments) and monetary policy stance (for debt instruments). So long as the overall macro-level indicators are promising, the issue will be one of profitability and financial soundness of actual companies they invest in. The soundness of the financial sector also needs to be factored in, along with the purely macro-economic indicators, to assess risks to macro-economic performance and the sustainability of returns. Such factoring in of financial stability considerations in country risk assessments is particularly important in an increasingly globalized setting of many EMEs. In addition to macro-economic and macro-prudential factors, factors like earnings growth, return on equity and other measures of corporate soundness and profitability are key considerations for global investors. Shifts in sovereign credit ratings—as a summary measure of credit risk derived from the country fundamentals and other factors—affect investor sentiment.

In addition a range of structural factors affecting the investability in EME assets play a key role. These include:

- Openness to various forms of capital flows.
- State of development of capital markets and the related financial market infrastructure.
- Structural changes in the sources of supply of capital.

First, a country's policies to open up and enhance the access of foreign investors to the equity and debt of its companies is a necessary first step to attract global investors seeking diversification and new opportunities for returns (see the section 'Factors Affecting Risk-Adjusted Returns' for further details).

Second, several structural factors governing security market infrastructure play a critical role in shaping the perceived returns and risks of investing in EMC equity securities. These include:

- *Corporate governance and transparency*: The Asian financial crisis highlighted the crucial importance of good corporate governance, transparency of management and majority shareholders actions affecting companies that foreigners invest in, and the accuracy of financial accounts presented to the investment community. The creation of effective regulatory and supervisory institutions and the formulation of appropriate policy framework for good governance in EMCs have been important factors in attracting portfolio equity in particular. There is some evidence, though not a whole lot, that foreign mutual funds investments in emerging markets are significantly linked to security-market infrastructure, shareholder rights and quality of accounting standards (see Aggarwal et al., 2003).

- *Market liquidity*: This is an important determinant of flows of portfolio capital into EMC equities. Global investors typically seek investments in which there are significant amounts of daily trading enabling them to buy and sell these assets without moving the price against them and also ensuring that they can enter and exit these investments easily as and when they desire to. Market liquidity is influenced by both the size and pattern of ownership of listed securities and the micro-structure of the markets, including the trading systems. The creation of a liquid security market with efficient trading arrangements is thus important to attract both domestic and foreign investment. There is evidence that equity-market liberalization, involving an opening up to foreign shareholders, is associated with significant increase in share prices and reduction in cost of capital (Henry and Lorentzen, 2003). Also, more protection of shareholders is strongly associated with the size, efficiency and stability of equity markets (see Ibid.).

- *Legal Infrastructure*: While transparency, good governance and market micro-structure are also important for developing debt markets, certain financial infrastructure components, such as insolvency regimes, trust and securitization laws require proper attention in order to develop corporate debt markets. In addition, the development of the government securities market calls for a conducive and effective framework for public debt management.

- *Macro-stability and macro-prudential surveillance*: Several broad structural features that affect the macro-economic and financial stability policy frameworks, such as the sustainability of exchange rate regime, the perceptions of financial system stability, including the debt-equity ratio of companies, public debt sustainability, efficiency and soundness of financial intermediation and so on, also play a significant role in shaping the overall perceptions of costs, risks and returns of investing in EMCs.

Third, structural changes in the sources of foreign capital can be critical. For all types of institutional investors in industrial countries, the share of foreign assets in their total portfolio is rising, reflecting a growing strategic focus of these investors on EMEs (see Global Financial Stability Report, IMF September 2005 and *Global Development Finance* 2006, World Bank). This could reinforce the impact of domestic capital market development policies in enhancing the depth and liquidity of the local financial market.

Finally, there are special factors such as privatizations, mergers, and other country- or region-specific one-off factors (for example, initial impact of accession to EU) that influence the type and level of capital flows.

Factors affecting risk-adjusted returns

The regional variations in growth and annual real exchange rate change in various EME regions are shown in Table 3.5 and in Table 3A(2)1 of this chapter.

Table 3.5 Average weighed annual GDP growth rates (%)

Weighed average annual real GDP growth rates	1991–96	1997–98	1999–2004	2005–07 (projected)
Africa	2.0	2.5	3.5	4.8
Americas	3.5	4.0	1.9	4.1
Asia	8.1	3.4	6.8	7.5
Europe	–2.9	1.8	4.4	4.9
Middle-East	5.3	3.7	3.9	5.7
Total EMF	4.3	3.3	4.7	6.1

Sources: Centennial Group, World Bank *WDI* (2006) and IMF's *WEO* (2006). Taiwan excluded, Serbia no data 1990–92, and Kuwait no data 1990–91.

Strong global growth and low inflation witnessed in 2005, despite further jumps in oil and non-oil commodity prices, continued in 2006. Emerging markets have faced unusually favourable external conditions, characterized by strong global demand, large terms of trade improvements and easier access to external financing. These circumstances were reflected in strong growth, large current account surpluses and moderate inflation in EMEs generally. In addition, stable or generally appreciating nominal or real exchange rates during in recent years—partly in response to the strong inflows of capital—added to the returns to foreign investors on EME assets. The number of upgrades of sovereign ratings by rating agencies far exceeded number of downgrades, contributing to strengthened external demand for EME assets and continued downward trend in credit spreads.

In the presence of such strong fundamentals that led to attractive relative returns, the monetary tightening in the US beginning 2004 has had only a limited impact on risk perceptions. However, the more synchronized tightening in late 2006 and early 2007 among industrial countries, and the prospective adjustments in the pattern of global current account imbalances, all seem to pose more significant downside risks for the global economy. This was already evident in the second quarter of 2006 and early 2007, when global financial markets experienced increased volatility and a sharp correction in the price of riskier assets. Some emerging market asset prices declined sharply, particularly in some of the more liquid local equity markets and in those currency markets that had appreciated the most. In debt markets, however, there was only a slight upward adjustment in the credit spreads, which have been at historic lows already. Thus the impact of recent turbulence seems well contained and transitory (see Box 3.1 for a further discussion of turbulence in emerging markets).

In 2006, emerging markets in particular broadly sustained the robust growth achieved in 2005; current account surpluses were expected to be broadly maintained, with an increase particularly in the Middle-East region on account of oil price increases, and inflation is expected to remain moderate in most EMEs. The relatively subdued reaction of inflation to commodity price

---

Box 3.1 Global imbalances, risk aversion and recent turbulence in emerging markets

While emerging market fundamentals and demand for EME assets remain strong, the effects of concerted monetary tightening in industrial countries on the demand for EME assets remain unclear. Also the sell off in mid-2006 by global investors, which affected some EME markets particularly sharply, has raised the issue whether this presages a generalized risk aversion leading to outflows of portfolio investment, or simply reflects transitory one-off adjustments in relative risk exposures.

An increase in risk aversion due to the perceived risks—uncertainty and shifts in inflation and exchange rate expectations, and possibly lower growth and corporate profitability, owing to possible downturn in economic activity in countries where monetary policy is tightening—could raise risk premiums and affect investor positioning in specific markets where investors feel over exposed. At the same time, large terms of trade improvements and continued moderate inflation in most EMEs may help to sustain strong growth and continued strong fundamentals overall.

The sell-off by global investors in the spring of 2006 was concentrated in local emerging markets, particularly equities and currencies, and to a limited extent in local currency debt markets; some of the EME equity prices that had risen sharply in 2005 witnessed sharp declines. Some of the higher yielding currencies that had been favoured by investors for carry trades saw significant sell off (IMF (2006b). This helped to reverse the sharp nominal and real appreciations in these currencies in 2005. A sell-off of portfolio local currency debt partly reversed the significant inflow into local currency debt markets in 2005, with sharp corrections in prices.

The evidence presented in IMF (2006b) and BIS (2006), suggest that the recent sell off in emerging market capital markets was modest relative to large inflows that had already occurred, and that recent increase in emerging market spread was small relative to the pronounced declines in spread that occurred since 2002. [Table on EME stock price increases in selected countries]. A recent analysis of the determinants of EME debt market spreads examines the time series evolution of spreads as a function of country fundamentals (measured by various country risk ratings) and external perceptions of global financial risk (measured by 3-month future Federal Reserve funds rate and its volatility). The analysis suggests that the EME spreads are well anchored in fundamentals, and that even sizeable increases in global risk may offset only slightly the reductions in the spread so far due to country fundamentals. This finding, combined with the evidence of significant structural improvements in local currency debt markets, including public debt management framework, and the prospects

(Box 3.1 continued)

(*Box 3.1 continued*)

> for continuation of strong fundamentals, all seem to suggest that the recent turbulence seems a one-off adjustment rather than a precursor of global risk aversion.

shocks, the greater role of EMEs in sustaining global demand, and generally favourable financial conditions of the corporate sector, both financial and non-financial, were some of the factors that contributed to continued strong macro-economic perform-ance globally and in EMEs in 2006.

The EME performance also benefited from improvements in the financial soundness of both banks and non-bank financial institutions (Bank for International Settlements [BIS], 2006; GFSR, April 2006). Banking systems in EMEs have generally strengthened overall (in terms indicators such as capital ad-equacy ratios, ratio of non-performing loans and so on) as a result of economic recovery and reforms, while debt-equity ratios of non-financial firms has declined. The capacity for making macro-economic and financial policy adjustments in response to various shocks impacting on the financial system has improved in many EMEs, which have built up their macro-prudential surveillance capabilities. As an indicator of their capacity for macro-prudential surveillance, 24 emerging and developing countries have started, over the last few years, issuing financial stability reports to com-plement their monetary policy-related reports.

In the future, perceptions of risks in EME investments could increase due to the uncertainties associated with the policy ad-justments and market reactions to the current and prospective global imbalances (and the associated shifts in inflation and exchange rate expectation). Nevertheless, the strength of funda-mentals in many EMEs and the recent structural changes in the EME capital markets together have the potential to stabilize the capital inflows to the EMEs with strong fundamentals.

In summary, the prospective continuation of strong funda-mentals in EMEs could serve to maintain broadly the risk-adjusted returns on EME assets at attractive levels seen in recent past, and thereby sustain the foreign investor appetite for these assets.

Structural and special factors affecting investibility and capital flows

While the continued strength of macro-economic fundamentals in EMEs clearly played a role in shaping the expected returns and perceptions of risk in all forms of EME assets, a range of structural forces have also been in play in shaping the demand for different categories of private capital inflows.

A large number of countries have opened up their capital markets to foreign investors during the last decade, both by allowing access of residents to foreign financial markets and by strengthening access of non-residents to domestic financial markets. As noted in Miniane (2004), the degree of capital account restrictions have been eased substantially, though at varying paces, in a wide range of countries during 1985–2000. The trend toward greater openness seems to continue as highlighted in IMF (2005). For example, in addition to relaxing non-resident's access to local money and securities markets, several countries have eased access of residents to foreign securities as part of policies to cope with strong inflows. These developments have allowed for a greater competition among countries for foreign investments and contributed to a reduction in concentration of capital inflows among countries noted earlier.

The local equity and debt markets have developed significantly in many EMEs on account of a range of structural reforms and supportive macro-economic environment. Various measures of market development—such as market capitalization to GDP ratio, bonds outstanding to GDP ratio and stock market turnover—have improved over the past decade. Although markets in many EMEs remain shallow, requiring further institutional development, overall EME equity markets have provided attractive opportunities for risk diversification (GFSR, June 2002) to global investors. The ongoing innovations and reforms in local and international debt markets for EMEs have also provided risk diversification opportunities (BIS, 2006). Some of these innovations, such as growing use of credit derivatives, strengthened public debt management arrangements, innovations in structured finance to design Islamic fixed income securities (see Box 3.2), all have raised the attractiveness of EME debt.

Box 3.2   Middle-East surpluses and Islamic securities

Recent analysis of financial market implications of growing surpluses in the Middle-East region—on account of energy price increases—conclude that current concentration of investments of oil funds in dollar assets, particularly offshore dollar bank deposits, could continue and only a slow diversification into other asset classes, including those denominated in other currencies, is likely to take place (IMF [2006a] Global Financial Stability Report).

The importance of Islamic Finance, particularly in the countries of the Middle-East raises the issue of whether the increase in oil surpluses could spur the demand for Islamic securities and Islamic investment products generally, and whether such securities could become a source of diversification for the investments of petrodollars.

Islamic financial instruments are financial contracts issued in accordance with the principles of Islamic Commercial Jurisprudence (Shariah principles). Some of the key principles include: prohibition of interest, sharing of risks to justify return, not incurring 'avoidable' or 'excessive' risks, avoidance of financial support to products and activities prohibited by Islam, transparency of contracts, and so on. Institutions offering Islamic Financial Services (IIFS) typically employ a Shariah Board constituting of Shariah scholars to seek *ex-ante* approval for the products and services to be offered in order to provide assurances that these are Shariah-compliant. The opinions/rulings (also referred to as fatwas) of Shariah Boards are further reviewed (and subject to approval) by a National Shariah Board in some jurisdictions (for example, Malaysia, Indonesia), and are left to market forces in others (Saudi Arabia, Dubai). Regardless of the institutional arrangements for the harmonization and implementation of Shariah rulings and standards, banking regulators will typically oversee the adequacy of the systems and controls in an IIFS to ensure Shariah compliance.

Consistent with the Shariah principles, Islamic finance instruments are either equity-like (based on various forms of profit sharing contracts, including partnership arrangements) or asset-based (based on purchases and resale of goods, ownership and leasing of assets, or forward purchases of goods for delivery, etc.). A range of Islamic investment products, such as non-tradable Profit Sharing Investment Accounts (PSIA)—based on profit sharing and loss-bearing contracts, known as *Mudarabha*—provided by IIFS, or tradable equity securities and mutual funds that meet specified screening criteria set up by Shariah boards, have existed for a long time. PSIA are fixed term products which provide returns linked to the profits of the overall asset portfolio of the IIFS (unrestricted PSIA) or to a specific investment portfolio (restricted PSIA). These are in principle similar to mutual funds, but are not tradable and constitute a significant source of funding for Islamic banks. The size and share of Shariah compliant stocks have

(*Box 3.2 continued*)

(Box 3.2 continued)

also grown rapidly in recent years. A large number of indexes—currently more than 40 under the Dow Jones Islamic Market Indexes (DJIMI) umbrella, and several indexes under the Financial Times Stock Exchange (FTSE) Global Islamic Index Series—are available to monitor Shariah compliant stocks in many jurisdictions. Globally, nearly 250 Islamic mutual funds operate managing about US$ 300 billion in assets. However, the availability of globally acceptable fixed income securities consistent with Shariah principle (known as *Sukuks*, or Islamic Bonds) is more recent (IOSCO [2004]). In particular, design of Shariah compatible short-term (money market) securities or government securities that yield a fixed income stream has been a major challenge in Islamic finance, owing to the Shariah prohibition of trading in debt, and this has constrained liquidity risk management by IIFS and liquidity management by central banks in jurisdictions with significant presence of IIFS. Recent innovations in Islamic Asset securitization have begun to overcome these limitations and the issuance of Islamic fixed income securities (*Sukuks*) particularly for project financing, has accelerated in recent years. Historically, many governments, notably Malaysia and Bahrain, have promoted Islamic bonds in their national jurisdictions. However, issuance of globally acceptable Islamic bonds has gathered momentum particularly since 2001, when Islamic Development Bank (IDB) and some national governments began securitizing Islamic contracts, particularly lease contracts (known as *Ijara* contracts).

Islamic Bonds or *Sukuks* are 'trust certificates' or 'participation certificates' that grant an investor a share of an asset along with the cashflows and risks commeneurate with such ownership. *Sukuks* represent 'certificates of equal value representing undivided shares in ownership of tangible assets, usurfruct and services, or in the ownership of assets of particular projects or special investment activity....' (Accounting and Auditing Organization for Islamic Financial Institutions [AAOIFI], Shariah Standard No. 17). *Sukuks* are classified according to the underlying Islamic contracts that underpin the securitization (*I Jara Sukuk, Musharakha Sukuk,* and so on). Issuance of *Sukuk* involves (*i*) creation of a Special Purpose Vehicles (SPVs) to own, service and operate specified assets, (*ii*) issue *Sukuks*, and (*iii*) pass on the proceeds to the originator and enter into income generating contracts using the assets (for example, leasing or trading, building and operating, etc.). Thus, ideally, *Sukuk* issuance requires strong secured asset laws and trust laws to ensure true sale and bankruptcy remoteness of SPV in order to safeguard investor interests. In practice, most *Sukuks* until recently have involved 'purchase undertaking agreements' by the originator, so that the underlying risks are related to the credit rating of the originator, rather than the quality of the underlying assets and SPV governance (Moody [2006]). Recent developments in global issuance of *Sukuks*, many issued

(Box 3.2 continued)

(Box 3.2 continued)

> for financing infrastructure projects are shown in Figure 3.9. This includes one of the largest issues—US$ 3.5 billion in—by Dubai Ports World to finance capital expenditures. The strong growth in issue activity in the Gulf region reflects both the boom in business investment and the availability of savings on account of energy price increases (*Financial Times*, 11 July 2006, p. 17). Reported *Sukuk* issues in the first half of 2006 was about US$ 12 billion, almost five times US$ 2.6 billion, closed in the same period of 2005. While Malaysia remained the leading issuer, issue activities by Gulf countries including Bahrain, United Arab Emirates (UAE), Kuwait and Saudi Arabia seem to be taking off. The innovations in Islamic finance, thus, augur well for efficient recycling of petrodollars.

Portfolio equity inflows benefited in particular from an expanded investor base, including a growing presence of retail investors through emerging market stock funds, in addition to strong growth in valuations (with emerging market stock prices performing exceptionally well during 2003–05). As a result, both international equity placements by EME issuers as well as foreign investment in local stock markets performed, well. A significant part of equity issues during 2005 was driven by IPO's, notably in China (World Bank, 2006).

Strong growth and reduced volatility of portfolio debt inflows into EMEs was attributable to the cumulative impact of a variety of structural factors affecting EME debt markets. These include: (*a*) growth in the Euro market for EME debt; (*b*) growth in credit derivatives applied to EME debt, allowing better risk diversification and, hence, stronger demand (and finer pricing) for EME debt; and (*c*) strengthened institutional arrangements for more active and effective public debt management, facilitated by a deepening of local currency debt markets and a widening of investor base for EME bonds.

Strengthened public debt management policies and structural demand from foreign investors have contributed to resilient markets for EME debt. For example, several EMEs have reduced currency mismatches and lengthened the maturities by strengthening local currency debt markets. Such markets have thus evolved into a major source of long-term finance in many EMEs.

In addition, a rise in allocations to EME assets by institutional investors in developed countries (pension funds, insurance companies and mutual funds) has contributed added depth and liquidity to many emerging markets. Active debt management to achieve desired trade-offs between cost and risks has played a key role in shaping the portfolio debt inflows. The specific measures to manage the trade-offs included: debt buybacks; pre-financing of borrowing needs to take advantage of liquid markets; and quick actions to stabilize the markets when markets faced selling pressures. These factors have improved the debt dynamics and contributed to reducing the spreads on EME debt.

Bank financing inflows to EMEs, mainly syndicated bank lending, was dominated by oil and gas projects and oil import financing. The strong growth recorded inflows of syndicated bank lending in some countries, noted in GDF 2006, being offset by outflows of bank financing from EMEs in many countries.

FDI inflows, which accounted for US\$ 316 billion or 64 per cent of total private capital inflows to EMEs in 2005 (compared to US\$ 167 billion in 2003), appear to be driven by a combination of traditional and new factors. The macro-economic and structural reforms as well as efforts of many countries to enhance private sector role in the economies have made the countries much more attractive to international companies; these companies are often investing large amounts to catch up. In high growth countries with large domestic markets like China, India, Russia and Brazil, the multinational companies are increasing their exposure to exploit market opportunities; indeed, many multinational companies realize that to remain a major global player they can not afford not to be present in fast growing EMEs, particularly the so-called BRICs (Brazil, Russia, India and China). In addition, most multinationals are investing in EMEs to source products at lower costs. Unlike the past, such investments now often go beyond investments in plants and include mergers and acquisitions of existing domestic players. And, finally, since the recent sharp rise in commodity prices, there has been a surge in investments in resource rich countries EMEs and other developing countries.

Summary of issues

Surge in private capital flows to emerging markets, particularly since 2002–03 continued in 2005. But, some of the factors that led to the buoyancy of capital flows were in retreat in the second half of 2006. The synchronized tightening of monetary policy in industrial countries, and the increases in commodity prices, particularly energy prices, have led to a cyclical build-up of risk aversion and inflation expectations. Despite recent turbulence, both portfolio equity flows and FDI have risen in 2006, but private debt inflows declined somewhat in the same year from a peak level reached in 2005. This reflected in part pre-financing by many sovereign and private borrowers in 2005 and early 2006 in anticipation of a future tightening of liquidity conditions in the financial markets.

Developments during the past 4–5 years highlight several key issues in managing capital flows:

1. Despite the buoyancy of capital inflows on account of the favourable combination of sound macro-economic performance, unusually accommodative monetary policies in major OECD economies, strengthened terms of trade and strong demand for EME assets, portfolio flows remain volatile as seen in the recent sell-off of equity positions in emerging markets. Nevertheless, the changes in debt management practices and greater depth and resilience of local debt and equity markets seemed to have limited market volatility. In particular, volatility in debt markets seems to have fallen relative to what was observed in recent years. Bank financing continues to remain volatile. These observations in turn raise three key issues:

   (*i*) What are the likely consequences of the potential unwinding of global imbalances on the size and volatility of private capital inflows to emerging markets? What are the likely implications for financial soundness, macro-economic stability and economic growth in EMEs?

   (*ii*) Does the recent turbulence and sell-off in emerging markets reflect one-off adjustments in relative risk exposures or presage a more fundamental shift in risk perceptions generally on account of global uncertainties?

(*iii*) Do emerging markets have adequate macro-prudential surveillance framework to monitor adequately the impact of global imbalances and of the shifts in capital flows on domestic financial soundness?

2. The continued strong growth in FDI in 2004 and 2005 was accompanied by some diversification of FDI among regions. FDI expanded strongly in resource-rich countries, which benefited from energy and commodity price increases, in some eastern and central European countries, which benefited from the improved investment opportunities and confidence deriving from the initial impact of their EU accession, and in Africa due to two large acquisitions in South Africa. Thus, a lot of FDI flow in these regions seems related to special, even one-off, circumstances, FDI remains concentrated in Asia, and regional differences remain important. East Asia, in particular China, continues to dominate. This raises the question: *What are the lessons of recent experience for the strategy to further improve and broaden access to FDI inflows?*

3. There is evidence that appropriate structural reforms to develop domestic financial markets can promote stable capital flows to finance long-term growth and limit the impact of volatility on financial soundness. This observation raises several policy issues:

(*i*) What is the appropriate scope and sequencing of reforms to build domestic capital markets?

(*ii*) Can capital market development strategies, with an emphasis on asset securitization, facilitate private finance of infrastructure development, which is a critical need in many emerging markets?

(*iii*) As the share of strategic investors grows, how could countries position themselves to attract larger shares or retain their relative shares?

(*iv*) What are the implications of growing importance of local currency debt markets for the relative shares of debt inflows to EMEs?

4. While private capital flows have been characterized by substantial concentrations by regions and countries, recent shifts in the structure of global imbalances due to oil price increases may have implications for the type and patterns of capital flows. In particular, the growing surpluses of oil exporting countries, particularly in the Middle-East, seems to have led to increased demand for 'Islamic securities', a form of structured finance transaction linked to ownership in tangible assets and equity claims, as a means to finance infrastructure and sovereign financing needs (see Box 3.2 for a discussion of Islamic securities). However, legal and institutional infrastructure for Islamic finance is still evolving. These developments in turn raise the following two issues:

(i) Would the sovereigns and firms issuing such securities play a key role in recycling oil surpluses?

(ii) What can be done to strengthen the financial infrastructure for issuing Islamic securities?

Figure 3.9 Global *Sukuk*

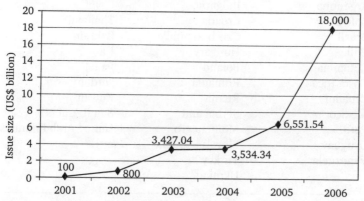

Source: Liquidity Management Center.

Note: The Liquidity Management Center lists a total of 77 issues since September 2001, with a current out-standing value of about 18 billion. Adding staff estimates for issues in the remainder of 2006, total outstanding could rise to about US$ 36 billion, mainly on account of what appears to be a huge surge in issuance in 2006.

Annex 1

List of emerging market countries

There is some debate as to how to define EMEs and, therefore, which countries should be included in any list of EMCs. For purposes of this chapter, we have used a relatively broad definition to include countries which are both of most interest to international investors at this time and which compete with each other in attracting international private capital flows. The list we have chosen corresponds to the list and definitions of EMCs used by international investors and also by journals such as *The Economist*. While most of these countries are middle- or upper middle-income countries, developing countries in Asia, Europe and Latin America, we also include some low middle-income and low-income countries (for example, China, India, Vietnam, Kenya, Nigeria, Bolivia and so on) which are capable of attracting significant capital flows, as well as the so-called 'tiger' countries in Asia which spawned the original club of the EMCs and whose economic policies are both emulated in and intertwined with the rest of emerging Asia.

Latin America	*Europe*	*Middle-East*
Argentina	Bulgaria	Egypt
Bolivia	Croatia	Thailand
Brazil	Czech Republic	Bahrain
Chile	Hungary	Iran
Colombia	Poland	Israel
Costa Rica	Romania	Jordan
Ecuador	Russia	Kuwait
Mexico	Serbia and	Saudi Arabia
Peru	Montenegro	United Arab Emirates
Uruguay	Slovak Republic	
Venezuela	Turkey	
	Ukraine	

Asia	*Africa*
Bangladesh	Algeria
China (PRC)	Morocco
Hong Kong, China	Tunisia
India	Cote d'Ivoire
Indonesia	Ghana
Korea, Rep.	Kenya

Malaysia	Nigeria
Pakistan	South Africa
Philippines	Uganda
Singapore	
Sri Lanka	
Taipei, China	
Vietnam	
Kazakhstan	

Annex 2

Data sources and definitions

1. FDI inflows are taken from line 78 bed of IMF's *International Financial Statistics* (*IFS*) year book (various issues); It is referred to in IFS tables as 'Direct Investment in Representative Economy, not included elsewhere (nie)', and represents increase in net inward investment by non-residents and includes equity capital, reinvested earnings, other capital and financial derivatives associated with various inter-company transactions between affiliated enterprises.

2. Portfolio debt net inflows is taken from line 78 bnd of IMF, IFS yearbook (various issues)'. It is referred to in IFS tables as 'portfolio investment liabilities, n.i.e, debt securities' and covers non-resident purchases of bonds, debentures, notes, and so on and money market and negotiable debt investments.

3. Portfolio Equity net inflows is taken from line 78 bmd. Of IMF, IFS yearbook (various issues); It is referred to in IFS tables as 'portfolio investment liabilities, n.i.e., equity securities' and covers non-resident acquisition of chares, stocks, participation and similar documents (for example, depository receipts) that usually denote ownership of equity.

4. Net Bank financing is calculated as the sum of line 78 bud (other investment liabilities, n.i.e., banks) and line 78 bqd (other investment assets, n.i.e., banks) and represents transactions with non-residents in currency and deposits, bonds and trade credits through the banking system.

5. Data for 2005 are staff estimates based on partial quarterly data reported in IFS and country publications.

6. Data reported here differ from other commonly cited sources— World Bank's *Global Development Finance*, IMF's Global

Financial Stability Report and World Economic Outlook—due to:

- differences in country coverage, and
- differences in the definitions and sources used in compiling portfolio debt and bank inflows.

For example, data in portfolio debt based on the IFS definition in this document roughly corresponds to net bond financing data used in World Bank's GDF (DT.NFL.PBND.CD, DT.NFL.PNGB.CD). For Bank inflows, we use net inflows from Banks plus net outflows to Banks as defined in IFS. As our list of EMEs include major financial centres, there can be massive recorded inflows that are offset by large outflows reflecting international inter-bank activity. Therefore, net figures are used to avoid distortions in measuring the true extent of inflows through the banking system; that is, resident outflows through the banking system are also deducted from net inflows, in addition to on lending and carry trade activities. As a result, net figures tend to be lower than the syndicated bank lending and other long-term net lending reported in GDF (DT.NFL.PCBK.CD, DT.NFL.PNGC.CD).

Table 3A(2)1   Real effective exchange rate by region (weighed by GDP)

	1995	1996	1997	1998	1999	2000	2001	2002	2003	2004	2005
Africa	114.1	112.7	119.8	118.8	104.1	100.0	96.9	90.4	96.3	101.2	103.7
Americas	97.1	98.3	105.4	106.1	102.0	100.0	102.2	95.2	87.8	88.5	92.2
Asia	93.8	100.6	105.0	105.5	100.7	100.0	103.2	101.3	95.0	92.5	92.7
Europe	99.7	115.1	123.5	112.7	93.2	100.0	113.6	115.8	114.8	121.6	132.4
Middle-East	93.4	95.9	100.3	102.1	97.5	100.0	100.8	95.7	88.7	83.1	81.3
EM Total	98.1	105.4562	111.0	108.4	99.3	100.0	104.6	102.8	99.0	100.0	103.9

Sources: Centennial Group, IMF, *IFS* and *WEO*, World Bank *WDI*.

Table 3A(2)2   Foreign direct investment by region (US$ billion), 1990–2005

	1990	1991	1992	1993	1994	1995	1996	1997	1998	1999	2000	2001	2002	2003	2004	2005
Africa	0.9	1.5	1.6	2.7	3.7	3.2	3.2	6.7	3.5	4.1	4.2	10.8	5.1	6.8	5.4	13.7
Americas	7.3	11.9	13.6	12.5	27.0	28.8	42.5	62.8	68.3	83.6	75.3	66.4	46.5	37.5	56.5	62.4
Asia	21.1	21.1	28.9	51.8	63.3	73.0	86.5	97.5	89.4	108.1	141.9	102.4	85.3	87.4	136.5	165.7
Europe	0.8	2.7	3.1	5.8	6.2	15.1	14.3	19.1	21.9	25.2	26.6	25.4	28.2	26.6	53.2	65.6
Middle-East	2.6	1.4	1.9	2.2	2.3	0.5	3.3	6.3	7.7	4.1	6.1	5.4	5.6	8.7	14.1	8.3
EM Total	32.7	38.5	49.1	75.0	102.5	120.6	149.8	192.4	190.9	225.1	254.1	210.5	170.7	167.0	265.7	315.7

Sources: Centennial Group, IMF (*IFS* and *WEO*), World Bank (*WDI* and *GDF*), Central Banks of India, Indonesia and Taiwan, Hong Kong Monetary Authority, Singapore Department of Statistics, CEIC and UNCTAD.

Table 3A(2)3   Portfolio capital inflows (debt plus equity) by region (US$ billion), 1990–2005

	1990	1991	1992	1993	1994	1995	1996	1997	1998	1999	2000	2001	2002	2003	2004	2005
Africa	0.1	0.6	3.8	0.8	3.1	2.9	4.5	11.4	9.9	13.8	1.8	-3.0	0.5	1.0	7.7	5.8
Americas	21.2	25.4	30.3	79.9	70.8	6.4	50.4	33.1	32.7	15.7	0.0	1.0	-9.6	4.5	-4.5	18.3
Asia	0.8	4.3	9.3	29.0	28.1	29.8	45.7	25.1	-1.8	90.2	73.0	25.9	13.8	77.8	78.8	111.5
Europe	0.7	0.7	3.2	10.7	4.7	5.1	7.9	24.6	5.6	5.7	-5.9	-0.5	9.8	10.4	39.4	37.2
Middle-East	0:5	0.2	0.2	0.3	0.5	0.9	2.0	2.5	0.1	2.2	5.1	1.8	0.8	1.3	4.0	4.8
EM Total	23.4	31.3	46.8	120.7	107.1	45.1	110.5	96.8	46.5	127.6	74.0	25.2	15.3	94.9	125.4	177.8

Sources: Centennial Group, IMF (*IFS* and *WEO*), World Bank (*WDI* and *GDF*), Central Banks of India, Indonesia and
   Taiwan, Hong Kong Monetary Authority, Singapore Department of Statistics, CEIC and UNCTAD.

Note: Hong Kong excluded before 1998.

Table 3A(2)4 Portfolio equity inflow by region (US$ billion), 1990–2005

	1990	1991	1992	1993	1994	1995	1996	1997	1998	1999	2000	2001	2002	2003	2004	2005
Africa	0.4	-1.4	-0.1	0.9	0.3	3.0	2.5	5.6	8.7	9.0	4.2	-1.0	-0.4	0.7	7.3	7.0
Americas	2.5	6.9	8.2	24.0	18.4	5.2	12.1	14.3	-2.2	-3.6	-0.6	2.5	1.4	3.3	-0.6	12.3
Asia	1.3	0.6	5.6	17.6	13.7	11.4	18.0	6.9	0.6	95.0	76.4	25.3	10.1	67.4	56.0	93.4
Europe	0.1	0.1	0.4	2.2	1.9	1.6	4.1	3.8	3.9	1.7	1.2	0.2	-0.3	0.3	5.8	5.7
Middle-East	0.0	0.0	0.0	0.3	0.5	1.0	1.4	2.2	0.3	2.2	4.7	0.5	0.5	0.6	3.6	4.2
EM Total	4.3	6.3	14.0	45.1	34.7	22.2	38.2	32.8	11.4	104.2	85.8	27.4	11.5	72.4	72.1	122.7

Sources: Centennial Group, IMF (*IFS* and *WEO*), World Bank (*WDI* and *GDF*), Central Banks of India, Indonesia and Taiwan, Hong Kong Monetary Authority, Singapore Department of Statistics, CEIC and UNCTAD.

Table 3A(2)5 Portfolio debt by region (US$ billion), 1990–2005

	1990	1991	1992	1993	1994	1995	1996	1997	1998	1999	2000	2001	2002	2003	2004	2005
Africa	-0.2	2.0	3.9	-0.2	2.8	0.0	2.0	5.8	1.2	4.8	-2.4	-2.0	0.9	0.2	0.4	-1.2
Americas	18.7	18.5	22.1	55.9	52.4	1.2	38.3	18.8	34.8	19.4	0.6	-1.5	-11.1	1.2	-3.9	6.0
Asia	-0.5	3.7	3.7	11.3	14.4	18.4	27.7	18.3	-2.4	-3.9	-1.3	1.3	3.7	10.4	22.8	18.1
Europe	0.6	0.6	2.8	8.5	2.8	3.5	3.7	20.8	1.7	4.1	-7.1	-0.7	10.1	10.1	33.5	31.5
Middle-East	0.5	0.2	0.3	0.0	0.0	0.0	0.6	0.3	-0.2	0.0	0.4	1.3	0.3	0.6	0.4	1.3
EM Total	19.1	24.9	32.8	75.6	72.4	22.9	72.3	64.0	35.1	24.3	-9.7	-1.6	3.9	22.6	53.3	55.7

Sources: Centennial Group, IMF (*IFS* and *WEO*), World Bank (*WDI* and *GDF*), Central Banks of India, Indonesia and Taiwan, Hong Kong Monetary Authority, Singapore Department of Statistics, CEIC and UNCTAD.

Table 3A(2)6 Net flow of bank financing by region (US$ billion), 1990–2005

	1990	1991	1992	1993	1994	1995	1996	1997	1998	1999	2000	2001	2002	2003	2004	2005
Africa	0.0	-0.8	-1.4	-0.7	0.4	2.8	0.0	-1.0	-0.6	-3.8	1.4	-2.6	-3.7	-8.6	-1.4	-0.5
Americas	4.1	2.1	5.3	-3.2	-3.1	3.8	-2.0	9.1	-6.9	-12.5	0.5	-11.9	4.0	-4.9	-0.7	-11.1
Asia	-3.6	7.1	9.4	10.3	9.7	15.8	10.8	-23.3	-76.6	-76.8	-68.5	27.0	31.6	3.4	42.2	-14.2
Europe	-5.4	-4.1	-0.6	1.1	-8.1	14.5	8.6	5.2	-0.7	-6.0	-5.3	-16.9	12.7	25.7	1.5	30.3
Middle-East	-3.5	-1.1	8.3	3.7	3.5	-1.4	-4.7	16.1	7.5	2.0	-2.8	4.0	1.6	1.7	-9.6	-2.5
EM Total	-8.5	3.1	21.1	11.3	2.4	35.4	12.6	6.0	-77.4	-97.0	-74.6	-0.5	46.2	17.3	32.1	2.0

Sources: Centennial Group, IMF (*IFS* and *WEO*), World Bank (*WDI* and *GDF*), Central Banks of India, Indonesia and Taiwan, Hong Kong Monetary Authority, Singapore Department of Statistics, CEIC and UNCTAD.

Table 3A(2)7 **Top 10 countries: Total FDI inflows into EMEs (US$ billion)**

FDI			
1994–95		*2004–05*	
China (PRC): Mainland	34.8	China (PRC): Mainland	67.0
Mexico	10.2	China, P.R.: Hong Kong	35.0
Singapore	10.1	Singapore	18.6
China, P.R.: Hong Kong	7.0	Mexico	18.0
Argentina	4.6	Brazil	16.7
Malaysia	4.3	Russia	15.0
Brazil	4.0	Poland	10.3
Indonesia	3.2	United Arab Emirates	10.0
Hungary	3.0	Czech Republic	8.0
Peru	2.9	Chile	7.2

Sources: Centennial Group, IMF (*IFS* and *WEO*), World Bank (*WDI* and *GDF*), Central Banks of India, Indonesia and Taiwan, Hong Kong Monetary Authority, Singapore Department of Statistics, CEIC and UNCTAD.

Table 3A(2)8 **Top 10 countries: Total portfolio inflows into EMEs (US$ billion)**

Total portfolio			
1994–95		*2004–05*	
Brazil	29.0	Taipei, China	24.1
Korea	11.7	China (PRC): Mainland	17.2
China, P.R.: Hong Kong	8.9	Korea	16.1
Argentina	8.1	Poland	12.9
Indonesia	4.0	Turkey	12.0
India	3.5	India	10.9
Thailand	3.4	Mexico	8.1
South Africa	2.9	Malaysia	7.2
Taipei, China	2.8	Hungary	6.5
Hungary	2.3	China, P.R.: Hong Kong	6.5

Sources: Centennial Group, IMF (*IFS* and *WEO*), World Bank (*WDI* and *GDF*), Central Banks of India, Indonesia and Taiwan, Hong Kong Monetary Authority, Singapore Department of Statistics, CEIC and UNCTAD.

Table 3A(2)8a   Top 10 countries: Debt inflows into EMEs (US$ billion)

Debt			
1994–95		*2004–05*	
Brazil	24.0	Poland	11.4
Korea	7.7	Korea	9.8
Argentina	5.2	Turkey	8.5
Thailand	2.4	Mexico	7.7
China (PRC): Mainland	2.3	Hungary	5.8
Indonesia	2.3	Malaysia	4.7
Hungary	2.3	Czech Republic	2.8
Philippines	1.8	Ukraine	2.4
South Africa	1.4	Indonesia	2.2
Taipei, China	1.0	Russia	1.8

Sources: Centennial Group, IMF (*IFS* and *WEO*), World Bank (*WDI* and *GDF*), Central Banks of India, Indonesia and Taiwan, Hong Kong Monetary Authority, Singapore Department of Statistics, CEIC and UNCTAD.

Table 3A(2)8b   Top 10 countries: Equity inflows into EMEs (US$ billion)

Equity			
1994–95		*2004–05*	
Brazil	5	Taipei, China	24.5
Korea	3.9	China (PRC): Mainland	15.6
India	3.5	India	10.9
Argentina	2.9	South Africa	6.8
Mexico	2.3	China, P.R.: Hong Kong	6.4
Taipei, China	1.8	Korea	6.3
Indonesia	1.7	Brazil	4.3
South Africa	1.5	Israel	3.7
Thailand	0.9	Turkey	3.5
Czech Republic	0.9	Singapore	3.5

Sources: Centennial Group, IMF (*IFS* and *WEO*), World Bank (*WDI* and *GDF*), Central Banks of India, Indonesia and Taiwan, Hong Kong Monetary Authority, Singapore Department of Statistics, CEIC and UNCTAD. Hong Kong excluded for 1994–95.

Table 3A(2)9 **Top 10 countries: Net banks flows into EMEs (US$ billion)**

	Net banks		
1994–95		*2004–05*	
Thailand	11.9	China, P.R.: Hong Kong	6.9
Singapore	3.1	India	6.8
Russia	2.5	Russia	6.5
Korea	2.2	Turkey	5.7
Saudi Arabia	2.1	Hungary	3.3
Czech Republic	1.9	Bahrain	3.2
Argentina	1.7	Romania	3.1
South Africa	1.7	Kazakhstan	2.3
Philippines	1.7	Croatia	2
Indonesia	1.2	Taipei, China	1.6

Sources: Centennial Group, IMF (*IFS* and *WEO*), World Bank (*WDI* and *GDF*), Central Banks of India, Indonesia and Taiwan, Hong Kong Monetary Authority, Singapore Department of Statistics, CEIC and UNCTAD. For Hong Kong, 1993 data used for 1994–95.

Table 3A(2)10 **Total capital inflows, long-term trend (average, US$ billin)**

	1985–90	*1991–96*	*1997–98*	*1999–2004*	*2005*
Africa	0.6	5.3	15.0	6.6	19.0
Americas	6.1	67.0	99.5	57.9	69.6
Asia	14.6	89.0	55.2	163.3	263.0
Europe	–3.4	15.1	37.8	42.6	133.2
Middle-East	–1.9	4.0	20.1	9.4	21.5
Total EMEs	16.1	180.5	227.6	279.8	506.3

Sources: Centennial Group, IMF (*IFS* and *WEO*), World Bank (*WDI* and *GDF*), Central Banks of India, Indonesia and Taiwan, Hong Kong Monetary Authority, Singapore Department of Statistics, CEIC and UNCTAD.

Note: Hong Kong excluded before 1998, save FDI.

Table 3A(2)11 **Total capital inflows, long-term trend (% of GDP)**

	1985–90	*1991–96*	*1997–98*	*1999–2004*	*2005*
Africa	0.26	1.86	4.73	1.85	3.30
Americas	0.76	4.75	5.23	3.34	3.07
Asia	1.25	3.98	1.86	4.34	4.85

(Table 3A(2)11 continued)

(Table 3A(2)11 continued)

Europe	−0.69	1.65	3.97	3.98	6.73
Middle-East	−0.49	1.02	3.72	1.42	2.25
Total EMEs	0.52	3.44	3.41	3.69	4.52

Sources: Centennial Group, IMF (*IFS*, BoP and *WEO*), World Bank (*WDI* and *GDF*), Central Banks of India, Indonesia and Taiwan, Hong Kong Monetary Authority, Singapore Department of Statistics, CEIC and UNCTAD.

Note: Hong Kong excluded before 1998, save FDI.

Table 3A(2)12 Capital inflows by type, long-term trend (average, (US$ billion)

	1985–90	1991–96	1997–98	1999–2004	2005
FDI	22.2	89.2	191.6	215.5	315.7
Tot Portfolio	4.9	76.9	71.6	77.1	177.8
Equity	1.1	26.8	22.1	62.2	122.7
Debt	3.9	50.2	49.5	15.5	55.7
Banks (Net)	−11.2	14.3	−35.7	−12.8	2.0
Total Capital Inflows	15.9	180.5	227.6	279.8	495.4

Sources: Centennial Group, IMF (*IFS* and *WEO*), World Bank (*WDI* and *GDF*), Central Banks of India, Indonesia and Taiwan, Hong Kong Monetary Authority, Singapore Department of Statistics, CEIC and UNCTAD.

Note: Hong Kong excluded before 1998, save FDI.

Table 3A(2)13 Capital inflows by type, long-term trend, period averages (% of GDP)

	1985–90	1991–96	1997–98	1999–2004	2005
FDI	0.72	1.70	2.87	2.84	2.82
Tot Portfolio	0.16	1.47	1.07	1.02	1.59
Equity	0.03	0.51	0.33	0.82	1.10
Debt	0.13	0.96	0.74	0.20	0.50
Banks (Net)	−0.36	0.27	−0.53	−0.17	0.02
Total Capital Inflows	0.52	3.44	3.41	3.69	4.42

Sources: Centennial Group, IMF (*IFS* and *WEO*), World Bank (*WDI* and *GDF*), Central Banks of India, Indonesia and Taiwan, Hong Kong Monetary Authority, Singapore Department of Statistics, CEIC and UNCTAD.

Note: Hong Kong excluded before 1998, save FDI.

Table 3A(2)14 **Foreign direct investment, long-term trend (average, US$ billion)**

	1985–90	1991–96	1997–98	1999–2004	2005
Africa	0.8	2.7	5.1	6.1	13.7
Americas	6.0	22.7	65.6	61.0	62.4
Asia	13.4	54.1	93.5	110.3	165.7
Europe	0.4	7.9	20.5	30.9	65.6
Middle-East	1.5	1.9	7.0	7.3	19.2
Total EMEs	22.2	89.2	191.6	215.5	326.6

Sources: Centennial Group, IMF (*IFS* and *WEO*), World Bank (*WDI* and *GDF*), Central Banks of India, Indonesia and Taiwan, Hong Kong Monetary Authority, Singapore Department of Statistics, CEIC and UNCTAD.

Table 3A(2)15 **Foreign direct investment, long-term trend, period averages (% of GDP)**

	1985–90	1991–96	1997–98	1999–2004	2005
Africa	0.34	0.93	1.61	1.70	2.38
Americas	0.76	1.61	3.45	3.52	2.75
Asia	1.15	2.42	3.16	2.93	3.06
Europe	0.08	0.86	2.15	2.88	3.31
Middle-East	0.40	0.49	1.30	1.12	2.01
Total EMEs	0.72	1.70	2.87	2.84	2.92

Sources: Centennial Group, IMF (*IFS* and *WEO*), World Bank (*WDI* and *GDF*), Central Banks of India, Indonesia and Taiwan, Hong Kong Monetary Authority, Singapore Department of Statistics, CEIC and UNCTAD.

Table 3A(2)16 **Total portfolio inflows, long-term trend (average, US$ billion)**

	1985–90	1991–96	1997–98	1999–2004	2005
Africa	−0.4	2.6	10.6	3.6	5.8
Americas	2.6	43.9	32.9	1.2	18.3
Asia	2.0	24.4	11.7	59.9	111.5
Europe	0.6	5.4	15.1	9.8	37.2
Middle-East	0.0	0.7	1.3	2.5	4.8
Total EMEs	4.9	76.9	71.6	77.1	177.8

Sources: Centennial Group, IMF (*IFS* and *WEO*), World Bank (*WDI* and *GDF*), Central Banks of India, Indonesia and Taiwan, Hong Kong Monetary Authority, Singapore Department of Statistics, CEIC and UNCTAD.

Note: Hong Kong excluded before 1998.

Table 3A(2)17 **Total portfolio inflows, long-term trend, period averages (% of GDP)**

	1985–90	1991–96	1997–98	1999–2004	2005
Africa	–0.15	0.92	3.36	1.02	1.01
Americas	0.32	3.11	1.73	0.07	0.81
Asia	0.18	1.09	0.39	1.59	2.06
Europe	0.13	0.58	1.58	0.92	1.88
Middle-East	0.01	0.18	0.24	0.38	0.51
Total EMEs	0.16	1.47	1.07	1.02	1.59

Sources: Centennial Group, IMF (*IFS* and *WEO*), World Bank (*WDI* and *GDF*), Central Banks of India, Indonesia and Taiwan, Hong Kong Monetary Authority, Singapore Department of Statistics, CEIC and UNCTAD.

Note: Hong Kong excluded before 1998.

Table 3A(2)18 **Equity inflows, long-term trend (average, US$ billion)**

	1985–90	1991–96	1997–98	1999–2004	2005
Africa	–0.1	0.9	7.2	3.3	7.0
Americas	0.5	12.5	6.0	0.4	12.3
Asia	0.7	11.2	3.7	55.0	93.4
Europe	0.0	1.7	3.9	1.5	5.7
Middle-East	–0.1	0.5	1.3	2.0	4.2
Total EMEs	4.3	26.8	22.1	62.2	122.7

Sources: Centennial Group, IMF (*IFS* and *WEO*), World Bank (*WDI* and *GDF*), Central Banks of India, Indonesia and Taiwan, Hong Kong Monetary Authority, Singapore Department of Statistics, CEIC and UNCTAD.

Note: Hong Kong excluded before 1998.

Table 3A(2)19 **Equity inflows, long-term trend, period average (% of GDP)**

	1985–90	1991–96	1997–98	1999–2004	2005
Africa	–0.05	0.30	2.26	0.92	1.22
Americas	0.07	0.88	0.32	0.02	0.54
Asia	0.06	0.50	0.13	1.46	1.72
Europe	0.00	0.19	0.41	0.14	0.29

(*Table 3A(2)13 continued*)

(Table 3A(2)19 continued)

	1985–90	1991–96	1997–98	1999–2004	2005
Middle-East	–0.04	0.13	0.24	0.31	0.44
Total EMEs	0.14	0.51	0.33	0.82	1.10

Sources: Centennial Group, IMF (*IFS* and *WEO*), World Bank (*WDI* and *GDF*), Central Banks of India, Indonesia and Taiwan, Hong Kong Monetary Authority, Singapore Department of Statistics, CEIC and UNCTAD.

Note: Hong Kong excluded before 1998.

Table 3A(2)20   Debt inflows, long-term trend (average, US$ billion)

	1985–90	1991–96	1997–98	1999–2004	2005
Africa	–0.2	1.8	3.5	0.3	–1.2
Americas	2.0	31.4	26.8	0.8	6.0
Asia	1.3	13.2	7.9	5.5	18.1
Europe	0.6	3.7	11.2	8.3	31.5
Middle-East	0.2	0.2	0.0	0.5	1.3
Total EMEs	3.9	50.2	49.5	15.5	55.7

Sources: Centennial Group, IMF (*IFS* and *WEO*), World Bank (*WDI* and *GDF*), Central Banks of India, Indonesia and Taiwan, Hong Kong Monetary Authority, Singapore Department of Statistics, CEIC and UNCTAD.

Note: Hong Kong excluded before 1998.

Table 3A(2)21   Debt inflows, long-term trend, period averages (% of GDP)

	1985–90	1991–96	1997–98	1999–2004	2005
Africa	–0.10	0.62	1.10	0.09	–0.21
Americas	0.26	2.22	1.41	0.05	0.26
Asia	0.11	0.59	0.27	0.15	0.33
Europe	0.12	0.40	1.18	0.78	1.59
Middle-East	0.05	0.04	0.01	0.08	0.14
Total EMEs	0.13	0.96	0.74	0.20	0.50

Sources: Centennial Group, IMF (*IFS* and *WEO*), World Bank (*WDI* and *GDF*), Central Banks of India, Indonesia and Taiwan, Hong Kong Monetary Authority, Singapore Department of Statistics, CEIC and UNCTAD.

Note: Hong Kong excluded before 1998.

Table 3A(2)22   Net bank flows, long-term trend (average, US$ billion)

	1985–90	1991–96	1997–98	1999–2004	2005
Africa	0.2	0.0	−0.8	−3.1	−0.5
Americas	−2.5	0.5	1.1	−4.2	−11.1
Asia	−0.9	10.5	−50.0	−6.9	−14.2
Europe	−4.4	1.9	2.2	1.9	30.3
Middle-East	−3.6	1.4	11.8	−0.5	−2.5
Total EMEs	−11.2	14.3	−35.7	−12.8	2.0

Sources: Centennial Group, IMF (*IFS* and *WEO*), World Bank (*WDI* and
    GDF), Central Banks of India, Indonesia and Taiwan, Hong Kong
    Monetary Authority, Singapore Department of Statistics, CEIC
    and UNCTAD.

Note: Hong Kong excluded before 1998.

Table 3A(2)23   Net bank flows, long-term trend, period averages (% of GDP)

	1985–90	1991–96	1997–98	1999–2004	2005
Africa	0.08	0.01	−0.24	−0.87	−0.09
Americas	−0.32	0.03	0.06	−0.24	−0.49
Asia	−0.08	0.47	−1.69	−0.18	−0.26
Europe	−0.89	0.21	0.23	0.18	1.53
Middle-East	−0.94	0.35	2.18	−0.08	−0.26
Total EMEs	−0.36	0.27	−0.53	−0.17	0.02

Sources: Centennial Group, IMF (*IFS* and *WEO*), World Bank (*WDI* and
    GDF), Central Banks of India, Indonesia and Taiwan, Hong Kong
    Monetary Authority, Singapore Department of Statistics, CEIC
    and UNCTAD.

Note: Hong Kong excluded before 1998.

Acknowledgement

The authors are grateful to Harpaul Alberto Kohli for his valuable assistance in collecting, organizing, analysing and presenting data on which this report is based.

Bibliography

Accounting and Auditing Organization for Islamic Financial Institutions (AAOIFI). 2004–05. *Accounting Auditing and Governance Standards*, Manama, Bahrain: AAOIFI.

Aggarwal, Rena, Leora Klappen and Peter D. Wysocki. 2003. 'Portfolio Preferences of Foreign Institutional Investors'. Policy Research Working Paper No. 3101, July 2003, World Bank, Washington, DC.

Bank for International Settlements (BIS). 2006. *Annual Report 2005–06*, June. Basel, Switzerland: BIS.

CEIC. Various Years. http.//www.ceicdata.com.

Henry Peter Blair and Peter Lombund Lorentzen. 2003. 'Domestic Capital Market Reform and Access to Global Finance: Making Markets Work'. In Robert E. Litan, Michael Pomerleane and V. Sundararajan (Eds), *The Future of Domestic Capital Markets in Development Countries*. Washington, DC: Brookings Institution Press.

International Monetary Fund. 2002. 'Global Financial Stability Report, World Economic and Financial Surveys', Washington, DC: IMF.

———. 2005. 'Annual Report on Exchange Arrangements and Exchange Restrictions', Washington, DC: IMF.

———. 2006a. 'Global Financial Stability Report, World Economic and Financial Surveys', Washington, DC: IMF.

———. 2006b. *Financial Market Update, Inter-national Capital Markets Department*, Washington, DC: IMF.

———. 2006c. *International Financial Statistics–Year Book*, Washington, DC: IMF.

International Monetary Fund and World Bank. 2003. *Guidelines for Public Debt Management: Accompanying Document and Selected Case Studies*, Washington, DC: IMF and World Bank August.

International Organization of Securities Commission (IOSCO). 2004. 'Islamic Capital Market Fact Findings Report, Report of the Islamic Capital Market Task Force of the IOSCO'. *IOSCO Public Document 170*. July.

Islamic Finance News. 2006. Volume 3, Issue 26, 4 August 2006. Available at www.islamicfinancenews.com. Kuala Lumpur, Malaysia.

Liquidity Management Center. Various Issues. Monthly Reports (September 2001–February 2006). Available at http://www.lmcbahrain.com

Miniane, Jacques. 2004. 'A New Set of Measures on Capital Account Restrictions'. *International Monetary Fund Staff Papers*, 51(2): 276–308, Washington, DC.

Moody's Investor Service. 2006. 'Shariah and Sukuk: A Moody's Primer, International Structured Financing', Special Report, London, 26 May 2006.

Pietro Garibaldi, Nada Mora, Ratra Sahay and Jeromin Zettlemeger. 2002. 'What Moves Capital to Transition Economies?', *IMF Staff Papers, Vol. 48, Special Issue*, May 2002, Washington, DC.

World Bank. 2006. *Global Development Finance (GDF)*, June 2006. Washington, DC: World Bank.

Outward Foreign Direct Investment from Emerging Economies: New Players in the World Economy?

4

HEINZ HAUSER

Introduction

For many years, emerging economies have commonly been perceived as target countries of foreign direct investment (FDI). Recent large-scale overseas investments by companies based in countries like China, India, Brazil, Mexico, Russia or South Africa have made it clear, however, that emerging economies also play an important role as origin countries of FDI. This chapter seeks to provide some background information on this phenomenon and formulates preliminary policy conclusions.

Stylized facts can be summarized as follows:

- Emerging economies have become an important source of FDI. Outflows grew particularly in the 1990s and reached US$ 133 billion in 2005 or about 17 per cent of world flows. Even excluding flows from Hong Kong (China) and offshore financial centres, outflows from developing and transition countries were close to US$ 90 billion. The outward FDI stock of developing and transition countries reached US$ 1.4 trillion in 2005, or 13 per cent of the world total (all data from United Nations Conference on Trade and Development [UNCTAD], 2006: 105–08).

- Because developing and transition countries invest heavily in other developing countries, mostly from the same region, their importance as source of developing countries' inward FDI is even more pronounced. The share of South–South flows in total FDI to developing countries rose from 16 per cent in 1995 to 36 per cent in 2003 (World Bank, 2006: 108). According to the UNCTAD Investment Report 2006, close to 50 per cent of the inward FDI stock of developing and transition economies comes from other developing countries. Especially for low-income countries, FDI from other developing countries takes the lion's share of all inward investments (UNCTAD, 2006: 117–21).

- For some emerging economies, outward FDI has become a quantitatively relevant phenomenon. Starting in the mid-1990s, outward FDI of emerging economies has gained strength, albeit with great volatility (Figure 4.1). Based on the average 2002–04, the following countries have experienced outward FDI of more than US$ 1 billion annually: Brazil, Chile, China (PRC), Hong Kong (China); (US$ 23 billion!), India, Korea, Malaysia, Mexico, Russia, Taipei, China (UNCTAD, 2005a). For countries like

Figure 4.1 Outward FDI of selected emerging economies

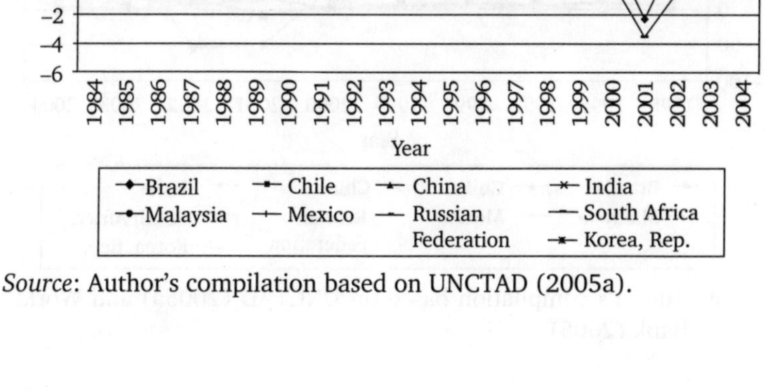

Source: Author's compilation based on UNCTAD (2005a).

Brazil (2004), Korea, Malaysia, Russia, South Africa
(2003–04), outward FDI is in the range (or above) of 50 per
cent of inward FDI (Figure 4.2).

- In some industries, multinational enterprises (MNEs) based
in emerging economies have become important players on
world markets. A recent Boston Consulting Group (BCG)
report identified, from an original set of more than 3,000
companies, a list of 100 global challengers from emerging
countries and analyzed their entry strategies and growth
potential (BCG, 2006). Major countries of origin of these
companies are China (44), India (21), Brazil (12), Russia
(7) and Mexico (6). They are active in a wide range of
industries, with 32 companies in the industrial goods sector,
18 in consumer durables, 15 in resource extraction, 11 in food
and cosmetics, six in technology equipment, six in telecom-
munication services and 12 in other sectors. According to the
2006 UNCTAD Investment Report (UNCTAD, 2006: 123),
MNEs from developing and transition countries are among
the top 20 players worldwide in all areas of economic

Figure 4.2 Outward FDI as a percentage of inward FDI

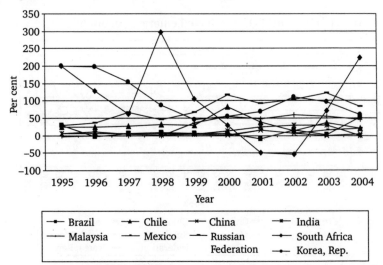

Source: Author's compilation based on UNCTAD (2005a) and World
Bank (2005).

activity, with some concentration in container shipping, steel and petroleum refining.

Before going into details, a cautious note on the availability and reliability of data is appropriate.[1] Information on outward FDI of emerging economies is incomplete and does not give a breakdown for industries or destination countries. The World Bank *Global Development Finance*, for example, calculates South–South FDI flows as residual, subtracting FDI outflows from high income to developing countries from total FDI inflows to developing countries (World Bank, 2006: 111). The paucity of data limits the extent to which general trends and conclusions can be derived from reported observations.

The main sources of information for this chapter are the World Bank *Global Development Finance* 2006 (World Bank, 2006), the UNCTAD World Investment Report 2005 (UNCTAD, 2005a), and the UNCTAD World Investment Report 2006 (UNCTAD, 2006)[2] for country data and trends. In addition, The BCG Report on the New Global Challengers (BCG, 2006), a Deutsche Bank (DB) Report on China's overseas FDI (Deutsche bank [DB], 2006), and a *BusinessWeek* lead article on 'The New Multinationals' of 31 July 2006 (Pete Engardio, 2006) provide useful information on markets and MNEs from emerging economies.

The remainder of the chapter is structured as follows: Section titled 'Outward FDI performance of emerging economies' discusses macro-economic trends of FDI from emerging countries, Section titled 'Determinants of the strong growth of FDI from emerging economies' summarizes determents of increased FDI flows from developing and transition countries, and Section titled 'New global players' highlights information on MNEs from developing countries and their impact on global markets. The next section titled 'The challenges ahead' points to some central challenges for policy makers in view of increased FDI participation of emerging economies.

It is also worth noting what the chapter does not address:

- Portfolio-investments of resource-rich countries: For some oil-producing countries, FDI has a strong element of portfolio-investment. Its main purpose is the spreading of risks. This category of FDI follows quite distinct motivations.

- The chapter does not discuss in sufficient depth China's FDI to secure oil and mineral resources. This activity is important quantitatively (in particular for African countries) and has substantial impact on world markets for resources. Nevertheless, it is a primarily Chinese phenomenon and follows quite different motivations.

To sum up: the chapter concentrates on macro-economic FDI flows and on firm activities in competitive product markets.

Outward FDI performance of emerging economies

Whereas the role of developing economies as origin of FDI was negligible in the early 1990s, the volume of their outward FDI showed impressive growth afterwards; for Asian countries since 1991 and for Latin America since 1997 (Figure 4.3). As with

Figure 4.3   FDI outflows from developing economies, and Southeast Europe and CIS (US$ billion)

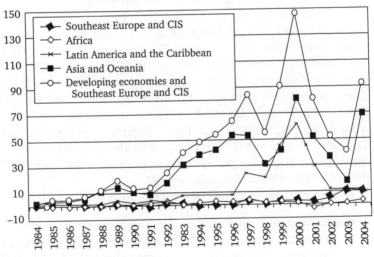

Source: UNCTAD (2005a: 8).

global FDI, the years 2001–03 saw a sharp decline, but FDI flows resumed their growth in 2004, although exclusively from Asian countries. The 2006 UNCTAD Investment Report contains no regional breakdown, but summary statistics indicate that the strong performance continued into 2005 (UNCTAD, 2006: 107).

According to the 2006 UNCTAD Investment Report, the outward FDI stock from developing and transition countries reached US$ 1.4 trillion in 2005, which corresponds to a share in world stock of 13 per cent (UNCTAD, 2006: 105). Nevertheless, these figures must be interpreted with caution. They are inflated by large transactions of Hong Kong (China)—roundabout transactions with the Peoples Republic of China (PRC)—and of offshore financial centres such as Bermuda, Virgin Islands and Cayman Islands. The 2006 UNCTAD Investment Report shows FDI flows from developing and transition countries net of Hong Kong (China) and offshore financial centres (UNCTAD, 2006: 108). They were negligible until 1987, increased to around US$ 10 billion to US$ 20 billion between 1988 and 1993, and reached US$ 30 billion to US$ 40 billion between 1994 and 2003. In 2004, they stood at US$ 70 billion and in 2005 close to US$ 90 billion—a clear indication of a strongly improved FDI position of emerging economies.

A further breakdown for regions and sectors shows two noteworthy concentrations (UNCTAD, 2006: 112–17): Asia is of growing importance as a source region for outward FDI flow and services dominate as sector. Asia's share of the total stock of FDI from developing and transition countries stood at 23 per cent in 1980, increasing to 46 per cent by 1990, and reaching 62 per cent in 2005. The vast majority is invested in neighbouring countries of the region. The share of services in the total of outstanding FDI stock of developing and transition countries 2004 reached 81 per cent and 71 per cent respectively, if one excludes Hong Kong (China). This compares to 67 per cent for developed countries which have a higher share of manufacturing FDI.

Albeit impressive on its own, these numbers underestimate the importance of emerging economies in FDI flows to the developing world. South–South flows are estimated by the World Bank to cover more than one-third of total inflows to developing countries (Table 4.1). Increased South–South flows provided partial compensation for the decline in FDI flows from high-income countries from US$ 130 billion in 1999 to US$ 82 billion in 2003. In addition, FDI flows from emerging economies tend to be less concentrated than those from high-income countries and reach poor countries in the respective area.

Table 4.1   South–South FDI as a share of global FDI to developing countries (US$ billion)

	1995	1999	2000	2001	2002	2003e
Total inflows (1)	90.3	163.5	154.7	159.3	135.3	129.6
From high income OECD (2)	48.1	95.4	93.7	84.8	55.1	59.4
From high-income non-OECD (3)	28.2	35.0	22.7	24.8	27.2	22.8
South–South FDI (1)–(2)–(3)	14.0	33.1	38.3	49.7	53.0	47.4
South–South FDI (per cent)	15.5	20.2	24.8	31.2	39.2	36.6

Source: World Bank (2006: 111).

Notes: The South–South estimates are based on 35 countries that account for 85 per cent of total FDI flows to developing countries. The estimates are based on the World Bank's classification of developing countries.

  e = estimate.

Determinants of the strong growth of FDI from emerging economies

FDI outflows from developing countries are concentrated by country of origin to a relatively small number of emerging economies and tend to be stronger for selected industries. Albeit, it is still a relatively recent phenomenon, some general remarks on its determinants are warranted.

Traditional FDI theory is a good starting point.[3] Firms need a specific or ownership advantage to support their competitive position on world markets. Ownership advantages can be located, among others, in specific technical or management knowledge, in preferred access to critical resources or in a brand which provides marketing advantages. The basic rationale for FDI strategies in a global market is to increase or protect profitability and/ or capital value, which can either lead to 'asset exploiting' or 'asset augmenting' strategies. The former concentrates on making best use of existing firm-specific advantages; the latter describes a strategy to tap into foreign pools of knowledge, be it technical (research clusters), managerial (introducing international standards of managing), or market-driven.

According to the investment development path theory,[4] the FDI position of a country is systematically related to a country's level and structure of economic development. In the first stage, there is likely to be very little inward and outward FDI, except inward investments in natural resources. In the second phase, inward FDI starts to rise (increase of per capita income and location-specific advantages), whereas outward investment remains low. Only at a later stage of development, outward FDI becomes a phenomenon of importance as domestic firms gain firm-specific competitive advantages and the required organizational capabilities. These general considerations are valid also for the more recent strong growth of FDI outflows from emerging economies. But, as the UNCTAD World Investment Report 2006 correctly notes, the length of the cycle seems to have shortened. Some emerging economies, notably China, India and Brazil, appear to be investing abroad at a very early stage of their investment cycle and their sources for firm-specific advantages seem to cover a wide range of competencies, including expertise and technology, access to resources, production and service capabilities, business models and cultural and institutional affinity.[5]

Against this background, what are the main drivers for the strong performance of outward FDI from emerging economies, and for the above-average growth of South–South flows in particular? Some of the major arguments include[6]:

- *Strong growth and maturing of domestic markets*: many emerging economies have large domestic markets with continued high growth. This provides a strong home base for international expansion. In addition, some of these markets, for example, China, are very competitive which puts their firms in a good position to enter foreign markets. With growing maturity of markets, firms expand internationally, with export sales first and followed by FDI to better exploit market opportunities. This is a normal development pattern and some of the large emerging economies have entered this sequence.

- *Regional patterns of trade and FDI*: From empirical research, we know that geographic proximity plays an important role in explaining bilateral trade and FDI flows. This is also true for emerging economies. Most South–South capital flows occur within the same geographic region, both because they follow trade[7] and because proximity, common language and cultural and ethnic ties reduce the risks of lending and investment. As the strong growing emerging economies are part of a larger developing area, China and India in Asia, Brazil in Latin America, South Africa in Sub-Sahara Africa, this phenomenon strongly supports South–South FDI.

- *The rise of RTAs*: RTAs have mushroomed since 1990 and activity has been particularly intensive in Asia, Latin America and Southern Africa. RTAs reduce trade barriers and spur FDI flows. They reinforce the underlying trend to strong regional activity.

- *Comparative advantage of emerging markets MNEs over industrial country competitors when investing in developing countries*: the greater familiarity of emerging markets' MNEs with technology and business practices suitable for low-income, developing-country markets and their home market experience in dealing with cumbersome regulations may give them an advantage over their rivals from high-income countries.

- *Liberalization and privatization policies in infrastructure of host governments*: the argument of greater familiarity with local conditions for successful business applies even stronger for infrastructure projects which have gained in importance in international FDI. Recent years have seen large infrastructure development programmes with participation of (foreign) private investors.

- *Differences in regional comparative advantages*: especially in Asia, there are still very large differences in wage levels and capital intensity of production between countries of the region. This creates opportunities for the outsourcing of labour-intensive parts of the value chain and strengthens incentives for international production, and hence FDI flows.

What are my expectations for the future? The reasons given earlier for strong outward FDI will continue into the following years. In particular, there are no signs that liberalization, particularly on a regional level, will cede to a backward movement to increased protectionism, and markets like Brazil, South Africa, China and India are becoming more mature and, hence, a larger number of their firms will embark on an internationalization path. In addition, the exchange reserve position of many of these countries has become quite comfortable and gives more leeway for outward FDI. China is a special case in question: with foreign exchange reserves in the range of US$ 1,000 billion, simple portfolio considerations speak for increased investment in real assets—instead of low-interest, short-term financing of the US trade deficits.

In order to get more detailed information, we put together FDI outflow data for nine countries which were chosen on the basis of their volume of outward FDI as well as their global or regional economic importance: Brazil, Chile, China, India, the Republic of Korea, Malaysia, Mexico, the Russian Federation and South Africa (Figure 4.1). For these countries, outward FDI activity did pick up at the beginning of the 1990s as it did in the rest of the world. Nevertheless, it has remained relatively limited and highly volatile in volume terms until today. As can be seen from Figure 4.1, the 'typical' level of outward FDI in this group of countries seems to lie between US$ 1 billion and US$ 5 billion. As a comparison, Japanese outward FDI reached more than US$ 30 billion in 2004 and that of the US, the world's biggest investor abroad, even exceeded US$ 229 billion in the same year.[8] These numbers put the positive interpretation of the foregoing discussion into a more cautious perspective. Although increasing and of some weight for South–South FDI flows, outward FDI of emerging economies is still far below their counterpart from highly developed countries. In addition, these flows are highly volatile and depend on large transactions of single firms. Nevertheless, I would keep the general conclusion that outward FDI of emerging economies is a phenomenon which needs attention for future FDI analysis.

When comparing the development of inward FDI to outward FDI, as done in Figure 4.2, it emerges that some of the countries in the group are just as important as sources of FDI as they are as FDI targets. Outward FDI as a percentage of inward FDI has fluctuated around 100 per cent since 2000 in the case of Russia, while it lay mostly above 50 per cent in the cases of Malaysia and the Republic of Korea. For Brazil, Chile, China, India and Mexico, outward FDI as a percentage of inward FDI, with few exceptions, was well below 50 per cent, while it fluctuated strongly in the case of South Africa.

The UNCTAD Outward FDI Performance Index gives also useful information on the relative position of the respective countries. It compares the share of a country's outward FDI stock in world FDI with the respective share of its GDP in world GDP.[9] A value of 1 indicates that the relative weight of outward FDI corresponds to its relative weight in GDP. Small, high-income or resource-rich countries have typically a value above 1, very large countries and low-income countries usually fall below 1.

In the years 2003–05, outward FDI performance index of UNCTAD (Table 4.2), Malaysia is ranked 20th (index value 1.39), Taipei, China ranked 21st (1.19), Chile ranked 27th (0.76), the Russian Federation ranked 28th (0.73), Brazil ranked 41st (0.42), the Republic of Korea ranked 59th (0.18), Mexico ranked 62nd (0.13), Turkey ranked 67th (0.10), China (PRC) ranked 71st (0.09) and India ranked 88th (0.04). These figures tell us that some emerging eco-nomies are already well integrated into international FDI flows. On the other hand, Mexico, India and China, three often-cited outward investors, are still well beyond their GDP share. One of the reasons for the low value of China and India might also be the fact that the index is calculated on the 3-year average of FDI stock, and that the more recent outward

Table 4.2   Outward FDI performance index, based on FDI stocks, average 2003–05

Rank	Economy	Index value
20	Malaysia	1.39
21	Taipei, China	1.19
27	Chile	0.76
28	Russian Federation	0.73
41	Brazil	0.42
59	Republic of Korea	0.18
62	Mexico	0.13
67	Turkey	0.10
71	China (PRC)	0.09
88	India	0.04

Source: UNCTAD (2006: 114).

FDI activities are not yet reflected in the respective values. But even taking into account the recent increase in FDI activity, these countries have great potential for more intensive outward FDI.

To summarize, the high-growth emerging economies have become an important source for FDI, starting in the early 1990s, and resuming growth since 2004. This should not come as a surprise, as these countries follow export-led growth strategies. FDI to optimize production and to enter new markets follows naturally. As this process has only started and countries like Brazil, China, India are still well below their potential, we will see continued strong growth of outward FDI from emerging markets in the years to come. This process will also be supported by the favourable foreign exchange reserve position of these countries.

New global players

Outward FDI from emerging economies is not only a macro-economic phenomenon, but also has micro-economic impacts. In some cases, MNEs from emerging economies start to shape global markets. They become important players who change the dynamics of competition worldwide.

Although, only a small number of MNEs based in emerging markets made it to the list of the world's top 100 non-financial Transnational Corporations (TNCs) of the UNCTAD's Investment Report 2006[10] (Hutchison Whampoa, Hong Kong (China) [ranked 17 by foreign assets], Petronas, Malaysia [ranked 59], Samsung, Korea [ranked 86] and CITIC Group, China (PRC) [ranked 94]), and only 18 out of a total of 141 cross-border mergers and acquisitions (M&A) deals, with a value of over US$ 1 billion, involved the acquiring firm to be based in a developing or transition country,[11] the influence can be felt in more specialized segments of the world economy. A non-exhaustive list of the Boston Consulting Group Report (2006: 5) includes:

- Forge, India—world's second-largest forging company.
- BYD Company, China—world's largest manufacturer of nickel–cadmium batteries and has a 23 per cent share of the market for mobile-hand-set batteries.
- Cemex, Mexico—has developed into one of the world's largest cement producers.
- China International Marine Containers Group Company, China—has a 50 per cent share of the marine container market.
- Embraco, Brazil—the world leader in compressors, with a 25 per cent market share.
- Embraer, Brazil—has surpassed Bombardier as the market leader in regional jets.
- Galanz Group Company, China—has a 45 per cent share of the microwave market in Europe and a 25 per cent share in the US.
- Johnson Electric, China—world's leading manufacturer of small electric motors.
- Ranbaxy Pharmaceuticals, India—is among the top 10 generic-pharmaceutical players in the world.
- Techtronic Industries, China—now the number-one supplier of power tools to Home Depots in the US.
- Wipro, India—has become the world's largest third-party engineering-services company (Infosys and Tata Consultancy Services, two other Indian technology services firms, complement the strong Indian segment in this industry).

The list could be enlarged by names such as China's Lenovo Group, which bought IBMs PC business, Brazilian brewer Ambev, Mexico's America Movil or Telefonos de Mexico, India's Tata Motors and Tata Steel and South African brewer SAB-Miller, all of which follow aggressive internationalization strategies. Add to that the Turkish Kok group holds substantial market shares in European TV sets and appliances markets and there are instances of industries where Haier and Hisense from China are important world market players. Huawei Technologies (China), which has become an important supplier of telecom equipment, won contracts from British Telecommunications for its US$ 19 billion programme to transform Britain's telecom network.[12]

There is little systematic information on the impact of new global players from emerging economies on the dynamics of world markets, which goes beyond the description of individual cases. The recent BCG Report (BCG, 2006) is, to my knowledge, the most comprehensive study done so far. I will, therefore, summarize some of the main results.

A global team of senior BCG consultants screened an original list of more than 3,000 companies from emerging economies and defined 100 top companies (RDE [Rapidly Developing Economies] 100) for further analysis (Table 4.3). Here are some of the main results:

- Asia is home to the majority with 70 companies, followed by Latin America with 18 companies and another 12 companies are based in Egypt, Russia and Turkey. China with 44 companies and India with 21 are disproportionately represented, when compared to their share in GDP of emerging economies.
- The RDE 100 is active in a wide range of industries, which include automotive equipment (12 companies), food and cosmetics (11 companies), fossil fuels (nine companies), consumer electronics (eight companies), home appliances (six companies), telecommunications services (six companies), technology equipment (six companies), engineered products (five companies), steel (five companies), non-ferrous metals (five companies) and IT services/business process outsourcing (four companies).

Table 4.3 The Boston Consulting Group list of top emerging global challengers

Company	Industry	Country
Aluminium Corporation of China (Chalco)	Non-ferrous metals	China
América Móvil	Telecommunication services	Mexico
Bajaj Auto	Automotive equipment	India
Bharat Forge	Automotive equipment	India
BOE Technology Group Company	Computers and IT components	China
Braskem	Petrochemicals	Brazil
BYD Company	Consumer electronics	China
Cemex	Building materials	Mexico
Charoen Pokphand Foods	Food and beverages	Thailand
China Aviation Corporation	Aerospace	China
China FAW Group Corporation	Automotive equipment	China
China HuaNeng Group	Fossil fuels	China
China International Marine Containers Group Company (CIMC)	Shipping	China
China Minmetals Corporation	Non-ferrous metals	China
China Mobile Communications Corporation	Telecommunication services	China
China National Heavy Truck Group Corporation (CNHTC)	Automotive equipment	China
China Netcom Group Corporation (CNC)	Telecommunication services	China
China Petroleum and Chemical Corporation (Sinopec)	Fossil fuels	China
China Shipping Group	Shipping	China

Chunlan Group Corporation	Home appliances	China
Cipla	Pharmaceuticals	India
CNOOC	Fossil fuels	China
Companhia Vale do Rio Doce (CVRD)	Mining	Brazil
COSCO Group	Shipping	China
Coteminas	Textiles	Brazil
Crompton Greaves	Engineered Products	India
Dongfeng Motor Company	Aerospace	China
Dr Reddy's Laboratories	Textiles	India
Embraco	Food and beverages	Brazil
Embraer	Aerospace	Brazil
Erdos Group	Textiles	China
Femser	Food and beverages	Mexico
Founder Group	Computers and IT components	China
Galanz Group Company	Home appliances	China
Gazprom	Fossil fuels	Russia
Gerdau Steel	Steel	Brazil
Gree Electric Appliances	Home appliances	China
Gruma	Food and beverages	Mexico
Grupo Modelo	Food and beverages	Mexico
Haier Company	Home appliances	China
Hindalco Industries	Non-ferrous metals	India
Hisense	Consumer electronics	China
Huawei Technologies Company	Telecommunications equipment	China

(Table 4.3 continued)

(Table 4.3 continued)

Company	Industry	Country
Indofood Sukeses Makmur	Food and beverages	Indonesia
Infosys Technologies	IT services/business process outsourcing	India
Johnson Electric	Engineered products	Hong Kong (China)
Koç Holding	Home appliances	Turkey
Konka Group Company	Consumer electronics	China
Larsen & Toubro	Engineering services	India
Lenovo Group	Computers and IT components	China
Li & Fung Group	Textiles	Hong Kong (China)
Lukoil	Fossil fuels	Russia
Mahindra & Mahindra	Automotive equipment	India
Malaysia International Shipping Company (MISC)	Shipping	Malaysia
Midea Holding Company	Home appliances	China
MMC Norilsk Nickel Group	Non-ferrous metals	Russia
Mobile Telesystems (MTS)	Telecommunications services	Russia
Nanjing Automobile Group Corporation (NAC)	Automotive equipment	China
Natura	Cosmetics	Brazil
Nemak	Automotive Equipment	Mexico
Oil and Natural Gas Corporation (ONGC)	Fossil fuels	India
Orascom Telecom Holding	Telecommunications services	Egypt
Pearl River Piano Group	Musical instruments	China

Perdigão	Food and beverages	Brazil
PetroChina Company	Fossil fuels	China
Petrobrás	Fossil fuels	Brazil
Petronas	Fossil fuels	Malaysia
Ranbaxy Pharmaceuticals	Pharmaceuticals	India
Reliance Group	Chemicals	India
Rusal	Non-ferrous metals	Russia
Sabanci Holding	Chemicals	Turkey
Sadia	Food and beverages	Brazil
Satyam Computer Services	IT services/business process outsourcing	India
Severstal	Steel	Russia
Shanghai Automotive Industry Corporation Group (SAIC)	Automotive equipment	China
Shanghai Baostell Group Corporation	Steel	China
Shougang Group	Steel	China
Sinochem Corporation	Chemicals	China
Sisecam	Building materials	Turkey
Skyworth Multimedia International Company	Consumer electronics	China
Sukhoi Company	Aerospace	Russia
SVA Group Company	Consumer electronics	China
Tata Consultancy Services (TCS)	IT services/business process outsourcing	India
Tata Motors	Automotive equipment	India
Tata Steel	Steel	India
Tata Tea	Food and beverages	India

(Table 4.3 continued)

(Table 4.3 continued)

Company	Industry	Country
TCL Corporation	Consumer electronics	China
Techtronic Industries Company	Engineered products	Hong Kong (China)
Thai Union Frozen Products	Food and beverages	Thailand
Tsingtao Brewery	Food and beverages	China
TVS Motor Company	Automotive equipment	India
UTStarcom	Telecommunications equipment	China
Vestel Group	Consumer electronics	Turkey
Videocon Industries	Consumer electronics	India
Videsh Sanchar Nigam (VSNL)	Telecommunication services	India
Votorantim Group Corporation	Process industries	Brazil
Wanxiang Group Corporation	Automotive equipment	China
WEG	Engineered products	Brazil
Wipro	IT services/business process outsourcing	India
ZTE Corporation	Telecommunications equipment	China

Source: BCG (2006: 7).

- The RDE 100 has shown very impressive economic results. It accounted for US$ 715 billion in revenue in 2004, with an average growth rate of 24 per cent per year from 2000 to 2004. It completed 200 publicly announced international transactions between 2001 and 2005, employed 4.6 million people of which 250,000–300,000 are engineers and scientists. These companies' collective stock market performance has been impressive. From January 2000 to March 2006, their total shareholder return (TSR) increased by more than 150 per cent, while the TSR of companies listed in Morgan Stanley's Emerging Market Index rose by 100 per cent and that of Standard and Poor's (S&P) 500 declined slightly.

- The majority of RDE 100 build on the home market strengths for their globalization strategy. The BCG report distinguishes six strategic models, of which four can be seen as variants of exploiting comparative advantages. They are: (*i*) Taking RDE brands global (home market products that have broad global appeal or are easy to customize for new markets); 28 companies active primarily in consumer electronics, household appliances, special foods, beverages, as well as automotive equipment. (*ii*) Turning RDE Engineering into Global Innovation (marketing innovative technology-based solutions that leverage their strengths in engineering and research); 22 companies active in telecommunications equipment, aerospace, automotive equipment, pharmaceuticals and technology services. (*iii*) Assuming Global Category Leadership (specialists and global leaders in one specific, relatively narrow product category); 12 companies involved mainly in manufactured industrial products, such as electric motors, compressors, power tools or shipping containers. (*iv*) Rolling out New Business Models to multiply markets (special knowledge in running complex logistics, in integrating acquisitions, or superiority along critical dimensions like supply-chain management or food processing lines); 13 companies in a variety of industries (cement, chemicals, food products, telecommunications services). The other two strategies are natural resource-based, either acquiring natural resources (with the majority of firms based in China) or monetizing natural resources of the home country (almost all the companies in this category are based in Brazil or Russia).

- Access to low-cost resources—including labour, property and equipment, raw materials and capital—is a major source of competitive advantage for RDE-based companies. This seems obvious, but needs closer scrutiny, as established MNEs from industrialized countries, in principle, have similar access to locations in emerging economies. Only the cost differential for activities in emerging economies between local and global MNEs creates comparative advantage. Some of the reasons for such cost advantages of local companies are: privileged access to energy and raw materials; familiarity with labour market conditions; and business models which are better adapted to the special conditions of emerging economies (for global MNEs, these operations are only a small part of their global activities, whereas they represent the core business for RDE-based players).
- Many RDE-based companies have surprisingly strong operating platforms. Their assets are often much younger than those of established competitors and they tend to be more flexible. In addition, some of the contenders have acquired special skills in operating long-distance supply chains.
- To cite from the closing thoughts of the report: 'We are fast entering a new era in which RDE-based challengers populate the world's largest industries. These challengers will be major players, reshaping many markets and forcing incumbent companies to respond' (BCG, 2006: 26)—an outlook I would fully subscribe to.
- Some additional thoughts on the motivation for emerging markets' firms to go international and on their impact on global markets' dynamics supplement the picture. What motivates MNEs from emerging markets to go global, although returns in their home markets are high, and what is its impact on global markets? Some of the motivations are fairly traditional and some of them have special relevance for emerging markets' firms.

- Securing energy and raw material supplies has been a traditional motivation for Western firms to operate globally, although in some cases these firms have begun to disinvest because energy and raw material markets have become more efficient and large resource-based investments have a high risk of state intervention. But the same has become a motivation for very large overseas investments by Chinese firms, which are mostly state enterprises. It seems that these deals are supported by political strategic interests of the Chinese government, and if continued these developments can influence world markets on two levels: first, there is an impact on the market for property rights in natural resources. State enterprises with a strategic interest tend to offer higher prices than purely private competitors, which can lead to shifts in ownership with global impact.[13] Second, and probably more important, is the risk that the government uses subsidized energy and raw material supply to strengthen the competitive position of their energy or raw material intensive industries—a strategy which is widely used in Russia and also found in China. This can have a sizeable impact on the global markets for some of the products like basic chemicals or steel.
- MNEs from emerging economies are in a similar position to their Western counterparts regarding market defence. If one looks at the history of Western MNEs, market defence has been a driving force in many cases. Competitors from neighbouring areas or countries, who threatened to enter the home market, were bought and with time this led to an ever-increasing expansion. In economic history, defensive takeovers were a widespread phenomenon, initially on a national scale, and with time they gained an international dimension. The consolidation of market structures in emerging economies is close to this development and part of regional FDI in emerging market areas has this defensive character.
- Regarding market expansion, it is difficult to distinguish precisely between market defence and market expansion, but there are examples which are relatively clear. In many modern

markets, you have to have a substantial global market share to remain competitive. Strong economies of scale or strong brand effects (which have become more important with modern communication) are responsible for this effect. Rapid expansion is a necessary precondition for success. MNEs from emerging markets in household appliances, specialized engineered products, IT industries are good examples. The production base is often concentrated in emerging economies but these firms operate in world markets. They change the competitive situation in developing and developed countries alike. The list of successful emerging markets' firms contains many examples from this category.

- Multiplying firm-specific advantages, again is a traditional motivation for internationalization which we also find in Western firms. With regard to outward FDI of MNEs from emerging economies, one could mention some specific features. More generally, emerging economies' MNEs seem to have a comparative advantage in dealing with legal systems of soft property rights. They follow a different legal and negotiation culture than many of their Western counterparts. Accordingly, they enjoy a comparative advantage in dealing with public-private partnership (PPPs) in infrastructure projects. Another example is the strong position of Indian firms in international markets for IT-based engineering and business consulting services.

To summarize this section: MNEs from emerging economies play an increasing role on global markets, and their number and impact will increase in the future. The motivation for the international expansion and the base for their firm-specific advantage shape the impact they will have on regional and global competition.

The challenges ahead

The focus of the chapter has been descriptive. Outward FDI from emerging economies, although still far below FDI activities of industrialized countries, has gained strength in the late 1990s and again since 2004. Given the impressive growth rates of emerging economies, the need of their industries is to globalize not only sales but also the production operations as well. The strong foreign exchange position of most rapidly growing emerging countries is not a spurious phenomenon of the last few years, but will be a constitutive element of international capital flows in the years to come. But FDI from emerging economies is not only a macro-economic issue of international capital markets, it also means far-reaching changes in market dynamics for many industries. Chapter 5 abounds with examples of firms which have become drivers of market change—and the list could easily be extended.

I am convinced that this is a very healthy development. Emerging economies stimulate growth in neighbouring developing countries and FDI projects provide much-needed development finance and production knowledge. Contenders from emerging markets increase competition on global markets and spur innovation with regard to products, processes and business models. Emerging economies are already important drivers of world economic growth and will remain so for the coming years. Globalization of these economies has started with trade and inward FDI, internationalization of production processes of emerging markets' companies, and hence increased outward FDI, is a natural complement.

But there are some major challenges down the road if one wants to fully reap the benefits of this development, which I would like to comment on briefly:

- FDI is sensitive to the quality of economic and political institutions of the host country. Even if the criteria might be somewhat different between developed and emerging country investors, we will experience increased competition for FDI. This has implications in two directions: on the one hand, the increased competition of countries for FDI will give strong incentives for welcomed market reform policies. There is good hope that development strategies which are firmly based on global integration will gain support. On the other hand, there is a downside to this process: countries which cannot, for whatever reasons, build sound political and economic institutions will lose out. There is a risk that the cleavage between strongly growing emerging economies and stagnant poor countries will increase—with negative implications for the world order. Hence, institutional capacity-building will become even more important in the future.

- Stronger competition of countries for FDI will increase the influence of business on politics. This is helpful if it means support for sound institutions and market-oriented economic policies. When it leads to corruption and to policies with highly negative impact on environmental or social outcomes, it has negative welfare effects and undermines the legitimacy of market-based systems. For an international market system to work properly—and more broadly based FDI flows contribute to this process—we need not only good governance in political systems, but also good governance in international corporations. The objectives and efforts of the Geneva-based World Business Council for Sustainable Development (WBCSD)[14] contribute to this goal.

- Trade and investment have a strong regional bias. From empirical trade theory we know that distance and cultural proximity play a decisive role for explaining the level of trade and investment flows between countries. In addition, we know that trade and investment are complementary. Regional integration in an area where we find strong emerging economies, contributes substantially to better exploiting the economic potential of internationally competitive firms. The weak regional integration in the developing world has hindered economic progress in the past. Regional economic cooperation has been substantially improved in Asia, parts of Latin America and South Africa, but much still needs to be done. The potential of FDI (and trade) flows between emerging developing countries for economic development could still be strongly improved. Unfortunately, long-standing political tensions, missing infrastructure for intra-regional trade and high barriers to trade are still important impediments to regional trade, which need concentrated political efforts for their removal.

- When it comes to FDI, many developed countries have a protectionist reflex, as a general political mood, but even more pronounced so when it comes to take-overs by emerging economies' MNEs. The (unsuccessful) China National Offshore Oil Corporation (CNOOC) bid for Union Oil Company of California (UNOCAL) set off strong nationalistic feelings in the US. Or the L.N. Mittal's bid for the European steel producer Arcelor was also not business as usual. A successful integration of emerging economies into the world economy necessitates an open FDI policy not only in developing countries but also in the industrialized world.

- The emergence of a large number of new global companies will increase the war for talents. Young professionals and companies are meeting on a global marketplace and, by far, not all university graduates—in developed and developing countries alike—are fit for global markets. The quality of educational systems will determine how far nationals of a country can profit from the new global economy. How firms can attract and integrate young talents from a variety of countries will become an important factor for comparative advantage and success.

Concluding remark

The emergence of MNEs from a number of rapidly growing developing countries marks the beginning of a new phase of globalization. It will change the landscape of the international economy. Whether we will reap the benefits from this new era to its potential depends on how we meet the political challenges in developed and developing countries and on how successful companies—contenders and incumbents—react to the new global environment.

Acknowledgements

The manuscript was prepared for the 2006 Global Meeting of the Emerging Markets Forum. At that time, the UNCTAD World Investment Report 2006, with its heavy emphasis on FDI from Developing and Transition Economies, was not yet available. In the following, I refer to the new UNCTAD report if suitable, but I cannot fully incorporate its rich empirical data and policy discussion.

I thank Christoph Böhler and Patrick Rudolph for their support in the preparation of the manuscript.

Notes

1. These difficulties can be attributed to differences in data coverage of FDI across countries, differences in methodologies and methods of data collection by host and home countries, and different time periods used for recording FDI transactions. Furthermore, it is not always obvious which transactions are to be considered as cross-border, because the highly intertwined ownership structures, with holding companies at different levels of a firm's hierarchy being located in different countries, makes attribution of home and host countries difficult. (Cf. UNCTAD [2005b]).
2. The UNCTAD Investment Report 2006 was not available at the time of the Emerging Markets Forum. The new information was incorporated for this publication.
3. Cf. UNCTAD (2006), Ch. IV.
4. Cf. Dunning (1981, 1986) for an early framework which links FDI theory with the development cycle.
5. UNCTAD (2006: 146–50).
6. Cf. also World Bank (2006), Ch. 4 and UNCTAD (2006), Ch. IV.
7. The WTO World Trade Report 2003 contains a detailed analysis of South–South Trade for the period 1990–2001. Cf. WTO (2004: 22–32).
8. Cf. UNCTAD (2005a: 303).
9. More precisely: The outward FDI performance (OND_i) of country i is given by $OND_i = \dfrac{FDI_i/FDI_w}{GDP_i/GDP_w}$, where FDI_i is outward FDI stock in country i, FDI_w world FDI stock, GDP_i GDP in country i and GDP_w world GDP. To avoid a bias from an unusually high level of outward FDI in 1 year, OND_i is always calculated on the basis of a 3-year period.

10. UNCTAD (2006), Annex Table A.I.11.
11. UNCTAD (2006), Annex Table A.I.7.
12. The examples are either from BCG (2006) or Pete Engardio (2006).
13. China's FDI in oil and mineral resource extraction in Africa is the most prominent example.
14. Homepage: Available at http://www.wbcsd.ch.

Bibliography

Deutsche Bank Research (DB). 2006. *Global Champions in Waiting. Perspectives on China's Overseas Direct Investment, Frankfurt am Main*, 4 August.

Dunning, John H. 1981. 'Explaining the International Direct Investment Position of Countries: Towards a Dynamic or Developmental Approach'. *Weltwirtschaftliches Archiv*, 117(1): 30–64.

———. 1986. 'The Investment Development Cycle Revisited'. *Weltwirtschaftliches Archiv*, 122(4): 667–75.

Pete Engardio. 2006. 'The New Multinationals. They're Smart and Hungry, and They Want Your Customers. Be Afraid. Be Very Afraid'. *Business Week*, 31 July: 41–49.

The Boston Consulting Group (BCG). 2006. *The New Global Challengers. How 100 Top Companies from Rapidly Developing Economies Are Changing the World*, The Boston Consulting Group, May 2006.

United Nations Conference on Trade and Development (UNCTAD). 2005a. 'World Investment Report 2005: Transnational Corporations and the Internationalization of R&D'. New York and Geneva: UNCTAD.

———. 2005b. *Introduction to Major FDI Issues*. Presentation at the 'Expert Meeting on Capacity Building in the Area of FDI: Data Compilation and Policy Formulation in Developing Countries'. Geneva: UNCTAD.

———. 2006. 'World Investment Report 2006: FDI from Developing and Transition Economies: Implications for Development'. New York and Geneva: UNCTAD.

World Bank. 2005. *World Development Indicators Database*. Washington, DC: World Bank.

———. 2006. 'Global Development Finance: The Development Potential of Surging Capital Flows', *Analysis and Outlook, Vol. I*, Review. Washington, DC: World Bank.

WTO. 2004. World Trade Report 2003. Geneva: WTO.

Outward Foreign Direct Investment from India

5

RAKESH JHA

Introduction

The world today is characterized by an increasing integration of economies and markets, with every nation seeking to benefit from the process of globalization. This is true even at the micro level where individual firms are rapidly expanding beyond domestic markets in an effort to participate in profitable growth opportunities in international markets. Globalization has led to the liberalization of trade and investment regimes. There has been an increase in competition from foreign firms through imports, inward FDI, non-equity forms of participation and various other means. Companies can no longer restrict themselves to the domestic market as a relatively secure source of profits. Competing at the global level requires firms to expand beyond domestic markets in order to achieve maximum efficiency. Increased access to markets and factors of production enables firms to operate efficiently and cater to an enlarged set of clients. Outward foreign direct investment (OFDI) can play an important role in enhancing the competitiveness of enterprises by providing access to strategic assets, technology, skills and natural resources. Two distinct sets of factors govern the flow of OFDI:

(i) *Macro-economic and policy environment*: favourable policy initiatives in the form of investment, trade and taxation treaties, and tax benefits are key drivers of investment flows. Further, factors such as saturated and highly competitive domestic markets may lead firms to develop capabilities and presence in overseas markets.

(ii) *Corporate specific factors*: rising costs in domestic markets, strategic considerations, global competitiveness, favourable conditions in foreign markets such as increased efficiency due to lower costs and greater access to cheaper natural resources drive corporates to invest abroad.

India has emerged as one of the fastest growing economies in the world and is drawing increasing international attention. The vast opportunities presented by Indian markets make India an important investment destination for international companies. Parallely, in recent years, investments by Indian enterprises in overseas markets have been increasing significantly. Overall economic growth, increasing competitiveness, improving quality, increasing corporate profitability, liberalization of regulations and improved availability of finance have resulted in a significant increase in OFDI from India. In recent times, driven by a fast-growing economy, healthy financial positions and the mindset to emerge as globally competitive, Indian firms have engaged in a large number of high-value outbound mergers and acquisitions (M&A).

Trends in OFDI

The evolution of OFDI flows from India can be divided into two distinct phases differing in terms of size, motivations and ownership patterns. While a restrictive policy environment marked the first phase, the second phase saw substantial liberalization of the policy regime. After the phase of restructuring in the late 1990s and the improved business cycle in recent years, Indian firms have emerged as more profitable and competitive. These factors along with greater access to finance led to a significant increase in outbound mergers and acquisitions during the second phase. The main characteristics of OFDI in the two phases are summarized in Table 5.1.

Table 5.1 Phases in the evolution of OFDI in India

Phase I (till 2003)	Phase II (2003 onwards)
1. Increased access to natural resources, markets and technology were the key drivers.	1. Apart from earlier reasons, OFDI driven more by strategic and market concerns.
2. The manufacturing sector was the most important driver of OFDI.	2. A variety of sectors contribute to OFDI, with the services sector emerging as an important contributor. Sectors such as pharmaceuticals and IT emerging as major players in cross-border mergers and acquisitions.
3. Indian companies were largely minority shareholders.	3. Indian equity participation is largely in the form of majority ownership.
4. Policy framework was restrictive and few sources of finance were available.	4. Policy framework liberalized; increased access to sources of finance along with significant internal revenues supported outbound deals growth.

Source: Author/ICICI Bank, Mumbai, India.

Prior to fiscal year (FY) 2000, FDI reported by India constituted only of equity flows. The Reserve Bank of India (RBI) revised the definition of FDI flows from FY 2001 to include three categories of capital flows under FDI:

(i) *Equity capital*: this includes equity in branches, shares in subsidiaries and other capital contributions.
(ii) *Reinvested earnings*: this includes retained earnings of foreign subsidiaries and affiliates.
(iii) *Inter-company debt transactions*: this includes inter-corporate debt transactions between associated corporate entities.

According to the United Nations Conference for Trade and Development, India's OFDI performance ranking improved from 80 in 2000 to 54 in 2004. OFDI increased from US$ 759 million in the FY 2001 to US$ 2,931 million in the FY 2006, an annual growth of over 55 per cent. During the first 9 months of FY 2007 alone, OFDI from India almost tripled as compared to FY 2006 to reach US$ 8,684 million. Outflows amounting to US$ 6,388 million occurred during October 2006 to December 2006 (Table 5.2).

Drivers of outward FDI

Increasing competitiveness, improved corporate governance, profitability and financial strength have been key drivers for the international expansion of Indian enterprises. The debt-equity ratio for corporate sector non-financial companies reduced from 1.3 in FY 1999 to 0.8 in FY 2005. For a set of about 2,900 companies (including financial sector firms), cash accruals increased from Indian Rupees (INR) 653 billion in FY 1996 to INR 1,938 billion for the period April–December 2006, an annual average growth of over 20 per cent. On a year-on-year basis, cash accruals for the period April–December 2006 increased by about 39.0 per cent. The quality of products and services by Indian firms has also seen significant improvement. Eleven Indian companies won the Deming prize (which is given to organizations that have achieved distinctive performance improvement through the application of quality management) between 2002 and 2006 as compared to only two between 1998 and 2001, and none prior to that.

Access to technology, distribution networks, skills, markets and brand names have been strategic considerations driving Indian enterprises to expand abroad. In addition, Indian firms are looking to secure natural resources and have invested in resource-rich countries like Russia, Sudan, Australia, Brazil and West and Central Asia. India serves as a prominent example of an economy where domestic firms have forayed abroad to

Table 5.2 Outward FDI from India (US$ million)

	FY2001	FY2002	FY2003	FY2004	FY2005	FY2006	April–December 2006
Equity	344	570	611	1,122	1,637	1,841	7,434
Reinvested Earnings	340	700	1,104	552	248	364	501
Other Capital	75	121	104	260	389	726	749
Total	759	1,391	1,819	1,934	2,274	2,931	8,684

Source: Reserve Bank of India (2006b).

establish their portfolio of locational assets as a source of increasing competitiveness. The main drivers of outward FDI from India are:

- High-growth sectors such as pharmaceuticals, Information Technology (IT) and auto ancillaries are poised at an inflection point. The pharmaceuticals sector, in particular, has witnessed an unprecedented increase in cross-border deal activity. With growth in domestic markets at more or less stable levels, firms in these sectors are looking to expand overseas operations and emerge as key global players.
- Strong equity markets, improved profitability and increased access to finance are major factors driving outbound mergers and acquisitions by Indian companies.
- As a consequence of rapid growth, Indian firms are increasingly benchmarking against global firms. Along with strong managerial expertise and improved efficiency, this has prompted Indian firms to compete at a global level.
- Strengthening established Indian brands abroad and building new brands are key drivers of overseas investments. A prominent example is the acquisition of Novelis by Hindalco, a company of the AV Birla Group, following which over 50 per cent of the group's business is expected to be generated in international markets. According to United Nations Conference on Trade and Development (UNCTAD), other examples of this strategy include Tata Motors' acquisition of Daewoo Commercial Vehicle Company (Republic of Korea), Infosys Technologies' acquisition of Expert Information Services (Australia), Ranbaxy Technologies' acquisition of RPG Aventis (France) and Tata Tea's acquisition of Tetley Tea (UK).
- Indian firms have placed increasing importance on acquisition of technology, knowledge and markets to improve competitiveness and move up the production value chain. The recent acquisition of Corus Group by Tata Steel is an example of this and will make Tata Steel the sixth largest producer of steel in the world. According to UNCTAD,

other examples of such deals are the acquisition of Nerve Wire (US) by Wipro, I-Flex's acquisition of Supersolutions Corp (US) and Wockhardt Ltd's purchase of a pharmaceutical company in the UK. Reliance Infocomm bought Flag Telecom (UK) for access to the undersea cable network. Firms are also setting up research and development centres at key offshore loca-tions to gain greater access to technology.

- Securing energy supplies have become a priority for Indian companies. Domestic oil companies such as Oil and Natural Gas Corporation Limited (ONGC) have increased their efforts to secure supplies of natural re-sources to meet the growing demand at home. Indian firms have been actively acquiring natural resources abroad. Hindalco's acquisition of copper mines in Australia, ONGC's acquisition of oil fields in Sudan and ONGC–Videsh's acquisition of a 20.0 per cent stake in the Sakhalin-1 oil and gas field in the Russian Federation are prominent examples of such ventures.

- Indian firms are looking to build a portfolio of locational assets to remain competitive internationally. Access to factors of production in various geographies leads to an intra-firm division of labour, allowing the production of distinct components of a product at places where they can be produced at least cost. This becomes a source of increased efficiency and competitiveness.

Sectors

More than half of India's outward FDI between fiscal 2001 and fiscal 2006 was concentrated in manufacturing, followed by non-financial services (Table 5.3). Reflecting the structural shift in the Indian economy towards the services sector, Indian software and service providers have emerged as important players in the overseas expansion by Indian firms. Indian business process out-sourcing (BPO) firms are increasingly looking to expand their

Table 5.3   Industry-wise distribution of approved outward FDI flows (US$ million)

	Manufacturing		Financial services		Non-financial services		Trading		Others	
	Amount	% share	Amount	% share	Amount	% share	Amount	% share	Amount	% share
FY2000	548.8	31.2	4.3	0.2	1,143.5	65.1	58.3	3.3	2.3	0.1
FY2001	370.7	26.8	16.6	1.2	876.5	63.4	89.2	6.5	29.1	2.1
FY2002	2,210.9	73.2	48.6	1.6	565.5	18.7	139.2	4.6	61.3	2.1
FY2003	1,056.7	71.9	1.8	0.1	280.2	19.1	69.9	4.8	61.7	4.2
FY2004	765.6	52.8	35.1	2.4	438.8	30.3	76.9	5.3	134.1	9.2
FY2005	2,026.4	72.3	9.2	0.3	548.2	19.5	69.1	2.5	151.3	5.5
FY2006	1,711.1	59.9	167.7	5.9	707.4	24.8	134.3	4.7	134.3	4.7
April–October 2006	2,402.8	39.8	5.8	0.1	2,250.0	37.3	390.8	6.5	985.6	16.3
Total	11,093.0	53.4	289.1	1.4	6,810.1	32.8	1,027.8	4.9	1,559.7	7.5

Source: Government of India (GoI), 2007.

client base in overseas markets by catering to firms not very keen on outsourcing business from its original location. Investments by IT firms were largely responsible for India emerging as the 10th largest investor in the UK at the end of 2004. Indian companies such as Tata Consultancy Services (TCS), Infosys Technologies and Wipro have operations in many foreign countries. Cross-border mergers and acquisitions have increased in recent years, particularly for entry into developed countries. The last year has seen a number of high-value outbound mergers and acquisitions led largely by the manufacturing sector. This has been driven by increased corporate profitability and financial reserves for Indian firms. The preference of Indian corporations is also shifting from minority-owned foreign affiliates to majority-owned ones.

In calendar year 2005, there were 136 outbound deals as opposed to 56 deals that were inbound. The first 6 months of calendar year 2006 have seen around 76 outbound deals valued at US$ 5.20 billion. Some significant deals in FY 2007 are shown in Table 5.4.

Destinations

The most important destination for outward FDI is the UK. It accounted for about 12 per cent of total cumulative outflows during fiscal years 2003–07 (till October), followed by Mauritius and the Netherlands which accounted for about 11 per cent and 10 per cent of the outflows. Investments in Russia and Sudan were largely in the form of acquisition of natural resources, whereas investments in the US were driven by strategic concerns and access to markets and technology. India is also emerging as an important investor in Europe. During the first 4 months of calendar year 2006, the largest proportion of outbound deals, by value, were made in Europe, which accounted for about 52 per cent of all outbound deals. It was followed by South America that contributed to about 39 per cent of the outbound deal value. The 20 most preferred destinations from FY 2003 through FY 2007 (till October 2006) are shown in Table 5.5.

Table 5.4 Major overseas acquisitions by Indian firms in FY 2007

Acquirer	Target	Region	Value (US$ million)
Tata Steel	Corus	UK	12,900
Hindalco	Novelis	USA	6,000
ONGC Videsh Ltd	Brazilian Oil Field	Brazil	1,400
ONGC Videsh Ltd	Omimex de Colombia	Colombia	850*
Tata Tea & Tata Sons	Glaceau	USA	677
Dr Reddy's Laboratories	Betapharm Arzneimittel	Germany	572
Suzlon Energy Ltd	Hansen Transmissions International	Belgium	565
Ranbaxy Laboratories Ltd	Therapia S.A.	Romania	324
Tata Coffee Limited	Eight O' Clock Coffee Co.	USA	220
Ballarpur Industries	Sabah Forest Industries	Malaysia	261
Subex Systems	Azure Solutions	UK	140
United Phosphorous	Advanta Netherlands Holdings	Netherlands	119

Sources: Grant Thornton and PricewaterhouseCoopers.

Note: * Through a joint venture with Sinopec group, China.

Table 5.5 Country-wise approved Indian direct investment in Joint Ventures (JVs) and Wholly Owned Subsidiary (WOS) (US$ million)

	FY 2003	FY 2004	FY 2005	FY 2006	April–October 2006	Total	% share
UK	34.5	138.5	71.9	158.3	1,335.9	1,739.0	11.9
Mauritius	133.4	175.6	149.4	332.7	741.4	1,532.4	10.5
Netherlands	15.9	30.2	30.7	284.6	1,005.5	1,366.9	9.4
USA	185.3	207.1	251.4	270.3	313.4	1,227.5	8.4
Sudan	750.0	162.0	51.5	63.0	118.1	1,144.7	7.8
Russia	0.2	1.4	1,076.2	1.2	3.0	1,081.9	7.4
Singapore	46.8	15.9	239.3	200.5	499.5	1,001.9	6.9
Cyprus	0.0	0.0	1.9	13.4	701.6	716.9	4.9
Australia	95.0	92.9	158.8	75.3	95.2	517.1	3.5
Brazil	5.2	5.0	17.2	420.1	6.7	454.2	3.1
UAE	12.6	32.1	41.9	141.0	205.3	432.9	3.0
Canada	2.3	0.7	0.8	3.5	397.8	405.1	2.8
Bermuda	29.0	142.5	221.3	2.6	0.0	395.3	2.7
Hong Kong	14.8	16.2	73.6	88.8	41.5	234.8	1.6
British Virgin	3.3	4.9	131.4	29.5	39.0	208.1	1.4
Belgium	0.3	9.2	1.1	69.4	86.4	166.3	1.1
Liberia	0.0	0.0	0.0	154.9	0.0	154.9	1.1
Switzerland	1.1	0.8	2.5	73.3	67.4	145.0	1.0
Kazakhstan	0.1	75.0	44.0	9.6	10.0	138.7	1.0
Indonesia	0.1	19.3	80.8	7.9	18.6	126.7	0.9
Others	142.4	321.9	158.5	459.2	317.4	1,399.5	9.6
Total	1,472.1	1,450.9	2,804.0	2,859.1	6,003.6	14,589.8	100.0

Source: Government of India (GoI), 2007.

Policies and regulatory framework

From a policy perspective, outward FDI received little regulatory support in India till 1990. This was largely due to the view that an emerging economy like India was capital-constrained and needed to conserve foreign exchange. The regulatory framework, therefore, favoured the import of capital rather than capital exports. Improvements in the regulatory framework and policies have played a vital role in increasing investments abroad. The changes were driven by the following factors:

- It was recognized that individual companies having the ability to expand abroad were constrained by the regulatory framework.
- Companies needed a portfolio of locational assets to remain competitive. Firms without a portfolio of locational assets are not able to optimally structure their production processes and gain from the efficiencies generated thereby.

This has led to the conclusion of bilateral investment treaties (BITs) and double taxation treaties (DTTs). India has concluded such treaties with more than 65 nations, encouraging firms to invest in these nations. Over the last few years, Indian firms are increasing their investments in software, biotechnology, automotive and oil sectors, and outward FDI from India is gaining importance. Policy with respect to outward FDI has been successively liberalized. Till 1991, JV enterprises with only a minority Indian equity were permitted. The main motive for outward FDI was export promotion and prohibited cash remittances towards equity participation, requiring it to be in the form of exports of Indian made capital goods and expertise.

During the 1990s, the government instituted an automatic approval system for outward FDI and successively raised the permissible investment limits. It also reduced other regulatory constraints in promoting Indian direct investment abroad. The years 2000–2005 have witnessed the introduction of significant policy changes. Also, the Reserve Bank of India (RBI) has been designated as the nodal agency for administering policy. After 2003, the overseas investment policy has been further liberalized with listed Indian companies being permitted to invest up to 35 per cent of their net worth in equity of foreign companies (having a shareholding of at least 10 per cent in an Indian company listed on a recognized stock exchange in India) listed on a recognized stock exchange. Indian corporates/registered partnership firms are allowed to invest in entities abroad up to 300 per cent of their net worth and the existing monetary ceiling of US$ 100 million has been removed. Further, the stipulation of a minimum net worth of INR 150 million for Indian companies engaged in financial sector activities in India has also been removed. In 2005, banks were permitted to lend money to Indian companies for acquisition of equity in overseas joint ventures, wholly-owned subsidiaries or in other overseas companies as strategic investment. In 2006, the automatic route of disinvestment was further liberalized. Indian companies are now permitted to disinvest without prior approval of the RBI in select categories. Further, to encourage large and important exporters, proprietary/unregistered partnership firms have been allowed to set up a JV/WOS outside India with prior approval of RBI.

Box 5.1   Selected changes to Indian overseas investment policy

- Since 2004, an Indian company with a satisfactory track-record has been allowed to invest up to 100 per cent of its net worth within the overall limit of US$ 100 million by way of market purchases for investment in a foreign firm. The provision restricting overseas investments in the same activity as its core activity at home was removed. Listed Indian companies, residents and mutual funds were also permitted to invest abroad in companies listed on a recognized stock exchange and in companies that have a shareholding of at least 10 per cent in an Indian company listed on a recognized stock exchange in India.
- Indian companies permitted to undertake overseas investments by market purchases of foreign exchange without prior approval of RBI up to 100 per cent of their net worth. Earlier, the foreign exchange purchase limit for overseas investments was 50 per cent of a company's net worth.
- Domestic companies located in Special Economic Zones (SEZs) permitted to undertake overseas investment up to any amount. The US$ 100 million ceiling under the automatic route was relaxed, provided the funding

(Box 5.1 continued)

(Box 5.1 continued)

was done out of the Exchange Earners Foreign Currency Account (EEFA) balances.

- The 3 years profitability condition requirement was removed for Indian companies making overseas investments under the automatic route.
- Overseas investments were allowed to be funded up to 100 per cent by American Depository Receipt (ADR)/Global Depositary Receipt (GDR) proceeds up from the previous ceiling of 50 per cent. Further, an Indian firm that had exhausted the limit of US$ 100 million in a year could apply to the RBI for a block allocation of foreign exchange subject to such terms and conditions as necessary.
- Overseas investments were opened up to registered partnership firms and companies that provided professional services. The minimum net worth requirement of INR 150 million for Indian companies engaged in financial sector activities in India was removed for investment abroad in the financial sector.
- In 2004, Indian firms were allowed to undertake agricultural activities, which was previously restricted, either directly or through an overseas branch, and are now permitted under the automatic route.
- In 2004, the monetary ceiling on Indian companies' investment abroad was further relaxed. Indian companies can now invest up to 100 per cent of their net worth without any separate ceiling even if the investment exceeds US$ 100 million. Furthermore, Indian companies can now invest or make acquisitions abroad even in areas unrelated to their business at home.
- In 2005, banks were permitted to lend money to Indian companies for acquisition of equity in overseas joint ventures, wholly-owned subsidiaries or in other overseas companies as strategic investment.
- In 2006, the automatic route of disinvestment was further liberalized. Indian companies are now permitted to disinvest without prior approval of the RBI in select categories. To encourage large and important exporters, proprietary/unregistered partnership firms have been allowed to set up a JV/WOS outside India with the prior approval of RBI.

Financing

Indian companies are scaling up the size of their overseas acquisitions. Many Indian firms have bought out companies abroad that are larger in size compared to them. A few examples include engineering major Punj Lloyd's acquisition of Singapore-based engineering firm SembCorp for US$ 640 million and oil drilling major Aban Loyd, which had a turnover of US$ 110 million in 2005–06, acquiring a 34 per cent stake in Sinvest ASA, a

Norwegian drilling company for US$ 446 million. Subex Systems Ltd recently acquired UK-based Azure Solutions Ltd., the world's largest revenue-assurance company, in a stock-plus-cash deal exceeding US$ 140 million.

The funding of M&A deals is increasingly being done through external funding as opposed to internal accruals, giving rise to the ability to fund larger deals. Stock-plus-cash deals and increasing institutional funding are the key sources of funds for large M&As. Indian companies have also engaged in leveraged buyouts and completed acquisitions by raising debt against the cash flows of the acquiree. Additionally, Indian companies have also accessed global financial markets for raising adequate funds. The issue of ADRs/GDRs and use of instruments like External Commercial Borrowings (ECBs) and Foreign Currency Convertible Bonds (FCCBs) have increased significantly in the past few years. External commercial borrowings rose from US$ 5 billion in FY 2005 to US$ 7 billion in FY 2006. In the nine months of FY 2007, ECBs stood at US$ 15.76 billion. Issue of ADR/GDRs increased by almost 417 per cent in 2006 to US$ 2.5 billion compared to US$ 613 million the previous year. Since May 2005, Indian banks have been permitted to finance overseas acquisitions by domestic companies. This has encouraged M&A undertaken by Indian companies, as Indian banks are more experienced with the domestic credit situation and have a better understanding of the local business environment.

Conclusion

Outward FDI from India has been growing at an impressive rate. Increasing competition, improved corporate profitability and governance together with the need for greater access to technology, markets and natural resources have led Indian enterprises to expand their overseas operations. Greater liberalization, improvement in the policy framework and increased access to various sources of finance have helped Indian firms in this process. As the outlook for the Indian economy remains robust and profitability of firms is expected to grow, Indian companies will be looking to scale up further and acquire meaningful market shares at the global level. India can be expected to emerge as an important investor in the global economy and the growth momentum of outward FDI from India is likely to continue.

Acknowledgements

The author acknowledges the assistance rendered by Rakesh Mookim and Karthik Hari of ICICI Bank in the preparation of this chapter.

Bibliography

Grant Thornton. 2006a. *Dealtracker Annual Issue 2005*. London: Grant Thornton.

———. 2006b. *Dealtracker Volume I 2006*. London: Grant Thornton.

———. 2006c. *Dealtracker Volume II 2006*. London: Grant Thornton.

———. 2007. *Dealtracker Annual Issue 2006*. London: Grant Thornton.

Government of India (GoI). 2007. Ministry of Finance, New Delhi.

PricewaterhouseCoopers. 2006. *Asia-Pacific M&A Bulletin Mid-Year 2006*. New York: PricewaterhouseCoopers.

Reserve Bank of India (RBI). 2006a. *Master Circular on Direct Investment by Residents in Joint Venture (JV)/Wholly Owned Subsidiary (WOS) Abroad*. Mumbai: RBI.

———. 2006b. *Monthly Bulletin June 2006*. Mumbai: RBI.

Sauvant, Karl P. 2005. 'New Sources of FDI: The BRICs'. *Journal of World Investment and Trade*, 6(5): 639–709.

United Nations Conference for Trade and Development (UNCTAD). 2004. *India's Outward FDI: a Giant Awakening?* Geneva: UNCTAD.

———. 2005a. *Case Study on Outward Foreign Direct Investment by Indian Small and Medium-Sized Enterprises*. Geneva: UNCTAD.

———. 2005b. *World Investment Report*. Geneva: UNCTAD.

Building National and Regional Financial Markets: The East Asian Experience

6

ANDREW SHENG

Introduction

In the year 2007 we marked the 10th anniversary of the Asian financial crisis. So where are we now? Where do we go from here? Or rather, why can't we move faster towards where we want to go?

Kristof and WuDunn (2001), writing in *Thunder from the East*: 'It (*the Asian crisis*) entailed a terrible human cost, but it is also helping to destroy much of the cronyism, protectionism and government regulation that had burdened Asian business. The crisis helped launch a political, social and economic revolution that is still incomplete but that ultimately will reshape Asia as greatly as the fall of the Berlin wall reshaped Europe.'

This chapter argues that despite its obvious successes, Asian bad habits and parochial thinking have not completely gone away, but the problems lay deeper than we all commonly realize. To move forward, we need to know where the roadblocks exist and how to move ahead.[1]

Where are we now?

The first good news is that the Asian economies have definitely recovered from the crisis and have regained not only their growth but also shown greater resilience in many ways. Recent IFI reports would suggest that, by and large, there is improved corporate governance, stronger supervision, healthier fiscal and balance of payments positions and higher reserves. In 2005, the Asian economies remained among the fastest growing region in the world, with the highest savings, in spite of higher energy prices. Overall, poverty has come down, although there still remain a large number of poor (Figure 6.1).

The second good news is that Asia has emerged almost naturally as the third area of trade integration, next to the European Union (EU) and the North American Free Trade Agreement (NAFTA) region in terms of size and importance. The process of regional integration is driven by trade integration (Table 6.1).

Over the last quarter century (1980–2005), intra-Asian trade has risen steadily from 34.6 per cent to 54.5 per cent of the region's total world trade. This is still lower than EU (66.2 per cent) but higher than that of NAFTA (45 per cent). Asia has emerged as the manufacturing global supply chain; initially centred around

Figure 6.1 Poverty in Asia

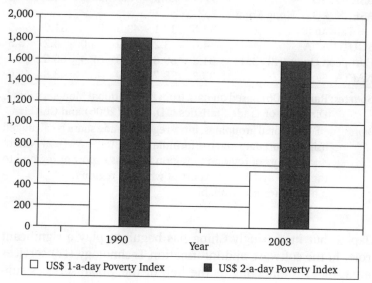

Table 6.1 Asian intra-regional trade (as % of total world trade)*

	1980	1985	1990	1995	2000	2005
Brunei Darussalam	80.1	77.3	81.7	79.5	74.2	75.0
Cambodia	n.a.	67.4	68.6	81.5	35.8	46.8
Indonesia	58.3	53.3	51.7	49.5	50.6	54.6
Lao PDR	n.a.	82.6	85.7	65.3	72.8	74.0
Malaysia	46.7	54.1	49.6	48.2	49.4	54.7
Myanmar	50.6	42.9	58.7	72.5	62.2	74.9
Philippines	33.8	36.0	32.8	37.5	39.7	52.7
Singapore	36.8	40.6	39.5	47.2	46.5	45.4
Thailand	38.1	42.7	42.6	43.7	44.9	49.5
Vietnam	n.a.	10.5	27.8	57.6	56.4	52.7
China	29.4	36.2	21.3	33.7	33.1	30.0
Korea	29.2	26.7	29.1	35.4	36.6	43.6
Japan	20.7	20.3	21.2	29.9	30.9	36.8
Association of Southeast Asian Nations (ASEAN) + 3 (Japan, China and South Korea)	30.2	30.2	29.3	37.3	37.0	38.2
Memo Items:						
ASEAN	17.9	20.3	18.8	23.9	24.5	24.0
ASEAN + 3 + Hong Kong + Taiwan	34.6	37.1	43.0	51.7	51.9	54.5
SOUTH ASIA	4.6	3.2	2.9	4.0	4.2	5.5
European Union (EU-25)	61.3	59.8	67.0	67.4	66.8	66.2
NAFTA	33.8	38.7	37.9	43.1	48.8	45.0

Sources: Rana (2006) based on data from International Monetary Fund, Direction of Trade Statistics C.D. Rom (2006) and CEIC.

Notes: * For regional groupings, intra-regional trade share is calculated using export data and the formula: $Xii/\{(Xiw + Xwi)/2\}$, where Xii is export of region i to region i; Xiw is export of region i to the world and Xwi is export of world to region i.
n.a. denotes not available.

Japan, but increasingly China has begun to play a significant role. In the software and Information Technology (IT) services area, India is emerging as the hub of the global services supply chain (Sheng, 2006d). In terms of Gross Domestic Product

(GDP), Asia had the smallest GDP level in 2004 of US$ 8.9 trillion, whereas NAFTA led with GDP of US$ 13.4 trillion and the EU following next with GDP of US$ 12.7 trillion. Asia had the largest population of 3.1 billion, whereas NAFTA and EU had 430 million and 460 million, respectively.

The third feature of Asian markets is the fact that its financial sector lags its manufacturing prowess and remains bank-dominated (Table 6.2). The larger banking sectors in Asia account for 80–177 per cent of GDP in terms of deposits, despite the fact that the Japanese banking system has withdrawn significantly from regional lending since the Asian crisis. The Bank for International Settlement (BIS) cross-border lending showed that the Japanese banking system pulled back about US$ 250 billion from a peak of US$ 375 billion in 1994 to US$ 125 billion by 2001 (Jeanneau and Micu, 2002). Part of the Japanese withdrawal has been compensated by the US and European investment in banks and bank branches in Asia, but the impact in Asia has not been significant in size and impact except in Korea.

Since the Asian crisis, Asian authorities have been extremely active in restructuring the banking system and trying to build capital markets. There are two distinct camps: the more sophisticated markets, such as Hong Kong, Singapore, Malaysia and Korea have been much more successful in reforming and deepening domestic bond markets and, to some extent, strengthening their equity markets, but the others are still struggling in their efforts. A common feature in the struggle to build domestic markets is the willingness to allow foreign financial intermediaries to help build these markets.

Using balance sheet data from Lane and Milesi-Ferritti (2006), it seems reasonably clear that Asia's success in its export-orientation had created a high level of net foreign asset position. Instead of the traditional view that emerging markets should run current account deficits and rely on foreign investment from developed markets, we have a situation where Asia is both an exporter of manufactures and services and also an important exporter of capital.

At the end of 2004, Asia had a net asset position of US$ 2.7 trillion or 30 per cent of its GDP, whereas Europe had a net liability

Table 6.2 Financial structure in selected countries, 1990 and 2004 (% of GDP)

	Bank deposits[a]		Equity market[b]		Bond market[c]		Insurance premiums[d]	
	1990	2004	1990	2004	1990	2004	1990	2004
ASEAN								
Brunei	n.a.	n.a.	n.a.	n.a.	n.a.	n.a.	n.a.	n.a.
Cambodia	4.0[3]	14.4	n.a.	n.a.	n.a.	n.a.	n.a.	n.a.
Indonesia	29.8	38.9	4.4	24.9	0.4	24.1	0.9	1.3
Lao PDR	4.0	17.3	n.a.	n.a.	n.a.	n.a.	n.a.	n.a.
Malaysia	52.1	88.7	100.7	152.6	69.8	89.3	3.0	5.5
Myanmar	7.9	8.9[5]	n.a.	n.a.	n.a.	n.a.	n.a.	n.a.
Philippines	24.1	48.4	20.6	30.6	22.1	28.7	2.0	1.5
Singapore	74.3	104.4	95.8	149.0	27.8	58.6	3.0	9.1
Thailand	56.8	79.7	29.2	72.3	9.7	38.9	1.7	3.5
Vietnam	10.9[4]	48.1	n.a.	n.a.	n.a.	n.a.	0.5[4]	2.0
ASIA—Others								
China	75.6	177.8	2.4[1]	40.3	8.5	29.4	0.8	3.2
Hong Kong SAR	205.6	299.3	107.2	486.3	1.5	28.3	3.0[1]	9.4
India	31.4	51.1	10.4	48.4	19.9	31.7	1.5	3.1
Japan	100.0	120.5	121.7	73.2	85.9	181.6	8.5	10.7
Korea, Republic of	32.6	68.8	48.2	56.1	34.1	74.9	11.0	10.1
Taiwan	n.a.	n.a.	107.6	135.3	17.0	58.3	n.a.	14.2

LATIN AMERICA							
Argentina	5.5[2]	2.7	28.2	9.8	15.4	2.4	2.7
Brazil	15.3[1]	6.7	46.9	2.2[1]	55.8	1.4	3.0
Chile	28.2	38.3	108.6	29.0	44.3	2.7	4.3
Mexico	14.1	10.6	21.9	21.1	24.2	1.1	1.8
OTHERS							
Russian Federation	12.9[2]	0.1[1]	43.1	0.4[2]	2.7	n.a.	2.8
South Africa	48.3	120.8	170.5	100.2	43.2	9.6	14.4
SELECTED OECD ECONOMIES							
Australia	49.0	40.6	108.4	35.6	52.9	7.3	7.8
Canada	43.5	46.9	106.4	72.3	75.5	5.4	7.1
Germany	53.8[1]	21.7	42.2	51.6	80.3	5.7	7.0
Switzerland	102.5	70.6	217.6	57.8	67.6	7.8	11.7
United Kingdom	87.8	85.2	123.0	36.8	43.9	9.6	13.8
United States	59.6	57.5	131.6	122.0	157.2	8.3	9.4

Sources: CEIC data; World Bank, Financial Structure Dataset, February 2006.

Notes: [a]Bank Deposits/GDP; [b]Stock Market Capitalization/GDP; [c]Public and Private Bond Market Capitalization/GDP; [d]Life and Non-Life Insurance Premium Volume/GDP.

[1]1992 data; [2]1994 data; [3]1995 data; [4]1996 data; [5]2003 data.

n.a. denotes not available.

position of US$ 1.2 trillion or 9.3 per cent of its GDP. NAFTA had a much larger net liability position of US$ 3.1 trillion or 22.9 per cent of its GDP. In other words, roughly two-thirds of the net liability position of NAFTA and EU are held by Asia. Looking at the gross asset position, however, the Asian position is much lower at US$ 8.6 trillion, whereas the EU and NAFTA positions are much larger at US$ 31.2 trillion and US$ 11.0 trillion, respectively.

The fourth feature is that despite stated policy initiatives of deepening regional bond markets, capital and debt markets are still relatively shallow and lack integration. There is no doubt that there is considerable political will in Asia to push for regional financial integration, such as the 2000 Chiang Mai Initiative (CMI) on regional swaps, the 2003 Asian Bond Market Initiative, the Asian Bond Fund Initiative (ABF1 and ABF2 created in 2003 and 2004, respectively) and more recently in 2005, the FTSE/ASEAN Index Series to help standardize market indices. In addition, efforts to revive the Asian Monetary Fund appear to surface in different forms.

The fifth feature is that the sharp rise in the Asian balance of payments surplus and foreign exchange reserves have served as a flashpoint of cross-Pacific debate. It is seen as the counterparty to the growing global imbalance, a code word for the US balance of payments deficit. The view from Washington is that excessive savings in Asia is causing the US to run a larger than necessary trade deficit (Bernanke, 2005). The solution is for Asia to adopt more flexible exchange rates (code word for upward revaluation). Asians, on the other hand, feel more comfortable with the status quo. A more benign view is that the relationship between Asia and the US is a Total Equity Return Swap (Dooley et al., 2003). Since Asian financial systems are not strong and deep enough to absorb its high level of savings, it is natural that surplus savings are placed in the deep and robust markets such as the US and Europe. The savings are recycled back into Asia in the form of foreign portfolio investment (FPI) and FDI, with the US and European financial intermediaries leveraging such investments to earn higher yields than the deposit and bond yields paid to Asian investors.

So, why is Asian financial development so patchy?

Problems of analysis

Having had the benefit of Claudio M. Loser's analysis of the Latin American (Chapter 7) experience in developing financial markets, one begins to appreciate that there are significant differences and similarities in comparing and contrasting the Asian and Latin American experience. The differences are commonly known—Asia has been much more trade-oriented and has, therefore, enjoyed faster growth with higher savings, whereas Latin America, under the inward-looking bias of the 'Raul Prebisch' approach in the 1950s, made the mistake of adopting an import-substituting industrialization strategy based on high debt and has, therefore, suffered a whole series of financial crisis since the early 1980s.

Loser identifies the following weaknesses in Latin American financial systems, which echo some of the problems in certain Asian economies:

- *Low savings rates*: it hindered the deepening of domestic financial markets in Latin America in the 1990s.
- *An unstable macro-economic environment*: it has been holding back financial system development, with chronic inflation, periodic external crises, and intermittent deposit freezes, imposing heavy losses on holders of financial assets.
- *Structural factors*: a range of structural factors, mostly micro-economic and institutional in nature, that deterred bank lending and creation of a strong credit culture.
- *Highly volatile capital inflows*: this was one of the key problems faced during the Asian crisis.

Seen from a global perspective, however, in the financial intermediation sphere, Latin America seems to have more similarities with Asia than the superficial differences of different growth rates. In terms of capital markets and financial intermediation, both regions are witnessing loss of domestic and global market share to New York and London. Latin American blue chips are more heavily traded as American Depository Receipts (ADRs) in New York than in their home markets. Both regions were heavily dollar-based, with several Latin American economies experimenting with dollarization. With the floating of the Chinese renminbi (RMB) and the Malaysian Ringgit (MYR), Asia is now experimenting with more flexible exchange rate regimes, but the dollar remains the key trading and financial transaction currency in the region.

In terms of policies and broad trends, I would say that the differences in views across the Pacific and with Europe are less stark or clear than the regular press portrays. There is general acceptance that globalization is inevitable, that flexible exchange rate regimes are here to stay and that capital account convertibility is a matter of time. The major difference of opinion is the speed of implementation of these policies, with the common proviso that domestic institutionaland structural conditions do not permit immediate liberalization without clear understanding of the risks associated with financial liberalization. In other words, Asia, like Latin America, faces the same cyclical and structural problems that are very much micro-economic and institutional in nature.

Hence, given the fact that the global community has had nearly 60 years of experience with economic development and crisis since Bretton Woods, why is it that we are still surprised by how slow and frustrating it is to change policies and the capacity of national economies to build robust and efficient financial markets that help economic growth with stability?

We are left with the classic Sherlock Holmes maxim of detection that 'when you have excluded the impossible, whatever remains, however, improbable, must be the truth.'

During the Asian crisis, it was fashionable to blame the Washington Consensus. As someone who has worked in Washington and accepted *mea culpa* in the policies and practices of the Washington Consensus, I have come to the realization that we must look deeper into what stands in the way of change.

Allow me to conjecture that the problems of analysing real-world problems, especially in the area of building financial markets, lay not in the practice of development economics but in the whole neo-classical paradigm of assuming away the most important pieces of the political economy conundrum. Keynes' dictum that 'practical men, who believe themselves to be quite exempt from any intellectual influences, are usually the slaves of some defunct economist' (1936) is still valid today in the analysis of market development and institutional building.

The first basic problem of the neo-classical paradigm was the emphasis on flow analysis. It took more than 50 years after the United Nations had published the first System of National Accounts before others finally begun to publish and use national balance sheets for serious analytical purposes (see Lane and Milesi-Ferritti, 2006). The emphasis on the two-gap analysis of fiscal and balance of payments deficits meant that balance sheet weaknesses were not the primary focus of analysis.

By assuming away the institutional framework as given, policies could be formulated without getting into the messy area of political economy, vested interests, bureaucratic inertia, corruption and other long-haul issues that had no easy short-term solutions. It was so much easier to focus on elegant policies supported by universally acclaimed theories that were logically impeccable but practically flawed.

The second basic problem was the emphasis on theoretical search for the right policies, rather than devoting greater resources on looking at the institutional context of policies. This emphasis on policy, using empirical models of behaviour, made bold and simplistic assumptions that the institutional framework of accounting, law and efficient judiciary and bureaucracy were in place for policies to be effected. As we all know, in many emerging markets, the quality of the property rights infrastructure were in many ways defective and policies that worked in market economies were in many instances ineffective when applied to emerging markets.

Indeed, the neo-classical emphasis on policies seemed to consider that when policies fail it was the countries and the institutional framework that were wrong, rather than the theory or the naïve use of theory that was wrong. Because the neo-classical theory is so logically complete there is a tendency for policy makers to assume that if only the market was complete policies will work better. Just as real-world practitioners realize that perfection is the enemy of the good, trying to impose completeness is enemy of the whole. Policy conditionality in recent years has been so demanding by number that in reality, the capacity of emerging markets to meet such conditionality is stretched to the limit.

To be fair, there has been a gradual but significant recognition of the importance of institutions and political realities in the formulation of policies. The September 2005 issue of the International Monetary Fund (IMF) *World Economic Outlook* (*WEO*) devoted a full chapter on 'Building Institutions'. The preliminary findings are music to the ears of those involved in institutional reforms. The same are listed:

- Openness is robustly associated with greater institutional quality.
- Greater accountability of the political executive is associated with higher institutional quality.
- A higher initial per capita income is associated with stronger institutions.
- The quality of institutions in the neighbouring countries and education levels are associated with better institutions, but there is some evidence that greater natural resource dependence is associated with weaker institutions.

The *WEO* report concluded that 'institutional change has to be designed and driven by countries themselves', but 'external factors can play an important supporting role.'

Furthermore, in a recent publication, the IMF Working Paper on Financial Globalization: A Reappraisal, there is an important insight that

the main benefits from successful financial globalization are probably catalytic and indirect, rather than consisting simply of enhanced access to financing for domestic investment.

There is now a rapidly growing literature showing that financial openness can—in many, but not all circumstances—promote development of the domestic financial sector, impose discipline on macro-economic policies, generate efficiency gains among domestic firms by exposing them to competition from financial entrants, and unleash forces that result in better government and corporate governance (Kose et al., 2006).

This new orientation towards greater appreciation of the institutional aspects of development still ignores the 'how'. It was one thing for brilliant macro-economists to give policy advice; it was another to get experienced market and institutional practitioners to teach emerging markets how to build or reform institutions. To say that there is 'no one size fits all' solution and that reforms do not succeed because of the 'lack of political will' is a cop-out. Anyone with a basic understanding of institutions would appreciate that every political structure, however, autocratic, does not have one view but a whole spectrum of views, and that every reform or change involves trade-offs between interests.

A key lesson, not well taken in during the post-crisis analysis of the Asian crisis, was the capacity and ability of the Asian bureaucracy to understand globalization and market forces. Having been groomed since independence to participate in mercantilist export growth, with fairly strong 'window guidance' towards integration with global markets, Asian policy makers became complacent and did not fully appreciate how global competition, financial innovation and changes in global standards, including standards of transparency, market practice and conduct, had profoundly changed the rules of the game. This lack of depth of understanding also impacted on the lack of capacity to manage the transition to fuller integration with the global economy.

Fortunately, there is already enough experience with institutional and market reforms in developed markets to know that there are common elements and principles of change management that could be more methodically applied to many emerging markets with greater chances of success. Change management is already a well-understood discipline in (corporate) managerial science, but has not been applied widely in the area of public institutional development. IFI support in this area has generally been under-resourced relative to the importance of building long-term public management capacity.

A major reason why institutional change is so much tougher than realized is because there are usually too many vested interests and conflicting views on the outcomes of change. Change managers understand that a first priority of institutional change is ownership or the creation of the common understanding of issues, common language of reform and, at least, sufficient acceptance of the trade-offs of change. This involves game theory, a greater grasp of local conditions and values, and is so much more inter-related and complex than providing macro-economic policy advice.

I shall illustrate this conundrum with the ongoing saga of developing bond markets in Asia. Here is an example where there is universal agreement within Asia that bond markets are both necessary and good, but progress is much tougher than realized at both the national and regional levels.

The titled book *Developing Bond Markets in APEC* (Parreñas et al., 2005) amply demonstrates the frustration of many policy officials and the private sector with progress to date. The Asian crisis led to one key consensus conclusion. The crisis was due to a fundamental liquidity and currency mismatch in the Asian financial system. Because Asian savings were predominantly in the banking system, there were two mismatches. The first is the banking system maturity mismatch—the deposit base was short-term, while a large part of the banking loans were used to finance projects with fairly long payback periods, such as real estate and infrastructure. The second mismatch was a currency mismatch, where borrowing became increasingly in foreign currency, while assets were in domestic currency. The two mismatches made Asia vulnerable to sharp capital withdrawals and flight. With high domestic savings, the obvious solution was the creation of deep and liquid bond markets. As Asian populations began to age, the demand for deeper bond markets to provide the investment channels for growing pension and retirement funds became also a demographic imperative.

However, despite this impeccable rationale and consensus, why are bond market developments so patchy in Asia? In China (PRC), India, Indonesia, Hong Kong (China) and Philippines, the bond market still accounts for only around 30 per cent of GDP, whereas the developed market average was around 60–80 per cent, with Japan and the US having levels exceeding 100 per cent of GDP due to their recent fiscal deficits (Table 6.2). One interesting point is that four markets—Singapore, Hong Kong, Malaysia and Taiwan—showed better improvements than others, but they were collectively not large enough to have a serious impact on the creation of regional markets. These markets also happened to be the most global in terms of trade as a share of GDP.

The Asia-Pacific Economic Cooperation (APEC) survey revealed a host of legal, fiscal, regulatory and systemic impediments. A key observation was that foreign bondholders still play a very small role in Asia's local currency market, with only 4 per cent in Japan and around 1 per cent in Hong Kong, Indonesia, Malaysia, Korea and Thailand. Intra-regional investments in Asian bonds were also insignificant. According to the IMF data survey, out of US\$ 9.1 trillion worth of cross-border investments in long-term debt securities at the end of 2003, Japan accounted for 15 per cent, Hong Kong 1.7 per cent and Singapore 0.6 per cent. The rest of East Asia accounted for another 0.3 per cent. These bond investments within Asia were also paltry. Japan invested only 0.8 per cent of its overseas investments in Asia, Hong Kong 14.4 per cent and Singapore 17.2 per cent.

These data confirmed that Asia preferred to put its overseas investments in the markets outside Asia, rather than within Asia. It demonstrated the superiority of the US and European financial intermediation skills and also the weaknesses of Asian financial markets.

The APEC study divided the major legal and fiscal impediments into three broad categories of restrictions, omissions and disparities. The restrictions include:

- Restrictions on foreign firm participation in local markets
- Exchange controls.
- Withholding taxes, stamp duties and levels of foreign ownership.
- Inadequacies in bankruptcy laws and property laws that affect securitization.

- Problems on asset transfers, especially to foreign asset holders.
- Problems in enforcement of court rights, including against state-owned enterprises and sovereign governments.

The omissions include:

- Inadequacies of creditor rights.
- Lack of clarity in settlement, custody, netting and transfer arrangements.
- Lack of recognition of trusts and onshore and offshore special purpose vehicles.
- Lack of clarity of master trading and repurchase agreements.
- Lack of clarity on taxation and other legal processes.

The disparities include:

- Differences in treatment of taxation, duties, refunds and administrative decrees.
- Arbitrary differences in creditor status and treatment in bankruptcy arrangements.
- Rules relating to usury or religious principles which may obviate repayment or recovery.
- Imprecise and conflicting laws.

In addition, the APEC study quoted another 28 different regulatory and systemic impediments to cross-border investment in Asian capital markets, ranging from technical matters, discriminatory treatment of foreigners, difficulties of market access, quality of infrastructure, illiquidity of markets, lack of supporting institutions, laws, regulations, supervision, oversight, standardization and so on.

For example, there is common agreement that a minimum condition for development of a domestic bond market is a benchmark yield curve. But this is not yet a reality in many markets in Asia, where trading in domestic government bond markets is still discontinuous and illiquid. Even in Malaysia, which has developed the domestic private bond market to 89.3 per cent of GDP, the government bond market does not have the same liquidity as, say, any European treasury market. Part of the reason is the dominance of one single holder of government bonds— the Employees Provident Fund relative to other investors.

Developing markets domestically face many vested interest issues, both from the private sector and the public sector. Although the private sector may prefer a good bond market as an alternative to the present bank-dominated system, they also like the personal relationship that arises from long-term banking relationships. After all, it is not unknown in Asia for large borrowers to end up with principal reductions in their debt repayment or eventually being able to buy back their defaulted loans at a discount. Large borrowers understood the principle that in a crisis, it was the banks that got into trouble for excessive exposure, not necessarily the borrowers.

Bond market development also cut through many jurisdictions, requiring huge coordination efforts between the central bank, the ministry of finance, the securities regulator and the companies' registry. There need to be major changes in the bankruptcy law. In addition, the banking system would have to develop skills in market making, while the master agreements, trading and settlement rules and processes need to be put in place. Very often, domestic banks do not have the risk management systems to control their market risks well, and at the same time they fear the entry of foreign banks that have all the skills and technology available to dominate the domestic bond and banking markets.

One of the key questions that domestic policy makers face is the degree of foreign bank and financial participation. Foreign banks can bring new technology, skills and access to foreign markets and resources. At the same time, domestic policy makers are wary because they also fear that the market share of foreign banks would increase considerably at the expense of domestic banks. Strong nationalist sentiment would constrain the speed of opening up.

As the World Trade Organization (WTO) begins to focus on a level playing field and greater liberalization to foreign entry, Asian financial markets will inevitably have to open up to greater regional and foreign participation. Nevertheless, there remains considerable home bias to banking. Despite having a common market in banking services, EU domestic banks have not totally lost their home markets in the core banking areas, although their ownership has become more European and international. At the same time, several leading US and one or two European investment banks have taken the lead to dominate the investment banking and securities business in Europe. This trend is also becoming evident in Asia, as leading investment banks in Asia are invariably non-Asian.

From what has been discussed, it seems abundantly clear that even though the technology and expertise to make bond markets happen is readily available, making the markets successful and liquid is much more difficult than policy makers initially estimated. Why were policy makers not able to overcome these institutional impediments? Since the Asian crisis, numerous ministerial task forces, conferences and seminars have been held at the national and regional (ASEAN, ASEAN+3 and APEC) levels to push for bond market development.

Recently available data showed that the quality of the financial infrastructure mattered in the development of bond markets. It was the bureaucratic capacity to implement policies and introduce institutional reform that was key. Table 6.3 shows indicators (not the cause) of such capacity.

One personal experience is sufficient to illustrate how even the widely touted Asian Bond Fund Initiatives have not attained the desired policy objective. The Asian Bond Funds were the culmination of the heroic efforts of the ministries of finance and central banks in ASEAN+3. However, the securities regulators were not brought into the planning process. The result was that the Bond Funds were launched in an environment where the Funds could trade actively in the two regional markets of Hong Kong and Singapore, but local rules and regulations in other markets regarding mutual funds did not allow for active trading within each country. The Hong Kong Securities and Futures Commission (SFC) therefore took the initiative to sign Letters of Intent with other regional securities regulators to try and achieve equivalence in regulatory standards to make the market in Asian Bond Funds less segmented and regionally tradable.

Table 6.3 Indicators on quality of financial infrastructure (0 to 10 scale, higher is better)

	Total score	Contract realization	Lack of corruption	Rule of law	Bureaucratic quality	Accounting standards	Freedom of press
Australia	9.06	8.71	8.52	10.00	10.00	8.0	9.12
Hong Kong	7.75	8.82	8.52	8.22	6.90	7.3	6.72
Indonesia	3.52	6.09	2.15	3.98	2.50	n.a.	2.86
Japan	8.67	9.69	8.52	8.98	9.82	7.1	7.92
Korea	6.73	8.59	5.30	5.35	6.97	6.8	7.36
Malaysia	6.55	7.43	7.38	6.78	5.90	7.9	3.90
Philippines	4.14	4.80	2.92	2.73	2.43	6.4	5.54
Singapore	7.58	8.86	8.22	8.57	8.52	7.9	3.44
Taiwan	7.50	9.16	6.85	8.52	n.a.	5.8	7.16
Thailand	6.50	7.57	5.18	6.25	7.32	6.6	6.02
Reference markets							
UK	8.93	9.63	9.10	8.57	10.00	8.5	7.78
USA	8.99	9.00	8.63	10.00	10.00	7.6	8.72

Source: de Brouwer et al. (2003).

Note: n.a. denotes not available.

One anomaly of the development of mutual funds and bond markets in Asia is that Asian regulatory authorities have unconsciously built up considerable barriers to cross-regional trading of financial products. In equity markets, the number of foreign listings in Japan has actually declined in the last 15 years. In the bond markets area, it is easier to get approval for a bond listed in the Irish Exchange to trade in Asia than it is to get approval for an Asian-issued bond. Similarly, a mutual fund registered in Luxembourg is more likely to be marketed throughout Asia, whereas a mutual fund issued in Hong Kong cannot be traded in Singapore and vice versa without greater regulatory equivalence.

Asian financial integration is proceeding much slower than the EU experience because there are still too many national currencies, national rules and regulations, and different market standards. If Asian markets have any chance of becoming more regional, it will require the willingness of Asian regulators and policy makers to become much less protective of their domestic markets from competition and be willing to remove impediments, barriers and disparities in their markets. The devil is clearly in the details.

In the words of John Kay (2004), the market is embedded in an elaborate social, political and cultural context and cannot function outside this context. Markets are adaptive and the behaviour of market participants is influenced by incentives and enforcement of rules and laws. The level of vested interests and the ability of policy makers to make institutional change therefore, depended, very much on the ability and capacity of policy makers to build consensus and make the necessary changes. This is clearly an under-researched and low area of attention in the literature of development economics and IFI advice.

There is, of course, more recent awareness of the inadequacies of the neo-classical paradigm. Nobel Laureate Robert Merton recognized in his seminal paper on financial innovation and institutional change (Merton, 1995) that the neo-classical paradigm was flawed because 'it is essentially an "institutional-free" perspective in which only functions (of prices and quantities) matter.' The institutional school propounded by Nobel Laureate

Douglass North and others tended to focus on the institutional structure and how it influenced behaviour. However, even though the neo-classical and institutional schools today recognize that both policies and institutions matter, they do not give you much insight on how to build or change these institutions.

This missing element of the role of management in the institutional and policy framework is clearly the dog that did not bark in Asia.

I come now to the discipline of management, which is much better developed in the corporate field than in the area of public governance. I contend that the lack of progress in institutional change in Asia, indeed in many emerging markets, is the lack of attention and understanding in academia, business, government and IFIs of the importance of managing change in public bureaucracies, particularly towards a government–market relationship that leads to sustainable development. In other words, we tend to emphasize too much on the easy areas of policy formulation and debate, at the expense of establishing and strengthening the institution framework and managing institutional change in order to create transparent, liquid and effective markets.

I would go further to say that even though now there is recognition at the IFI level that institutional effectiveness is important for growth, focusing on corruption is looking at the symptoms rather than the roots of the institutional barriers to growth. The bond market example illustrates that even if there is no shortage of political will, the management knowhow of how to effectively make the institutional changes necessary for effective market trading is still lacking. It is, in practice, a massive coordination job; one of balancing huge vested interests, building coalitions, changing laws, standards and ultimately market and bureaucratic behaviour. Neo-classical theory assumed that implementation of policies is costless and that there is no principal–agent problem between the policy maker and the bureaucracy. We know from the lessons of the Asian crisis and the post-crisis implementation of structural change that this assumption is naïve, but also flawed and costly if not damaging to the reformers.

As the late management guru Peter Drucker recognized (1985:13):

It became clear fairly early in the post-World War II period that management is the crucial factor in economic and social development. It was obvious that the economists' traditional view of development as a function of savings and capital investment was not adequate. Indeed, savings and investment do not produce management and economic development. On the contrary, management produces economic and social development, and with it savings and capital investment.

It is a pity that many development economists did not pay too much attention to this advice.

The fall of the Berlin Wall brought the triumphalism of free markets, but it was a triumphalism of policies, not institutions. It took the Asian crisis to recognize that institutions and corporate governance matter, and only recently was there recognition that public governance to complement markets is crucial to the function of markets. Indeed, as Francis Fukuyama so insightfully pointed out that building the appropriate bureaucracy that complements markets is a part of the larger issue of 'state-building', which 'is one of the most important issues for the world community because weak or failed states are the sources of many of the world's serious problems, from poverty to AIDS to drugs to terrorism' (Fukuyama, 2004).

Hence, I come back to the major theme of this chapter. The difficulties faced in the creation of financial markets in Asia, indeed in Latin America and elsewhere, are not the shortage of right policy advice or the shortage of money, technology and the like. It is the lack of understanding that theory is always theory, and institutional change is not just about theory and policies, but also about managing social change effectively. We need to be able to walk the talk. We need to focus on how to help the emerging markets do it.[2]

Because markets and institutions are embedded in the social, cultural and political environment that they grow in, we cannot organically transplant markets and new institutions without tissue rejection. We need to create the DNA of market change through the education and establishment of right class of entrepreneurs, managers and technical experts who can make that market come alive. Deep and liquid markets in Europe and the US were not created overnight and we cannot realistically expect such markets to become instantly deep and liquid in Asia. Indeed, with globalization and standardization, we would expect the European and the US markets to achieve network effects of 'winner-take-all' dominance, even as Asia begins to build its own liquidity in absolute terms.

Hence, I come back to a realization that we need to go back to basic principles of political economy to admit that we need to start with building effective bureaucracies in Asia which understand how to balance the government's role in a market economy. To illustrate, the attempt so far in building markets was top-down in approach, whereby the policy and institutional designs often involved only the public sector and did not fully consult the private sector. The foreign sector, which has the expertise and the motivation to expand the market were often excluded in the decision process. The domestic players are often unwilling to build competitive markets that erode their own franchises and market share. The result is that domestic private sector participants or state-owned enterprises often play along the 'liberalization' game, whereas in practice they have little or no incentive to innovate or change unless forced by crisis.

Moreover, the Asian crisis brought home the need for global standards of accounting, governance, transparency and even social conduct. Once global standards of accounting and transparency are imposed, domestic players are exposed in terms of hidden losses, inefficiencies and competitive weaknesses. There is, therefore, every incentive for the vested interests to resist opening up and/or to buy time for internal change to prepare for global competition. For the market to work effectively, we need effective public bureaucracies that can simultaneously educate, regulate, lead and motivate change. To do this, it will also need leadership from academia, the business community and the media to work together to facilitate change.

As Fukuyama (2004) points out correctly:

It is true that government in the developing world is often too large and bloated in the scope of functions they seek to carry out. But what is most urgent for the majority of developing countries is to increase the basic strengths of their state institutions to supply those core functions that only governments can provide.

Asian bureaucracies need to recognize that complementing and facilitating effective markets is a core function in today's global economy.

Once that is recognized, the next step is to strengthen and motivate the bureaucracy to effectively exercise that core function. Policy thinkers need to accept that in the real world bureaucracies have monopolistic positions and functions that markets cannot change easily. We need to accept the fact that unless the bureaucracies fulfil that function effectively, the markets cannot function effectively.

To be fair, there is sufficient awareness that Asia, like many other emerging markets, has to move towards global standards, processes and practices because of global competitive forces. The elites have also become aware that markets are the way to go, but are uncomfortable that free markets create winner-take-all situations and therefore lead to social instability. Hence, the state or rather the bureaucracy, complemented by civil society such as non-governmental organizations (NGOs), may be the only way forward to deal with market failures, such as environmental degradation, social inequality, terrorism and natural disasters.

Herein are the horns of the institutional dilemma. It is a fact that in emerging markets many public bureaucracies are under-paid, under-motivated and under-managed. Why should they help facilitate change when all it does is to appear to benefit the private sector? If the existing bureaucracies, for various reasons, are unwilling or unable through under-resourcing, inertia, ignorance, corruption or lack of incentives to move effectively to make the necessary social, institutional and policy changes, then these market failures will not be tackled. And if the bureaucracies cannot change, the market cannot change and perform effectively.

This chapter is not about the blame game, but about the need to become aware of the very real problems facing emerging markets in building an effective market economy, both domestically and regionally. We have moved beyond the policy game into the real world of institutional and social change. If we accept that development is about social change, then we have to accept that institutions are the instruments of change. However, if Asian bureaucracies as institutional instruments become the end and not the means of social development then Asia will neither create sustainable growth with equity, nor rise to play its rightful role in the global economy.

I end this chapter with a note about the role of the key players, including the IFIs. The Bretton Woods Institutions have played a crucial role in the development process. They are the intellectual custodians of the development ideals, guarding the flame of global change with stability. They have helped the process of globalization and acted as effective teachers, stewards and referees of the growth of emerging markets. But they have also been the channels through which the neo-classical paradigm has imposed both its benefits and its costs.

We have reached a stage in the global economy where the neo-classical paradigm has been turned on its head. The emerging markets are now the providers of liquidity for the developed markets. The developed markets and the IFIs are no longer the most important sources of finance for development. Neither are they willing to be the lender of last resort for emerging markets.

Hence, changing the global imbalance requires not only changes in the consumption pattern of emerging markets but also the way in which the institutions of emerging markets have to evolve to create a balanced and mutually sustainable global market. To push the old medicine of appropriate macro-economic policies is necessary but not sufficient. The IFIs must review their own roles in the development process and draw lessons as to how to help emerging markets make that important institutional change. Their own institutional capacity to help that change should be reviewed.

At the national and regional levels, the elite must accept that the transition to global markets is inevitable. The question is time and pace of change. The burden of change is to accept sunken costs now, reform the institutional framework as soon as possible, or to delay that change and pay the price of crisis.

The private sector has a crucial role to play in this evolutionary change. The business leadership has to rise above parochial interests and work with the policy makers to make the necessary transition to globalization. Opening up should not be the 'can-opening' mantra of foreign businesses backed by foreign governments. It should be the joint efforts of both domestic and foreign businesses to demonstrate to the community that they share common goals in economic development and that they have corporate social responsibilities.

The developed part of Asia, being richer and more advanced in institutional capacity, has to play a much larger role to help the developing part of Asia in its institution-building. Regional and global cooperation share the same objective: how to ensure that member weaknesses do not become a systemic problem. We need to cooperate and share resources, financial, human and knowledge, in order to strengthen ourselves against the inevitable stresses and strains that come from globalization.

To sum up, structure follows strategy. If the strategy is to accept that globalization and markets will bring both benefits and costs/risks to emerging markets, then the priority is to change the structure/institutions that fit this strategy. But changing structures itself requires vision, mission, resources and the determination to make that change. This is about leadership. Who in Asia has the vision, mission and the will to make that change is a question that is beyond the scope of this chapter.

Acknowledgements

The author is grateful to Pieter Bottelier, G.L. Tan and others for very helpful comments and Sharmila Sharma for research in the preparation of this chapter, but bears total responsibility for any opinions, errors and omissions.

Notes

1. Asia in this chapter is defined as the 10 members of the ASEAN, China (PRC), Hong Kong SAR, Japan, the Republic of Korea, Taipei, China plus India. The 10 ASEAN members are Brunei Darussalam,

Cambodia, Indonesia, Lao PDR, Malaysia, Myanmar, Philippines, Singapore, Thailand and Vietnam.

2. It is interesting that the new management language follows exactly the Chinese maxim 'Listen not what a man talks, but watch how he walks' (the word for 'walk' is the Chinese word for 'act').

Bibliography

Asian Development Bank. 2005. *Key Indicators 2005: Labor Markets in Asia: Promoting Full, Productive and Decent Employment*, Manila: Asian Development Bank.

Asian Development Bank, World Bank and Japan Bank for International Cooperation. 2005. *Connecting East Asia: A New Framework for Infrastructure*, Manila, Washington D.C. and Tokyo: Asian Development Bank, World Bank and Japan Bank for International Cooperation.

Bernanke, Ben. 2005. *The Global Saving Glut and the U.S. Current Account Deficit*, New York: Board of Governors of the Federal Reserve Bank System.

CEIC. Various Years. Available at http://www.ceicdata.com

de Brouwer, Gordon. 2003. 'Financial Markets, Institutions and Integration in East Asia'. *Asian Economic Papers*, 2(1): 53–80.

de Brouwer, Gordon, Masahiro Kawai and Jay Rosengard. 2003. 'National Markets and Institutions to Support Financial Development in East Asia'. *Conference on Institutional Development in East Asia*, 31 October–1 November 2003, Bangkok.

Dooley, Michael P., David Folkerts-Landau and Peter Garber. 2003. 'An Essay on the Revived Bretton Wood System'. NBER Working Paper No. 9971, National Bureau of Economic Research, Cambridge, MA.

Drucker, Peter F. 1985. *Management: Tasks, Responsibilities, Practices*, New York, NY: Harper & Row.

Fukuyama, Francis. 2004. *State Building: Governance and World Order in the Twenty First Century*, Washington, DC: HarperCollins.

Goto, Junichi and Kawai, Masahiro. 2001. 'Macroeconomic Interdependence in East Asia'. *International Conference on Economic Interdependence: Shaping Asia-Pacific in the 21st Century*, 22–23 March 2001, Tokyo, International Monetary Fund and World Bank.

International Monetary Fund (IMF). 2005. *World Economic Outlook*, September 2005. Washington, DC: IMF.

———.2006. 'Financial Globalization: A Reappraisal', IMF Working Paper, Washington, DC.

Jeanneau, Serge and Marian Micu. 2002. 'Determinants of International Bank Lending to Emerging Market Countries'. BIS Working Papers No. 112, Bank for International Settlements, Basel.

Karacadag, Cem V. Sundrarajan and Jennifer Elliot. 2003. 'Managing Risks in Financial Market Development: The Role of Sequencing'. In Litan, Robert, E., Michael Pomerleano and V. Sundrarajan (eds), *The Future of Domestic Capital Markets in Developing Countries*, Washington, DC: Brookings Institution.

Kay, John. 2004. *The Truth About Markets: Why Some Nations Are Rich But Most Remain Poor*, London: Penguin Books.

Keynes, John Maynard. (1936–42). *The General Theory of Employment, Interest and Money*. London: Macmillan.

Kose, M. Ayhan, Eswar Prasad, Kenneth Rogoff and Wei Shang-Jin. 2006. 'Financial Globalization: A Reappraisal'. IMF Working Paper No. WP/06/189, International Monetary Fund, Washington, D.C.

Kristof, Nicholas and Sheryl WuDunn. 2001. *Thunder from the East: Portrait of a Rising Asia*, First Vintage Book Edition. New York, NY: Vintage Books.

Lane, Philip R. and Gian Maria Milesi-Ferritti. 2006. 'The External Wealth of Nations Mark II: Revised and Extended Estimates of Foreign Assets and Liabilities, 1970–2004'. IMF Working Paper No. WP/06/69, International Monetary Fund, Washington, D.C.

Loser, Claudio. 2006. *Financial Markets in Latin America*, Washington, DC: Emerging Markets Forum.

Merton, Robert C. 1995. 'Financial Innovation and the Management and Regulation of Financial Institutions'. NBER Working Paper No. 5096, National Bureau of Economic Research, Cambridge, MA.

Nijathaworn, Bandid. 2006. *East Asian Financial Markets: Some Thoughts on the Way Forward*, Bangkok: Bank of Thailand.

Parreñas, Julius Caesar, Kenneth Waller and Newin Sinsiri. 2005. *Developing Bond Markets in APEC: Towards Greater Public–Private Sector Regional Partnership*, Singapore: Institute of Southeast Asian Studies.

Rana, Pradumna B. 2006. 'Economic Integration in East Asia: Trends, Prospects and a Possible Roadmap'. Working Paper Series on Regional Economic Integration No. 2, Office of Regional Economic Integration, Asian Development Bank.

Sa, Sopanha and Guérin, Julia. 2006. 'Recent Developments in Monetary and Financial Integration in Asia'. *Financial Stability Review*, 8: 111–29.

Severino, Rodolfo C. Jr. 1999. Regionalism: The Stakes for Southeast Asia, *ASEAN Faces the Future: A Collection of Speeches by Rodolfo C. Severino, Jr., Secretary-General of the Association of Southeast Asian Nations*, pp. 31–40, Jakarta: ASEAN Secretariat.

Shanmugaratnam, Tharman. 2001. *An Asian Wall Street*. Singapore: Monetary Authority of Singapore.

Sheng, Andrew. 2006a. 'The Art of Reform: Applying Lessons from Suntze to Asia's Financial Markets'. *Finance and Development*, 43(2): 20–23.

———. 2006b. *Financial and Monetary Integration in East Asia*, mimeo, University of Malaya.

———. 2006c. 'Infrastructure Reform as a Precondition to a Stable Regulatory Framework in Asia'. Paper presented at the 'APEC Policy Dialogue Workshop on Financial Sector Reform', July 3–4, 2006, Shanghai, Asia-Pacific Economic Cooperation.

———. 2006d. *The Asian Network Economy*, Washington, DC: World Bank.

———. 2006e. *ASEAN Integration to Meet Global Challenges*, Malaysia: Ministry of Finance, Malaysia.

World Bank. 2006. *Financial Structure Dataset, February 2006*, Washington, DC: World Bank.

Ziegler, Dominic. 2003. 'The Weakest Link: A Survey of Asian Finance'. *Economist*, 6 February 2003.

Financial Markets in Latin America 7

CLAUDIO M. LOSER

Introduction

Financial system development makes important contributions to economic performance. A well-functioning financial system channels financial resources and capital to productive use, and spurs economic growth. In turn, excessive regulation and government intervention can severely interfere with the proper functioning of financial institutions.

For many years, and through the 1990s, limited access to bank credit and uncertainty about macro-economic and financial stability imposed serious constraints on Latin America's growth and contributed to high volatility. As these facts became increasingly recognized, many countries of the Western Hemisphere took steps to reform and liberalize their financial systems, including reductions in government controls. Financial liberalization spurred credit growth during the early part of the 1990s, but bank lending slowed after a series of banking crises in the mid-1990s. Subsequently, bank restructuring and regulatory reforms were introduced to help strengthen banking systems in a number of countries. Such reforms have generally been successful in increasing financial intermediation and in improving economic performance. In the process of reform, however, there was a need to attain a balance between appropriate liberalization and adequate government prudential and policy regulation concurrently. Failure to accomplish a proper balance has lead to financial crises such as those that recently hit several countries like Argentina, Dominican Republic, Mexico and Uruguay a few years ago.

Investment and finance have also become a global matter, and, for developing and developed economies alike, countries must integrate their domestic financial systems into the emerging global system. With an eye on that ultimate objective, many countries are coordinating their liberalization and integration efforts with neighbouring countries. The best-known examples of sub-regional cooperation and integration efforts are the Asia-Pacific region and the European Union (EU). A number of institutions in the Americas are also supporting the move towards financial integration, although at much earlier stages of the process.

This chapter seeks to explain how financial sector developments have been related to the structural characteristics of Latin American economies, and to highlight some of the financial sector failures that have affected Latin America's macroeconomic performance. The analysis presented here provides evidence of the need to strengthen Latin America's efforts to ensure financial system soundness and promote deeper financial intermediation.

Key characteristics of Latin American financial systems

In order to understand the Latin American financial system, it is worth exploring its market structure, profitability and the trends towards dollarization observed over the last decade.

Market structure

Latin American financial systems are largely bank-based, with mostly small and illiquid security markets. Banking systems are highly concentrated, intermediation margins are high, and the scale of bank lending is low relative to economic activity. Banks have had a comparative advantage in the collection and processing of information that is central to financial intermediation, precluding market-based finance (Table 7.1).

In most Latin American countries, the private sector's use of bond and equity markets to raise finance remains limited, relative

Table 7.1 Indicators of capital market size (US$ trillion)

	Stock market capitalization	Public debt	Private debt	Bank assets	Bonds, equities and bank assets	As per cent of GDP	GDP
World	41,967	23,422	36,282	63,473	165,130	370	44,595
European Union	9,556	6,674	12,024	30,975	59,229	460	12,879
United States	17,009	5,922	18,152	9,324	50,398	405	12,456
Japan	7,543	6,608	2,037	6,647	22,835	501	4,557
Emerging Market Countries	6,385	3,176	1,610	10,895	22,066	184	12,014
Of which:							
Asia	4,409	1,485	1,189	7,323	14,405	265	5,433
Europe	296	553	74	803	1,725	79	2,190
Latin America	972	1,014	277	1,374	3,638	149	2,448
Share of Latin America in Total (% of total)	2.3	4.3	0.8	2.2	2.2		5.5

Sources: IMF (2007) with data from World Federation of Exchanges; BIS (2006); IMF (2007b, 2007c).

to its recourse to banks, although, in some countries, pension reforms have begun to encourage broader capital market development. Despite their prominence, banking systems remain relatively small compared with GDP, and the depth of intermediation is particularly low. Deposit-to-GDP ratios are less than 50 per cent, compared with typical ratios of 90 per cent in East Asian emerging markets.[1] Moreover, bank credit represents only a fraction of bank assets. In most countries, except Chile and Ecuador, lending represents no more than a third of bank assets. Again, except in Chile, the ratio of bank credit to economic activity remains much smaller than in the bank-based financial systems of the advanced economies of the euro area and Japan, or of the Emerging Market Economies (EMEs) of Asia (Table 7.2). Furthermore, lending is directed to a large extent to consumer credit, rather than investment, which tends to be financed from retained earnings or non-bank and foreign sources.

Table 7.2   Bank assets (US$ trillion and as % of GDP)

	Bank assets	As % of GDP
World	63,473	142
European Union	30,975	241
United States	9,324	75
Japan	6,647	146
Emerging Market Countries	10,895	91
Of which:		
Asia	7,323	135
Europe	803	37
Latin America	1,374	56

Source: IMF 2007a.

The pattern of credit growth in Latin America has been marked by boom–bust cycles. Credit growth was particularly rapid in the early 1990s, but collapsed in many cases after banking crises in the mid-1990s and has since remained subdued. Argentina, Brazil and Mexico all follow this pattern, although in Mexico the growth of other sources of financial intermediation has partly compensated for the lack of bank activity. Chile has managed to achieve a more even pattern of credit growth because of its longer track record of macro-economic stability and early financial sector reforms, but, more recently, other countries have also achieved greater stability. In any event Latin America made significant progress regarding financial liberalization (Figure 7.1), in periods where the process of reform was much faster than in other areas of the world (Figure 7.2).

Figure 7.1 Latin America: Financial liberalization (index 0 to 1)

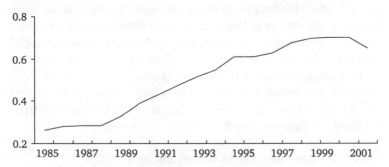

Source: Inter American Development Bank, 2003.

Figure 7.2 Financial liberalization (including capital account and domestic financial markets)

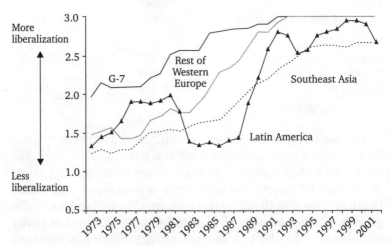

Source: Kaminsky and Schmukler (2003).

Over this period, a rising share of bank balance sheets has been absorbed by government securities. During the second half of the 1990s, after serious banking crises, many banks in Latin America shed non-performing loans and obtained, in exchange, sizeable portfolios of government bonds. For public banks, this typically occurred through restructuring, with bad credits being replaced by government securities—for example, in Mexico after the 1994 banking crisis. In the private sector, this shift was often a reaction to experience with high default rates on lending to households and corporations and to a tightening of supervisory standards after setbacks to stabilization and reforms in the mid-1990s. As banks shared in the costs of these crises, they sought to hold significant amounts of high-yielding, apparently safer government bonds. For example, Argentina's banks' holdings of such bonds more than doubled in 1995; and in Brazil, about a third of banks' assets were invested in government bonds by 2000.

The process of bank restructuring that occurred during the 1990s led to rising foreign ownership of Latin American banking systems. During this process, legal and regulatory limitations on the activities of foreign banks were relaxed or eliminated in most countries. Foreign banks gained market shares, mostly by taking control of domestic banks in need of fresh capital and new management rather than opening new institutions. In Brazil, for example, foreign banks grew from an insignificant presence in the mid-1990s to hold one-fifth of deposits and provide one-fourth of credit by the end of 2000. In Argentina, Chile, Mexico, Paraguay, Peru and Venezuela, foreign banks owned more than half of banking-system assets by 2000 (Table 7.3).

A few large banks typically account for a large share of the system's assets. Bank restructuring that occurred during the 1990s also led to increasing concentration. Typically, more than two-thirds of bank assets are concentrated in the 10 largest institutions, which hold about 70 per cent of deposits and provide 75 per cent of credit. However, the largest institutions often remain in government hands. This is particularly true of Brazil, Argentina and Uruguay where a few public banks still account for a significant share of banking-system assets and credit. Many Latin American public banks were endowed with the role of providing credit to targeted segments of the economy, often

Table 7.3 Selected Latin American countries: Structure of banking systems

	Argentina	Brazil	Chile	Colombia	Ecuador	Mexico	Paraguay	Peru	Uruguay	Venezuela
Institutions										
Number of banks	71	135	28	32	40	35	22	15	23	39
Concentration—Top 10 banks					(in per cent)					
Share of total assets	62	70	76	67	82	95	79	95	87	81
Share of total deposits	71	77	78	68	79	90	79	96	85	36
Share of total credit	66	70	80	65	78	93	59	94	88	64
Foreign bank participation										
Number of banks*	28	27	18	11	—	20	17	12	16	21
					(in per cent)					
Share of total assets	54	28	60	21	—	82	81	64	35	68
Share of total deposits	48	21	47	20	—	82	86	62	34	67
Share of total credit	46	25	45	21	—	77	74	62	35	72

Sources: Based on Singh et al., 2005, National central banks and bank supervisory agencies; and IMF staff calculations.

Notes: * Domestic banks with foreign participation or control. Offshore banks are not included.
This table considers only deposit-taking universal banks. Data are for 2000, except for Uruguay and Mexico, for which 2002 data are used.

poorer regions and sectors that had been left outside conventional channels of financing (for example, housing, regional development, agriculture). Such operations remain important, although questions have been raised about the cost-effectiveness and governance of such activities, and alternative mechanisms—including community-based micro-finance—are being developed to deliver credit to such sectors.

The high degree of concentration suggests a lack of competition among banks, which may be a concern. Economies of scale may be important in containing costs and taking advantage of new information technologies. A lack of competition may also result in excessively high prices or quantity rationing for customers. In small, advanced economies too, the banking system is often highly concentrated, but banks typically face strong competition from securities markets and non-bank financial intermediaries, as well as offshore markets. In Latin America, however, financing from securities markets is usually available to only a limited range of top-quality corporate borrowers.

Reforms to introduce private pension systems provided an important impetus to financial system development in Latin America during the 1990s. Chile was the first to replace a state-run, 'pay-as-you-go' pension system with a privately managed, individually funded system in 1981. Its lead was subsequently followed in Argentina, Bolivia, Brazil, Colombia, Ecuador, Mexico and elsewhere. These pension funds can, however, be vulnerable targets for governments looking for financing. For example, Argentina's pension funds suffered heavy losses after being forced to invest sizeable shares of their portfolios in government paper after the collapse of the economy in 2001–02.

Bank profitability

Latin American banks' profitability improved during the 1990s, but their returns on assets and equity remain below those in industrialized countries. This has occurred despite high interest margins on private lending. Interest spreads on lending to the private sector have declined somewhat during the past decade but remain high by international standards. Intermediation margins averaged more than 50 percentage points in Brazil, Peru and Uruguay during the 1990s.[2] In part, the weak profitability performance reflects a continued reliance on interest earnings, both from lending and from government bonds. Other sources of income, such as commissions from asset management and fees from securities trading, remain limited.

In times of high inflation, bank revenues from bonds indexed to the overnight interest rate exceeded the less frequently adjusted interest rate paid on deposits, providing banks with easy profits. Although incentives for cost reduction have increased since inflation was brought down across the region, banks' operating costs remain high, about one-third higher than in banks in advanced countries, as productivity in the sector is lower, in part due to strong unionization in the sector. Non-performing loans have been an additional burden on bank costs. Although restructuring since the mid-1990s—including by the government swapping bad loans for public securities—improved the quality of bank lending, non-performing loans continue to represent a large share of loan portfolios.

Dollarization

In a number of countries, a large and rising share of both bank deposits and credits have been denominated in US dollars. For example, in Bolivia, dollar deposits rose from 65 per cent of total deposits in 1990 to 74 per cent in 2001 and to about 95 per cent in 2003. In some countries, formal dollarization was deliberately used to provide a nominal anchor for the economy. In 1991, Argentina adopted a currency board guaranteeing full convertibility between dollars and pesos, and intermediation was increasingly denominated in dollars until the collapse of the regime in 2002. Ecuador in 1999 and El Salvador in 2001 chose full dollarization to bolster price stability. Of course, conditions were different in both countries. In Ecuador, dollarization was imposed as a way to come out of a major currency crisis, while in the case of El Salvador, the actions were taken to preserve stability, that had been achieved already, while helping reduce interest rates and accelerate the process of integration with the rest of the world.

Some countries avoided dollarization altogether or were able to reduce it. Brazil, and to some extent Mexico, prohibited most holdings of foreign currency deposits for non-transaction purposes, while Chile and Colombia have used strict prudential guidelines to reduce the incentives to hold foreign currency deposits. Placing a ban on foreign currency deposits or discouraging their use, however, also served to encourage the shifting of financial assets offshore. Deposits held by Argentines and Venezuelans in the US far exceed the countries' broad money. For all of Latin America, IMF data suggests that total financial assets (excluding international reserves) held abroad amounted to some US$ 480 billion in 2005, about 23 per cent of GDP, and somewhat below the level of broad money.

In recent years, there has been a trend that runs against dollarization. With the Emerging Markets Bond Index (EMBI) spread down to less than 160 basic points (bps), fixed-income investors have moved away from investing in Latin America public sector external debt into local market instruments. This trend has been positive in developing or strengthening local debt markets in Latin America and is allowing governments to reduce the currency risk of their debt portfolios. At the same time, there has also been increasing investment in corporate bonds and particularly in equity, where markets are still shallow in the region.

Underlying weaknesses

The features of the Latin American financial systems today reflect a series of underlying weaknesses common to most countries in the region.

- Low Savings rates hindered the deepening of domestic financial markets in Latin America in the 1990s. However, low bank intermediation co-existed with a wide range of savings rates; and, similarly, loan ratios and savings rates did not seem to be consistently determined by per capita GDP.
- In most Latin American countries, an unstable macroeconomic environment has been a critical factor holding back financial system development. Chronic inflation,

periodic external crises and intermittent deposit freezes imposed heavy losses on holders of financial assets. Even after success in bringing down inflation across Latin America, inflexible exchange rate regimes and excessive fiscal deficits continued to undermine confidence and bring instability. High unremunerated reserve requirements reduced banks' available resources. Similarly, a number of countries have resorted to financial transaction taxes, which have tended to discourage financial intermediation.

- Latin American banks have also had to cope with a range of structural factors, mostly micro-economic and institutional in nature, that deterred banks from engaging in lending to the private sector: frequent crises destroyed the old client base and new customers had no credit record; inadequate auditing and accounting standards and practices hampered banks' ability to monitor both financial and non-financial companies; legislative frameworks typically did not support the enforceability of creditors' rights once loans became overdue.[3]
- Latin American financial systems have had to cope with highly volatile capital inflows. Private inflows rose from a yearly average of US$ 10 billion during 1983–90 to US$ 62 billion by 1998, before declining to about half that amount in recent years. Until recently, capital inflows were accompanied by rapid expansions of bank credit and consumption booms—and strong contractions and busts when they reversed. With limited resources from reserves and official sources, domestic policies became pro-cyclical and reduced the capacity of the government and banks to react to crises. Only in recent years have private inflows been accompanied by significant current account surpluses, as external markets for Latin American exports boomed and governments tended to follow more prudent, and thus less pro-cyclical, fiscal policies.

Banking crises and reforms

Over the past 10 years, banking-system fragilities contributed to a series of financial crises. A first wave of crises hit several

Latin American countries during the mid-1990s, starting in 1994 with Bolivia, Brazil, Mexico and Venezuela, followed by Argentina and Paraguay in 1995 and Ecuador in 1996. Banks were restructured and/or recapitalized, at great fiscal cost, while regulatory systems were overhauled. In many cases, the reforms were successful, but in others it was not the case. A second wave of crises hit several banking systems, including those in Ecuador in 1999, Argentina in 2001, Uruguay in 2002 and the Dominican Republic in 2003. Bolivia experienced banking-system stress more recently, in 2003–04, but since then financial conditions in the region have improved.

Past experience clearly demonstrates the potential for rapid contagion across borders. In the wake of the 1994 Mexico crisis, Argentines were seen as particularly exposed because of questions about the government's ability to defend the currency board. Similar forces put the banking system of Uruguay in danger, after the Argentine financial system collapsed in 2002. Micro-economic influences, such as poor bank management and prudential regulation and bank supervision, were also responsible for bank problems in a number of countries.[4]

Latin American crises were typically not as expensive to resolve as those that afflicted Asia in 1997–98. The most costly crises in Latin America (in Argentina, Ecuador, Mexico and Venezuela) cost around 20 per cent of GDP to resolve, about one-third to one-half the costs of dealing with the crises in Indonesia, Korea and Thailand.

To deal with these banking crises, governments across Latin America implemented a series of banking-system reforms aimed at resolving weak banks and strengthening regulation and supervision, including mergers, restructurings, privatizations, stronger prudential regulations, including on/offshore operations, and accounting regulations were strengthened, and foreign participation was liberalized.

Financial integration

Financial integration in Latin America has been strongly linked to integration on other fronts. Integration through trade and FDI has been an important determinant of the integration in banking and cross-listing of equity. Two features have been notable since the liberalization process of the 1990s. Large international banks have increased their presence in the region (as noted earlier), and firms have gained the ability to increase their sources of funding by tapping international capital markets directly, mostly through the listing of Depositary Receipts (DRs) on foreign stock markets. Through these mechanisms, firms have been allowed to issue cheaper debt abroad and foreign banks have been allowed to penetrate financial markets, including the administration of pension funds and insurance companies.

Advances in formal regional financial cooperation have been very limited among the Latin American countries. Aside from North American Free Trade Agreement (NAFTA), where agreements are in place to proceed with the integration of the financial markets of Canada, Mexico and the US, there has not been much progress in regional financial service liberalization beyond approval of protocols. However, some initiatives are worth noting, such as certain efforts to integrate stock markets, as well as the creation of sub-regional development banks in Central America (*Banco Centroamericano de Integración Económica* [BCIE]), the Andean area (*Corporacion Andina de Fomento* [CAF]), the Southern Cone (*Fondo Financiero para el Desarrollo de la Cuenca del Plata* [FONPLATA]) and Carribean Community (CARICOM) (Carribean Development Bank [CDB]). In recent months, the Southern Common Market (MERCOSUR) countries have also announced their intention to establish a new development bank, Banco del Sur, as an alternative to existing regional and IFIs. However, no detailed plans are yet known about the initiative, except for the fact that the financial support would be mainly provided by Venezuela, Brazil and Argentina.

Some CARICOM countries have moved towards a regional stock market with cross-listing and trading in securities on existing stock exchanges. The small islands of the Organization of Eastern Caribbean States (OECS) have a long-functioning common currency and a common central bank. Meanwhile, at a regional level, *Asociación Latinoamericana de Integración* (ALADI) developed a reciprocal payments system to finance trade among members in 1966. The system, designed to overcome foreign exchange obstacles to trade, is currently facilitating only a small proportion of total regional trade. One of the areas in which the issue of financial integration is attracting attention is the Central American Common Market (CACM). While some efforts have been made in Central America, efforts are needed to move towards consolidated regulation with common standards across countries.

In the end, other than the increased participation of foreign banks in different countries and the trading of securities in developed countries through Real Estate Investment Trusts (REITs), little progress has been achieved in regional integration. Institutional features in individual countries have precluded adequate cooperation in this regard. Policies such as eliminating controls for foreign agent participation or creating specific agreements among countries can serve as a basis for financial integration. However, such agreements have been few. Future financial integration can also be enhanced by adopting international best practices regarding accounting standards, disclosure and sharing of information, and tax regimes. Even if full harmonization of regulations is reached, however, problems with key national institutions and macro-economic instability can hinder the process of financial integration, both with the developed world and within the region. Protection of property rights and legal stability are needed to attract regional and international players into Latin America.

Acknowledgements

This paper was prepared as background for the Forum of Emerging Economies (Jakarta, September 2006). It constitutes a survey of existing material produced by a number of institutions, particularly the IMF, IADB, INTAL, CAF, and the World Bank. Specifically, this document draws heavily on the following works: Stabilization and Reform in Latin America: A Macroeconomic Perspective on the Experience Since the Early 1990s. Anoop Singh, et. al. (International Monetary Fund,

Occasional Paper #238, 2005); Beyond Borders: The New Regional-
ism in Latin America, Inter-American Development Bank, (2003);
Recovering Growth in Latin America: Trade, Productivity and Social
Inclusion, RED, CAF, (2005). Important comments made by Harinder
Kohli and Graciana del Castillo have been incorporated into the text.
However, any mistakes and misquotes are the responsibility of the
author of this note.

Notes

1. Even though financial intermediation rose in recent years, it took
   Mexico 5 years after the 1994 crisis before bank intermediation was
   reactivated and then loans were mostly for consumption. 10 years
   latter, consumer credit is less than 4 per cent of GDP (as compared
   to 8 per cent in Chile and 17 per cent in the US). In Uruguay, 4 years
   after the banking crisis bank lending is short term and basically for
   consumption.
2. Spreads are about 13 per cent in Latin America while the average
   in emerging Asia and the industrialized countries is about 3 per
   cent. High spreads existed before financial liberalization and were
   the consequence of non-remunerated reserve requirements and, to
   a lesser extent, private crowding out by the public sector. Taxes on
   financial intermediation, imposed as a quick way of the crisis, also
   contributes to the high spreads.
3. According to calculations by Galindo et al. (2002a, 2002b), if Latin
   American countries could increase the effective protection of
   creditors to the level of the developed countries, their financial markets would deepen on average 15 additional percentage points.
   Creditors' rights and law enforcement are lagging even in comparison
   with other regions with legal frameworks of the same origin (for
   example, some Asian countries).
4. The banking crisis in Uruguay was not only the result of contagion.
   In addition to the fiscal and macro-economic problems that affected
   the banks negatively, there was plain fraud in two large banks and
   supervision was lax. Regarding contagion, problems arose because
   a number of banks were holding Argentine bonds to back non-
   resident deposits. When the supervision authorities required that
   they exchange such bonds for loans to creditworthy companies, the
   companies were unable to do so because of a freeze on banking
   system transactions (*corralito*) in Argentina.

Bibliography

Bank for International Settlement. (BIS). 2006. Annual Report 2005–2006. Basel, Switzerland: BIS.

Collyns, Charles and G. Russell Kincaid. 2003. *Managing Financial Crises: The Recent Experience of Latin America*. International Monetary Fund Occassional Paper #217, Washington, DC.

Corporacion Andina de Fomento (CAF). 2005. 'Recovering Growth in Latin America: Trade, Productivity and Social Inclusion', Reporte de Economia y Desarrollo. Caracas, Venezuela: CAF.

Galindo, Arturo, Alejandro Micco and César Serra. 2002a. 'Determinants of Cross-Border Banking Activity: The Role of Economic and Legal Relationships', Mimeo, Washington, DC: Inter-American Development Bank.

Galindo, Arturo, Alejandro Micco and Guillermo Ordoñez. 2002b. 'Financial Liberalization and Growth: Empirical Evidence', Mimeo, Washington, DC: Inter-American Development Bank.

Inter-American Development Bank. 2003. *Beyond Borders: The New Regionalism in Latin America*. Washington, DC: Inter-American Development Bank.

International Monetary Fund (IMF). 2006. *World Economic Outlook (WEO)*, September 2006. Washington, DC: IMF.

———. 2007a. Global Financial Stability Report, April 2007, Washington, DC.

———. 2007b. *International Financial Statistics (IFS)*, June 2006–August 2007. Washington, DC: IMF.

———. 2007c. *World Economic Outlook (WEO)*, April 2007. Washington, DC: IMF.

Kaminsky, Graciela and Sergio Schmukler. 1999. 'On Booms and Crashes: Stock Market Cycles and Financial Liberalization', Mimeo. Washington, DC: World Bank.

———. 2003. 'Short-Run Pain, Long-Run Gain: The Effects of Financial Liberalization'. NBER Working Paper No. 9787, June, Washington, DC.

Singh, Anoop, Agnès Belaisch, Charles Collyns, Paula De Masi, Reva Krieger, Guy Meredith and Robert Rennhack. 2005. 'Stabilization and Reform in Latin America: A Macroeconomic Perspective on the Experience since the Early 1990s'. International Monetary Fund Occasional Paper #238, Washington, DC.

World Bank. 2007. *World Development Indicators (WDI)*. Washington, DC: World Bank.

Latin American and East Asian Trade Strategies 8

Luis Miguel Castilla

Introduction

This chapter seeks to establish that the most successful countries in sustaining growth and improving living standards have been those which actually broadened their participation in global markets. The East Asian experience suggests that export-led growth and outward-oriented policies, among other policies, account for the significant growth achieved by these countries. A key factor in their success is a trade agenda complemented with other policies designed to improve the competitiveness of the domestic economy; through these policies, productivity is improved and sustainable growth is ensured. In general, through a coherent selection and combination of multilateral, bilateral or regional trade schemes, a positive impact on development can be achieved. Nevertheless, important challenges remain, especially concerning the compatibility of different trade options.

This chapter is organized into five sections (including this introduction). The section 'Latin American and East Asian Development Tracks' presents a brief account of the main determinants behind the contrasting development performances of Latin America and East Asia. Having identified the importance of trade policy and export-orientation as determinants of productivity improvement, the section 'Trade strategies: A Comparison between Latin America and East Asia' compares the trade regimes followed by Latin America and East Asia. This account includes a review of trade policies since the mid-1980s, when unilateral trade liberalization was pursued, until the most recent proliferation of bilateral free trade agreements between developing and industrialized economies. The debate on the co-existence of multilateralism and regionalism is also briefly covered. The section titled 'Fostering Stronger Trade Relations Between Latin America and East Asia: Challenges and Opportunities' outlines the opportunities and challenges associated with the broadening of trade relations between Latin America and East Asia, including China. Finally, the section 'Concluding Remarks' presents concluding remarks, which focus particularly on the need to accompany trade policy with a productive transformation agenda, to ensure that the benefits of trade materialize.

Latin American and East Asian development tracks

Latin America has made considerable progress during the past two decades in areas such as macro-economic stability, greater openness to trade and international capital flows, as well as in the consolidation of democracy. In spite of this, the region has not grown enough to close a development gap that dates back to the 1950s; income distribution is extremely uneven, and social exclusion is a common element to many Latin American countries. In other words, economic growth has been disappointing, and its fruits have not been shared equitably, nor have they reached the destitute in any significant way.

Observed growth rates are relatively low when analyzed from three points of view: (*i*) Latin America's average growth in the 1990s was lower than in the 1960s and 1970s; (*ii*) other developing regions, such as East Asia, had higher growth rates; and (*iii*) growth in Latin America was substantially lower than the needed rate to improve the living conditions of most of its inhabitants. In the first place, per capita Gross Domestic Product (GDP) growth in Latin America between 1990 and 2003 was only 1 per cent per annum, considerably below levels posted during the 1960s (3.3 per cent) and 1970s (2.4 per cent).[1] Second, Latin

America's growth levels lagged behind those of East Asia, with per capita income growth averaging only one-fourth of the rate reached by those Asian countries over the past four decades. This means that while East Asia's per capita income increased seven folds in a 40-year span, Latin America did not even succeed in doubling its per capita GDP.[2] And third, the poor growth exhibited in the 1990s meant that no significant reductions in poverty could be expected, as compared to the 1960s and 1970s when high growth rates resulted in major social improvements.

Figure 8.1 illustrates Latin America's pronounced divergence in per capita income. A comparison with the US reveals a growing differential in per capita income between the US and Latin America over the past 50 years. When East Asian countries are considered, there is an evident convergence between per capita income of these countries and the US, while Latin America's per capita income diverges.

Latin America's disappointing growth performance is largely due to its unsatisfactory record in factor accumulation and productivity growth. In their study of the differences in growth between Latin America and Southeast Asia between 1960 and 2002, De Gregorio and Lee (2003) found that half of this differential can be attributed to factor accumulation.[3] Investment in physical capital has remained low in Latin America over the past two decades (20 per cent of GDP), whereas it has increased in Southeast Asia (30 per cent of GDP) and in Organisation for Economic Co-operation and Development (OECD) countries (22 per cent). This low level of investment can be traced, in part, to Latin America's poor capacity to generate domestic savings; according to Economic Commission for Latin America and the Caribbean (ECLAC) (2003), average domestic savings in the region declined as a percentage of GDP from 22.8 per cent in the 1980s to barely 17.7 per cent during the 1998–2001 period. Contrastingly, domestic savings in Southeast Asia accounted for more than 35 per cent of GDP during the 1990s.

Low productivity is another reason why Latin America has not been able to achieve sustained growth. Total factor productivity (TFP) has not grown as vigorously as in the 1960s and 1970s; this has widened Latin America's productivity gap with the rest

Figure 8.1 Income convergence/divergence, 1950–2000

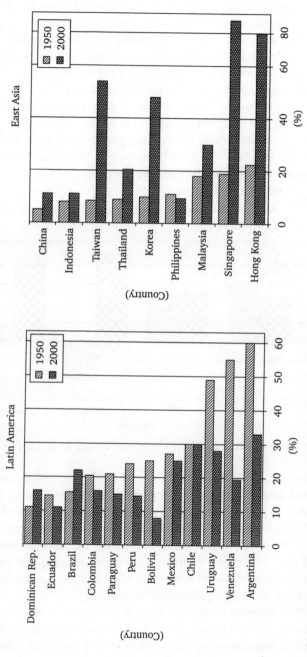

Source: Own elaboration, based on Penn World Tables 6.1 (2002).

of the world. Although productivity declined in other developing regions as well, it continued to expand at a noteworthy rate in the developed world as well as in most East Asian countries, with positive growth rates during the 1980s and 1990s. As shown in Figure 8.2, after a relatively strong expansion in the 1960s, productivity in Latin America slowed and was actually negative during the so-called 'lost' decade of the 1980s. Since then, productivity has recovered, partly due to the reforms that were put in place in the 1990s. In contrast, productivity grew at much faster rates in East Asia, greatly exceeding Latin America's TFP average growth during the last two decades.

Figure 8.2 Average total factor productivity (TFP) growth in Latin America

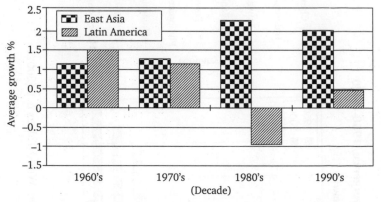

Sources: De Ferranti et al. (2003) based on Loayza et al. (2002).

Figure 8.3 shows TFP trends for individual countries between 1991 and 2000, which display important differences among them. Countries like Argentina, Chile and the Dominican Republic reported annual average productivity growth of over 2 per cent; on the other hand, in Colombia, Venezuela, Ecuador, Honduras, Paraguay and Jamaica, productivity fell. In contrast, TFP growth rates in Singapore, South Korea and Malaysia were considerably higher than most Latin American countries.

A key component of the East Asian development experience has been that its growth model, which has been outward-oriented and export-led, suggesting a positive relationship between openness

Figure 8.3 TFP growth in selected countries, 1990–2000

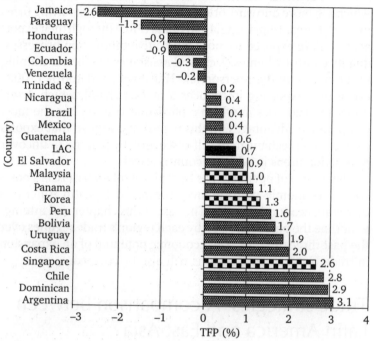

Source: Loayza et al. (2002).

and growth. According to traditional theory, openness is desirable because it aligns domestic and international prices, allowing a more efficient resource allocation. Other channels through which openness positively affects growth are those associated with endogenous growth theory; these include technological diffusion, learning by doing, use of economies of scale, among others. There is a large body of literature which demonstrates that cross-country income per capita variations can be explained by differences in the degree of openness, and that the level of openness is positively associated with real GDP growth.[4]

The debate regarding the effect of export growth on GDP growth and development, in general, has been spurred by recent studies of developing countries at the firm level. In fact, there is evidence that firms in tradable sectors tend to be more productive and more technologically advanced; this does not necessarily imply that exports have a positive effect on productivity, but rather that firms which are already productive are the ones which are more outward-oriented.[5] For example, exporting firms in South Korea, Taipei, China and China (PRC) through their export activities are exposed to more innovative production processes, quality control schemes, technical assistance and better training programmes for their personnel.[6] Hausmann and Rodrik (2003) argue that exporting introduces a market signal, which determines the activities in which a particular country has the most comparative advantages. In this regard, it is argued that exports can act as a mechanism of self-discovery, by helping to uncover production areas in which a country excels.[7]

The degree of openness has helped to explain East Asia's noteworthy economic performance, compared to Latin America's moderate economic results. The rest of this chapter will attempt to outline the paths followed by each region's trade regimes over the past three decades. The economic potential of an expansion in trade between both regions will also be covered.

Trade strategies: A comparison between Latin America and East Asia

In the last decades, most developing countries, including Latin America and East Asia, have been committed to broadening their participation in international trade, following the global trend towards liberalization. Within the General Agreement on Tariffs and Trade (GATT)/World Trade Organization (WTO) framework, industrialized countries reduced their tariffs significantly and eliminated a large part of their non-tariff barriers. Developing economies also undertook important reforms in this regard, abandoning protectionist policies in favour of export-led growth. In general, the global process towards liberalization resulted in a growing economic interrelation among countries through the trade of goods and services, capital and even immigrant flows. As a result, global exports from developing economies, as a percentage of GDP, have doubled in the past 40 years.

Despite these trade liberalization efforts, the impact of these reforms on development has been largely disappointing. In the case of Latin America, greater openness has not resulted in sustained growth and, as shown in Figure 8.5, its participation in world trade has actually declined. In contrast, East Asia boasts a consistently increasing share in global markets. This situation is partly due to each region's particular pattern of specialization (as outlined), and to the growing productivity gap between Latin America and East Asia.

Imports from developing economies are subject to trade barriers applied by both industrialized countries and other developing countries. Despite significant progress in global trade

Figure 8.4   Exports performance

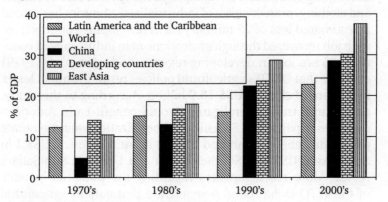

Source: Own elaboration, based on World Bank (2005).

Figure 8.5   Share of world exports

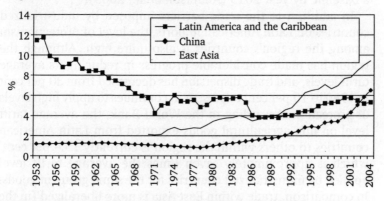

Source: Own elaboration, based on World Bank (2005).

liberalization, developed countries continue to impose high levels of protection in important sectors, particularly in agricultural products and medium-technology manufactures such as textiles and apparel. Although average tariffs are relatively low, trade regimes in industrialized economies are characterized by the imposition of peaks (tariffs over 15 per cent), tariff escalations (tariffs that rise according to the degree of processing of the imported good), and various forms of non-tariff barriers.

According to the World Bank and the International Monetary Fund (IMF) (2002), trade barriers impose important costs for developing countries. For example, in the specific case of textiles and clothing, protectionism of industrialized countries has caused an estimated loss of 27 million jobs in developing countries; for each job recovered through protectionism in industrialized countries, 35 are lost in developing regions. Anderson et al. (1999) estimate that OECD's agricultural policies result in annual losses in welfare of close to US$ 18.9 billion. According to this study, agricultural trade liberalization would benefit Latin American countries in particular. Specifically, liberalization would generate per capita benefits of around US$ 30 in Latin America, US$ 1 in South Asia, US$ 4 in Southeast Asia and US$ 6 in Sub-Sahara Africa. More recent updates regarding the potential benefits of the WTO Doha round demonstrate that cuts in agricultural domestic support as well as the elimination of subsidies for agricultural exports in industrialized countries would represent global real income gains of up to US$ 120 billion, compared to a baseline by year 2015 (Anderson et al., 2005).

In addition to the trade barriers imposed by industrialized countries on Latin American imports, the level of protectionism among the region's countries is also quite high. Although the region has made considerable progress in reducing its average tariff levels, and trade dispersion has decreased from 30 per cent in 1980 to 10 per cent at present, it continues to apply high levels of protection. According to the World Bank, the average tariff level on non-agricultural goods exported from Latin American countries to others within the region is currently 15.4 per cent, which is approximately seven times the average tariff level applied by industrialized countries for the same group of goods. In comparison, trade within East Asia is more liberalized (in the case of non-agricultural products), since a lower average tariff level is applied to intra-regional East Asian imports. However, East Asia imposes higher tariffs on agricultural goods, whether they are imported from countries within or outside the region; Latin American agricultural products are actually taxed with lower tariffs (Table 8.1).

Table 8.1   Average tariff by type of goods and by region (%)

Exporting region	Importing region		
	East Asia	Latin America and the Caribbean	Industrial countries
Agricultural goods			
East Asia	31.0	15.5	30.5
Latin America and the Caribbean	42.1	14.8	20.4
Industrial countries	33.3	20.1	15.3
Non-agricultural goods			
East Asia	8.2	15.1	5.1
Latin America and the Caribbean	4.3	15.4	2.1
Industrial countries	7.4	8.5	1.0

Source: World Bank (2003).

Trade patterns

Manufactured goods have been the fastest-growing exports; in the 1960s, they represented close to half of total trade, and now they amount to nearly 80 per cent of total goods traded. Moreover, fast-growing emerging economies have been gaining ground in the manufactured goods global market, at the expense of other developing economies. For example, China and Southeast Asian countries have sustained high growth rates in manufactured exports over the past three decades. In contrast, Latin American, manufactured export growth, after expanding at a fast pace between the mid-1980s and early 1990s, have posted a more moderate expansion during the last decade (Figure 8.6).

These trade patterns are consistent with particular comparative advantages (Figure 8.7). The fact that Latin America has lost participation in the markets for manufactured goods, partly

Figure 8.6 Performance of manufacturing and exports

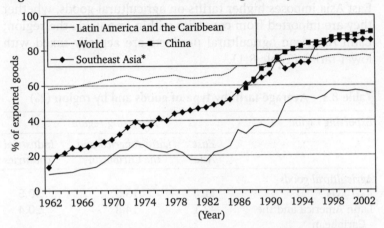

Source: Own elaboration, based on World Bank (2005).
Note: * The Southeast countries are Korea, Singapore, Philippines and Thailand.

Figure 8.7 Comparative advantages

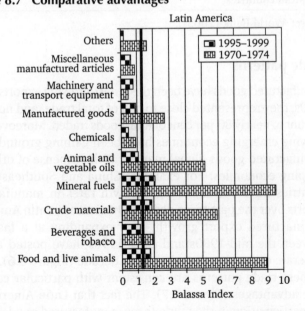

(*Figure 8.7 continued*)

(Figure 8.7 continued)

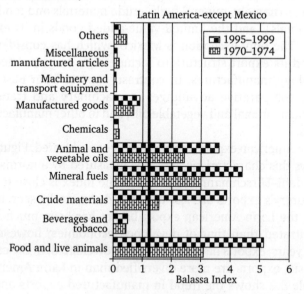

Latin America-except Mexico

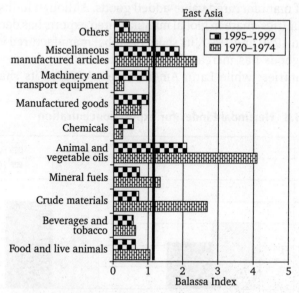

East Asia

Source: Own elaboration, based on UN (2005).

Note: Measure of relative export performance by country and industry, defined as a country's share of world exports of a good divided by its share of total world exports.

reflects its comparative advantage in terms of its abundant natural resources (namely, mineral fuels, crude materials and food and live animals), and the limited value-added goods in its export basket. The only exception is Mexico, which has considerably changed its export structure to include high and intermediate technology manufactures. In contrast, exports from East Asia exhibit comparative advantages in machinery and transport equipment, animal and vegetable oils, and in other manufactured articles.

Latin American exports are also highly concentrated. Figure 8.8 displays this characteristic, which is measured by a normalized Herfindahl–Hirschmann index. When the index is close to one, the country's exports are less diversified. As can be seen in the graph, the Latin American export basket has been much more concentrated than that of developed economies; however, in recent years, exports have become more diversified. In the case of East Asia, exports are more diversified than in Latin America.

Table 8.2 shows the trend in manufactured exports and the share of manufactured value-added goods. Although industrialized countries' share in global manufactured exports has declined between 1980 and 1997, its share of global manufactured value-added goods has increased. The situation differs for developing countries: while Latin America has increased its share of

Figure 8.8 Herfindahl index for export concentration

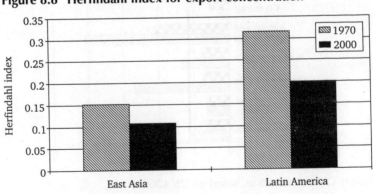

Source: Own elaboration, based on UN (2005).

Table 8.2   Participation in manufactured exports and manufactured value-added goods by regions, 1980 versus 1997

	Participation in global manufactured exports (%)		Participation in global manufactured value added goods (%)	
	1980	*1997*	*1980*	*1997*
Industrial countries	82.3	70.9	64.5	73.3
Developing countries	10.6	26.5	16.6	23.8
Latin America	1.5	3.5	7.1	6.7
Southeast Asia	6.0	16.9	7.3	14.0
China	1.1	3.8	3.3	5.8

Source: *United Nations Conference on Trade and Development* (UNCTAD) (2002).

global manufactured exports, its share of global manufactured value-added goods has declined. In contrast, the increase in manufactured exports in Southeast Asia and in China has been accompanied by a larger share of manufactured value-added goods in global markets. Although most Latin American countries have increased their manufactured exports, they continue to be net importers of these goods and have not been able to move up the value chain.

The rise in medium- and high-technology manufactured exports respond to the fact that many of these goods are part of international production chains (that is, trade patterns respond to the fragmentation degree of production processes).[8] Currently, about 40 per cent of global trade is intra-industrial (trade of similar goods between countries). In developing countries, the main form of intra-industrial trade is vertical, given that trade occurs within the same production chain (for example, in the vehicle-assembly industry). Table 8.3 displays these patterns in intra-regional trade.[9] It is worth noting that, generally, different regions tend to trade more intra-industrially among themselves, than with the rest of the world. For example, 35.5 per cent of intra-industrial trade in the European Union (EU) is vertical, 29 per cent in the case of North America and 24.2 per cent in East Asia. In contrast, the share of intra-industrial vertical trade

Table 8.3   Typology of intra-regional trade by trading blocs (% of total intra-industrial trade)

Regions	Inter-industrial	Others (not classified)	Horizontal Intra-industrial	Vertical intra-industrial
European Union	38.31	1.53	24.66	35.51
North American Free Trade Agreement (NAFTA)	27.97	19.44	23.58	29.01
Mexico	36.33	10.93	10.07	42.67
MERCOSUR	67.63	0.52	15.97	15.87
Andean Community	80.79	0.47	8.16	10.59
East Asia	62.93	4.96	7.95	24.15

Source: Zignago (2005).

in Latin America (perhaps with the exception of Mexico) is comparatively low (10.6 per cent in the Andean Community and 16 per cent in *Mercado Común del Sum* [MERCOSUR]).

These patterns reflect the growing importance of global production chains. This is the result of the reductions in transportation costs, and the improvements in domestic absorption capacities (particularly those related to human capital stocks), which have enabled technological diffusion and enhanced location advantages in certain emerging economies. International production sharing has also been associated with a rising degree of intra-regional trade in parts and components that are produced and assembled into final goods within Asia, particularly in East and Southeast Asia. For example, developing Asia's share of world trade in parts and components rose from 16 per cent in 1992 to 32 per cent in 2003, surpassing North American Free Trade Agreement's (NAFTA) share.[10] Although components are traded within developing Asia, the ultimate destination for most assembled products remains outside the region, mainly in the EU and the US markets.

In sum, while global trade of goods is increasingly being driven by the dynamic trade of manufactured goods from Southeast Asia and China, most Latin American countries (particularly in South America) continue to export mainly primary goods or natural resource-based manufactures. To a large extent, these differing trade patterns reflect relative comparative advantages and productivity differentials, which have enabled countries such as China and other East Asian economies to actively participate in global production chains. Furthermore, the persistence of trade barriers has also inhibited a larger penetration of Latin American goods in global export markets.

Trade strategies in Latin America and East Asia

Unilateral liberalization: Trade liberalization has been pursued by most developing countries for the past two decades. The debt crisis of the 1980s, and the ensuing external restrictions, revealed the limitations of import substitution policies pursued by most Latin American countries. These policies were abandoned when adjustment programmes were put in place, and most countries in the region began to dismantle their protectionist regimes to participate in the world economy in a different way. The prevailing strategies until the early 1980s had promoted industrialization through high-tariff barriers and quantitative restrictions; the new regimes fostered development through increased and improved participation in the world economy. Export growth and access to new markets took on a strategic sense. It was no longer a matter of protection against imports, but of developing competitive, tradable sectors.

Initially, trade liberalization was unilateral and was basically designed to address the external restrictions imposed on the region at that time. As Table 8.4 shows, tariff levels were drastically cut. Consistent with these measures, openness (measured as the ratio of exports plus imports to GDP) increased considerably (Table 8.5).

Unilateral trade liberalization in East Asia was similar to the Latin American experience. The elimination of tariffs on capital and intermediate goods, as well as the reduction of non-tariff barriers in the 1980s, played a prominent role in igniting and then sustaining trade growth in the period from 1980 to 1998.[11]

Table 8.4 Average tariffs per region (%), 1980–99

	1980–85	1986–90	1991–95	1996–99
Latin America	30	22	15	11
OECD	18	10	9	8
East Asia	28	18	19	16

Source: de Ferranti et al. (2003).

Table 8.5 Trade openness by decade (%)

	1980	1990	2000
Latin America	31.7	40.6	48.3
Andean countries	37.3	41.5	41.9
MERCOSUR	17.8	19.1	28.1
OECD	37.3	38.1	45.6
Southeast Asia	88.4	119.7	137.3
China	21.5	39.7	54.5

Source: Own elaboration, based on World Bank (2005).

This built on previous policy developments, such as the establishment of export processing zones for manufacturing and special economic zones throughout East Asia. In addition, technological advances which lowered transportation costs also spurred Asia's trade. In fact, an increase in trade efficiency, as well as the reduction of trade costs, may have had a more powerful effect on trade than trade liberalization itself.[12] Actually, East Asia applied higher tariff levels (16 per cent), on average, than Latin America (11 per cent) during the 1996–99 period. Instead, higher trade efficiency was achieved through various trade facilitation measures, such as the application and diffusion of improved telecommunications in international transactions; the development of port infrastructure and improvements in customs procedures, among others.

Regional integration schemes: Efforts to integrate Latin American economies date back to the 1950s, when a free trade area was established between South America and Mexico (known as the Latin American Integration Association), and a common market was created in Central America. However, these frameworks—and those that followed them, such as the Andean Community—exhibited the same flaws as national development strategies. Economic integration caused national import substitution strategies to be reproduced at the regional level. Thus, countries promoted 'inward-looking' integration, raising protectionist barriers and stimulating regional or sub-regional industrial integration projects. As might be expected, integration made little progress in this initial period. The economies of the region were closed not only to the rest of the world, but also to their regional partners. Moreover, given the similarities of their productive structures, Latin American countries were more resistant to negotiate with their neighbours than with the rest of the world.

However, this situation changed in the early 1990s, when an important re-activation of some of the old integration frameworks took place, and new ones were established, such as MERCOSUR.[13] These new efforts to promote further integration between neighbouring countries were more effective than previous ones. Tariff and non-tariff barriers were eliminated, intra-regional trade grew rapidly, and relations between economic agents in various countries were significantly strengthened. Openness produced a new type of integration, referred to as 'open regionalism'.[14]

In this new context, the existing integration schemes in Latin America acquired greater vigour and rapidly achieved important objectives such as the liberalization of reciprocal trade. During the first stages trade dynamism included the active participation of business sectors which had previously adopted a passive role in integration strategies promoted by their governments. At this point, integration was seen as a way to effectively enhance Latin America's participation in the world economy.

Despite these efforts, regional markets have not been as active as it was expected; they represent only a limited fraction of the countries' total trade, although this may vary according to specific countries.[15] In addition, trade flows within regional groups are generally dominated by trade between the largest countries. Moreover, since the late 1990s, regional integration schemes have become sluggish. MERCOSUR is still affected by the adverse consequences of the financial crisis that hit the region at the end of the 1990s. There has also been a systematic failure to meet integration targets, and the institutional framework, including settlement dispute mechanisms, continues to be fragile. As a result, MERCOSUR's credibility has diminished among economic agents, who have begun to doubt the stability and consistency of the scheme. In the Andean Community, for various reasons, the integration process has also been hindered, in part by the political turbulence in certain member countries.

In the case of East Asia, an increasing bias towards intra-regional trade has been observed since the mid-1980s, which coincided with the proliferation of intra-regional Foreign Direct Investment (FDI), and unilateral trade liberalization in some countries of East and Southeast Asia.[16] The expansion of FDI and FDI-related intra-industry as well as intra-firm trade that led to greater integration within Asia and the growth of intra-regional trade, all began before the recent boom of preferential trade agreements involving Asian developing countries; a situation quite unlike what was seen in Latin America.

The Asian Free Trade Agreement (AFTA) of the Association of Southeast Asian Nations (ASEAN), was set to encourage trade liberalization during the 1990s along two tracks which coalesced into a framework of 'open regionalism'. One track implied an ambitious reduction of most tariffs from around 20 per cent to 5 per cent in 2005, and another one encouraged members of AFTA to reduce tariffs applied to the rest of the world, to reach a target of 10 per cent by 2005. These measures were implemented under the assumption that ASEAN countries needed a simultaneous deepening and opening of their economies in order to face outside competition. This would allow them to become sufficiently competitive to cope especially with China which, at that time, was negotiating its incorporation to the WTO. Nevertheless, the Asian financial crisis changed the nature of this process. In 1997, as the financial crisis unfolded, AFTA's liberalization path was modified; the target date for the first track was advanced to 2002 and the reduction of tariffs to the rest of the world was postponed. As a result, AFTA became more closed to the rest of the world and more open among its members, thus strengthening the process of regionalism.

Regardless of this push for further regionalism, the large list of exceptions granted within AFTA produced a counter-productive reaction from some of its members who were interested in free trade (Desker, 2004). Singapore, being a major international trading hub, was a natural opponent to this reformulation of AFTA, as well as Thailand, which was greatly affected by the financial crisis of 1997. Both countries believed that because AFTA did not allow a rapid increase in regional trade, the ideal venue was to pursue bilateral agreements with countries beyond ASEAN (Hiwatari, 2003). Although countries have been encouraged to consider trade deals with other neighbours, progress in this front has been limited. This reflects the diversity of approaches within ASEAN countries, in terms of economic development and trade competitiveness, and also regarding their perceptions of the value of an East Asian regional bloc (Smith, 2004).

In view of these experiences, it seems necessary to rethink regional integration, to focus on the achievements so far, especially the liberalization of reciprocal trade, and to further develop new markets. The Latin American experience has revealed that the elimination of tariffs does not remove all the barriers to trade, and that many of these barriers—technical rules, customs obstacles and limitations on infrastructure, among others—are much more difficult to correct than tariffs barriers. Regional integration has to be seen as a long-term effort. Existing treaties, or those that may emerge from increased coordination, must be provided with a solid legal and institutional framework of a regional scope. The credibility of integration and the participation of economic operators depends upon the honouring of commitments, the execution and continuity of the initiatives taken, and the existence of effective dispute settlement mechanisms.

Moreover, as the East Asian experience shows, the heterogeneous nature of the countries involved in regional integration schemes, the characteristics of intra-industry trade and the role of FDI in fostering intra-regional trade are also important determinants to the potential success of regional integration initiatives. In addition, more than trade liberalization per se, a more effective push was given to intra-regional trade through the improvement of infrastructure and the adoption of trade facilitation measures.

Participation in the multilateral sphere: Most developing countries are active members of the WTO where global free trade is pursued under a non-discriminatory, reciprocal basis. The multilateral system under the WTO is very different from the old system under GATT; WTO's area of expertise has been broadened to include issues such as trade in services and intellectual property. Also, respect for the rules is more stringent and rigorous, partly due to the strengthening of dispute settlement mechanisms. In contrast, GATT limited its field of action to trade in goods and had given developing countries a series of privileges in the form of special and differential treatment that the WTO later limited.

For developing countries, the shift from a more flexible GATT system to a more demanding WTO clearly involved important commitments. First, countries agreed to consolidate tariffs, such as fixed ceilings, which prevented an increase in tariffs without negotiating equivalent concessions with the affected WTO countries. Second, most developing countries agreed to execute their trade policy in conformity with the WTO multilateral guidelines, which cover a broad range of areas, such as export subsidies, trade-related investment policies, sanitary and phytosanitary requirements and the application of antidumping and countervailing measures. Consequently, WTO membership contributed significantly to the strengthening of economic reforms and to further economic openness. Member countries could also rely on a stable legal framework to expand their markets, promote their trade interests and assert their rights.

The ongoing multilateral negotiations, grouped into what is known as the Doha Development Program (DDP), will prove whether multilateralism is effective for developing countries. These ambitious negotiations will define WTO's role as an institution capable of promoting liberalization and the growth of world trade. One of the key issues included in these negotiations is the expansion of markets for agricultural products, industrial goods and services. Also, there is an attempt to improve WTO regulations so that they may be better adjusted to the reality of international trade and to the differences between WTO members, particularly regarding their size and their specific interests and concerns. However, the Doha negotiations are currently stalled due to the inability of negotiating countries to agree on measures to further liberalize agriculture, considered to be the most protected sector worldwide.

The experience of developing countries in Latin America and East Asia can shed some light on the present debate regarding the compatibility between multilateralism and regionalism. Recent experience reveals that it is possible to participate actively and constructively in different trade negotiation schemes, to use the existing negotiating fora effectively, and to promote particular trade interests where successful dialogue may take place. However, the relation between regional initiatives and the multilateral trade system is not trivial. Although the WTO has tried to establish criteria that may allow regional initiatives and multilateral rules and obligations to co-exist in harmony,[17] there is no consensus about the desirability of this co-existence. It is argued that preferential trade agreements, which grant trade preferences only to members are, in principle, incompatible with the WTO system, which is based on non-discrimination, and on the unrestricted application of the Most Favoured Nation (MFN) clause. Therefore, it is contended that regional agreements should not exist because they are contrary to the spirit of the multilateral system. However, this has not prevented the proliferation of regional agreements; Latin America and East Asia have been very active regions in this respect.

The number of regional agreements reported to the WTO has grown exponentially during the last decade: around 200 regional agreements were in place in the first months of 2005 (Crawford and Fiorentino, 2005). Moreover, practically all WTO member countries have negotiated this type of agreement, which is a relatively new development. For example, although up to the early 1990s, the US only used the multilateral system to conduct its trade relations, it is now an enthusiastic defender and promoter of preferential trade agreements. Japan, Hong Kong, Singapore, South Korea and other Asian countries had also kept regionalism at arm's length; however, they are now active participants of regional agreements. In fact, Southeast Asia is one of the areas where regional initiatives are being actively implemented. Some of these have emerged around China, Japan and South Korea, the largest economies of the region. In Europe and Latin America, regionalism has also been pursued for many years. The EU has historically been the most effective trading bloc; it has grown continuously and has created a wide network of free trade agreements with its neighbours and with countries beyond the region.

In any event, regional preferential trade agreements are part of the existing framework of international trade relations, which will not change in the foreseeable future. Therefore, a way has to be found for these agreements to co-exist in harmony within the multilateral system. To do this, the multilateral system must regain its effectiveness and credibility. If the current stalemate continues and the WTO fails to adapt to the new realities of world trade and fails to address the needs of its members—especially those of developing countries, which are the most vulnerable—regional agreements will not be considered as complementary, but rather as alternatives to the multilateral system. Consequently, it is important to define, in a practical sense, the relation between regionalism and multilateralism, and to establish an appropriate framework for its constructive development.

Bilateral trade agreements: As outlined earlier, there has been a proliferation of preferential trade agreements. These include bilateral trade agreements between developing and industrialized countries (North–South agreements), as well as agreements among developing countries (South–South agreements). In response to the sluggishness of multilateral trade negotiations, East Asian trading partners were led to consider liberalizing trade on a reciprocal basis. In this case, bilateral agreements, viewed from a strategic perspective, allow 'like-minded' countries to make more progress on a wider range of issues, and in a shorter period of time; this would be hard to accomplish within the diverse and complex WTO environment (Heidrich, 2006). Before 1998, only three preferential trade agreements involving East Asian developing countries were notified to the WTO. By 2005, 13 additional agreements had been presented, and a large number of other agreements are currently under negotiation.

Another interesting fact is that not all preferential trade agreements have been intra-regional; this demonstrates that Asia is increasingly interested in 'cross-regional agreements', with economies across the Pacific, for the most part, but also with the rest of the world. Furthermore, Asia's emerging giants, China and

India, are also seeking to be a part of this trend. The fact that many of the new preferential trade agreements extend beyond the Asian region, underscores the importance of extra-regional markets, particularly with respect to the export of final products. These cross-regional agreements are driven by factors such as energy security, access to minerals and other natural resources (as will be argued next for the case of Latin America and China), and countries' efforts to 'lock in' reforms, by making them part of a formal trade treaty with a major developed country or region. Moreover, many of these agreements are politically motivated and countries seek to strengthen diplomatic alliances by providing economic benefits to their partners (Heidrich, 2006).

In the case of Latin America, there is also a growing interest in the pursuit of bilateral trade agreements with the region's main trading partners. In the early 1990s, Mexico began negotiations for a free trade agreement with the US, which Canada joined later. These countries signed the NAFTA, the first agreement of this type between the industrialized and the developing countries. NAFTA inspired the launch, shortly afterwards, of a hemispheric integration initiative of a broader scope, the Free Trade Area of the Americas (FTAA). However, this process reached an impasse a few years ago, and its prospects today are still uncertain.[18]

NAFTA was presented as a modern agreement, which included guidelines for tariff reductions, trade in goods and in services (which covers a wide range of economic activities), and investments, an area until then excluded from the external trade agenda of Latin American countries. Therefore, NAFTA rules were attractive to countries embarking on the modernization and liberalization of their economies. As the negotiations for an agreement with the US began, Mexico experienced a considerable increase in FDI and in trade with the US. In fact, NAFTA has become the standard for the bilateral negotiations which have recently surfaced between numerous Latin American countries and the US.

Most countries in Latin America have begun to negotiate broader bilateral agreements with their main trading partners. Such is the case of Mexico, which also negotiated bilateral agreements with the EU, Japan, and other countries and regions. Chile followed suit, implementing an ambitious strategy of

Figure 8.9(a)   Latin American import from East Asia, by countries, 2004

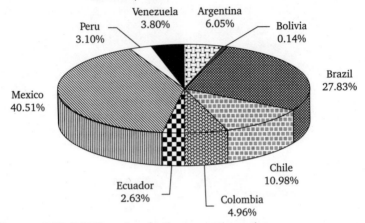

Source: IMF (2005) and author's own construction.

Figure 8.9(b)   Latin American export from East Asia, by countries, 2004

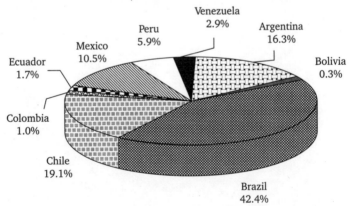

Source: IMF (2005) and author's own construction.

these regions from 1980 to 2004 strongly exceeded Latin America's trade flows with the rest of the world, which increased five-fold during that period. The trade balance between East Asia and

Table 8.6 Trade flows between East Asia and Latin America (US$ million)

		1980	1990	2000	2004
East Asian Exports (Free on Board [FOB]) to:	LAC	3,098.4	5,617.4	27,639.9	40,610.1
	Andean	242.3	322.3	2,193.6	4,074.3
	Argentina	264.5	169.7	1,785.9	1,684.0
	Brazil	543.7	439.5	4,741.6	7,750.3
	Chile	151.6	378.5	2,187.8	3,057.8
	Mexico	188.4	1,210.9	7,286.0	11,282.4
East Asian Imports (Cost Insurance and Freight [CIF]) from:	Latin America and Caribbean (LAC)	1,768.3	6,429.9	13,230.8	36,523.9
	Andean	254.7	585.8	1,700.3	3,917.5
	Argentina	232.3	937.3	1,856.7	5,468.1
	Brazil	464.6	2,902.2	4,155.9	14,234.7
	Chile	228.7	708.8	2,775.6	6,398.0
	Mexico	209.9	626.4	1,824.3	3,514.9

Source: IMF (2005).

Table 8.9 Percentage of Latin American imports from East Asia, by product, 2004

Imports	LA-9	Andean	Argentina	Brazil	Chile	Mexico
Food and live animals	1.1	1.3	1.5	2.2	1.8	0.6
Beverages and tobacco	0.0	0.0	0.0	0.0	0.0	0.0
Crude materials, except fuels	1.6	2.1	3.2	4.2	1.7	0.7
Fuels, lubricants, etc.	2.0	0.8	1.8	7.3	2.0	0.7
Animal, vegetable oils, fats, wax	0.2	0.3	0.6	0.7	0.1	0.1
Chemicals	5.0	8.5	15.5	9.2	4.8	2.3
Manufactured goods	9.3	18.3	11.6	10.1	11.9	7.1
Machines, transport equipment	63.8	44.0	50.1	53.3	32.3	74.6
Misc. manufactured articles	15.6	24.1	15.7	13.0	45.3	11.9
Unclassified goods	1.3	0.7	0.0	0.0	0.0	2.1

Source: Own elaboration, based on UN (2005).

Note: The table was constructed following Sitc. Rev. 3 trade classification.

marked by the import of manufactures from East Asia and the export of natural resources from Latin America, reflecting a clear pattern of inter-industrial trade, based on particular comparative advantages. Lastly, export growth with East Asia reflects a real market expansion for Latin America.

Trade between Latin America and China

Trade links between Latin America and Asia cannot exclude a specific analysis of China's performance, given that this country's trade liberalization has altered global trade patterns. China's record growth in the last 30 years has placed it in a key position within the world economy. Some predictions even suggest that China could, in less than two decades, displace the US as the world's largest economy.[20] China's economic accomplishments have been based on high rates of domestic investment, accompanied by significant trade liberalization, which have had a considerable effect on global trade and FDI flows. In fact, China's international trade grew 17 times between 1980 and 2003 and represented an average of 4.8 per cent of world trade in the 2001–03 period. China also received about a third of global FDI flows.[21]

China's unprecedented growth has had a substantial effect on other emerging economies, such as those in Latin America. In the first place, China is increasingly affecting commodity markets, by becoming a key driver of global demand. China's growth rate in import volume for several primary commodities, such as iron, copper and soyabeans, greatly exceed the import growth rate of these goods in all industrialized economies. In fact, China has become the world's leading importer of vegetable oil, wood and pulp, iron, aluminium, among others. This explains the current persistence of high international commodity prices. Moreover, an increasingly large portion of the growing demand in China is being supplied by Latin American economies. For example, 62 per cent of Argentina's vegetable oil exports (it is the third largest exporter in the world) and over a fifth of Brazil's iron exports (the largest exporter in the world) are to China (see Table 8.10).

Chinese manufactures are also aggressively penetrating the consumer markets of the main industrialized economies, competing with—and in some cases substituting—the supply from other developing countries. Additionally, Chinese manufactures are being increasingly imported by developing countries; therefore, China has become a significant competitor in domestic markets. Trade liberalization in China and its broader participation in mature markets due to the gradual removal of quotas on Chinese imports constitute important challenges for countries with similar manufacturing export baskets, especially for countries with abundant low-skilled labour. For example, Chinese competition has increased, as expected, in the US textile and apparel market for some Central American countries, as well as in markets for low- and medium-technology manufactures. In fact, some US and Japanese automobile and auto-parts assembly facilities are relocating from Mexico to other countries which offer lower costs, in view of Chinese competition.

These economies could meet strong competition from China only through the production of higher value-added goods, by upgrading technological content—which promotes product differentiation—and by reducing costs in production processes and in transportation of exports. In fact, infrastructure investment and trade facilitation have been critical determinants in China's increasing competitiveness within the US market. Important differentials in the quality of infrastructure between China and Latin America are explained by very significant differences in investment (9 per cent of GDP in China versus 2.5 per cent in Latin America). Moreover, regarding logistics and trade facilitation, especially customs, China, as most East Asian economies, possesses a competitive edge with respect to Latin America. For example, an imported good takes, on an average, 7.5 days to clear customs in China, whereas it takes 17 days in Ecuador and 7.3 in Peru (World Bank, 2000).

Broader bilateral trade flows between Latin America and China are also limited by the imposition of trade barriers, especially non-tariff ones, by the Chinese government on agricultural imports from Latin America. These barriers, which primarily consist of rigorous sanitary and phytosanitary standards, limit export penetration in the Chinese market. Therefore, efforts to expand trade must reduce non-tariff barriers. Further progress in this regard could be achieved through the negotiation of bilateral trade agreements with China. In fact, Chile is the only Latin American country that has signed a free trade agreement with China. Mutual economic benefits are expected, since both nations' export baskets are complementary. A bilateral trade agreement between other Latin American countries and China could also reduce the frequent application of contingent measures, such as anti-dumping charges and safeguards, on Chinese imports.[22] The strengthening of trade links between China and Latin America also requires the development of efficient mechanisms for the exchange of commercial and technical information and trade opportunities in key sectors.

In sum, there is a great potential in broadening trade relations between China and Latin America (especially South America). From the perspective of Latin America, the desirability of doing so hinges upon diversifying trading partners and taking advantage of complementary export baskets. However, the region also needs to effectively deal with competitive pressures, both in domestic and international markets; this requires that an active trade strategy oriented at reducing trade barriers be accompanied with an agenda to improve competitiveness. From the perspective of China, the attractiveness of furthering trading ties resides in the enlargement of markets for Asian goods and the provision of needed natural resources, particularly raw materials.

Concluding remarks

As has been argued throughout this chapter, successful emerging economies have been able to broaden existing and potential markets, by pursuing aggressive trade liberalization agendas. However, while global trade in goods is increasingly being driven by the dynamic trade of manufactured goods (with an increasingly larger value-added content) from East Asia, most Latin American countries continue to export mainly primary goods or natural resource-based manufactures. To a large extent, these

8. Fragmentation is defined as the distribution of the productive chain among several countries. The production site and the subsequent value-added stages are determined according to the particular comparative advantages of each country.
9. The focus is on intra-regional trade, given that it concentrates the main thrust of intra-industrial trade. By contrast, within extra-regional trade, the share of intra-industrial trade is generally low.
10. Athukorala and Yamashita (2005).
11. The East Asian financial crisis led temporarily to a more protectionist stance in some Asian countries, as will be discussed later.
12. Engman (2005).
13. MERCOSUR was established in 1991. Its member countries, Argentina, Brazil, Paraguay and Uruguay, set an ambitious time table of tariff reductions, which was completed by 1994, with some exceptions.
14. IADB (2002)
15. In MERCOSUR, for example, even though reciprocal trade has increased, the sub-regional market only represents 13 per cent of its members' total exports (after exceeding 25 per cent in the late-1990s). On the other hand, although intra-Andean Community trade has doubled among member countries, it only represents 10 per cent of this region's total exports.
16. Thee (1991 and 2003).
17. GATT Article XXIV contains the rules that govern the formation of customs unions and free trade areas.
18. The FTAA process could not resist the opposing views of some of its key actors, mainly the US and Brazil. In what should have been the final stage of negotiations, the divergent positions of these two countries on the content of the FTAA and its relation to WTO negotiations delayed the process. These differences were particularly evident in 2003, when the US formally declared that it was not willing to negotiate some issues in the FTAA framework which, in its opinion, should be dealt within the WTO (namely, domestic aid for agriculture, subsidies for agricultural exports and anti-dumping regulations). This position triggered an immediate reaction among Brazil and other MERCOSUR countries. They decided to exclude areas considered by the US as top priority, such as services, investments, government purchases and intellectual property. On view of this, countries agreed to negotiate 'minimum' common commitments and allow countries to negotiate broader agreements among themselves; this was called a 'light' FTAA.
19. Understood as the sum of total imports and exports.

20. China has grown at an average annual rate of 9 per cent in the last 3 decades, and represents a 4 per cent share of world GDP. It is also worth mentioning that Chinese GDP per capita has risen from less than 4 per cent of US GDP per capita in 1982 to over 12 per cent in 2002.

21. China is the country that creates most confidence among international investors (Kearney, 2004).

22. Although the desirability of a free trade agreement with China would certainly depend on each country's specific defensive and offensive interests.

Bibliography

Anderson, Kym, Francois, Joseph F., Hertel, Thomas W. and Martin, Will. 1999. 'Agriculture and Non-Agriculture Liberalization in the Millennium Round'. Policy Discussion Paper No. 0016. University of Adelaide. Adelaide.

Anderson, Kym, William J. Martin and Dominique van der Mensbrugghe. 2005. 'Market and Welfare Implications of Doha Reform Scenarios'. In Kym Anderson and William J. Martin (eds), Agricultural Trade Reform and the Doha Development Agenda, Washington, DC: World Bank.

Athukorala, Prema-chandra and Nobuaki, Yamashita. 2005. 'Production Fragmentation and Trade Integration: East Asia in a Global Context'. Working Paper in Trade and Development 2005–07, Division of Economics, Research School of Pacific and Asian Studies, Australian National University, Canberra.

Aw, Bee Yan, Sukkyun Chung and Mark J. Roberts. 2000. 'Productivity and Turnover in the Export Market: Micro-level Evidence from the Republic of Korea and Taiwan (China)'. World Bank Economic Review, 14(1): 65–90.

Crawford, Jo-Ann and Roberto V. Fiorentino. 2005. 'The Changing Landscape of Regional Trade Agreements'. WTO Discussion Paper No. 8.

de Ferranti, David, Lederman, Daniel and Perry, Guillermo and Suescún, Rodrigo. 2003. Trade for Development in Latin America and the Caribbean. Washington, DC: World Bank.

De Gregorio, José and Jong-Wha Lee. 2003. 'Crecimiento y Ajuste en el Este Asiático y América Latina'. Working Paper No. 245, Central Bank of Chile, Santiago, Chile.

Desker, Barry. 2004. 'In Defense of FTAs: From Purity to Pragmatism in East Asia'. *Pacific Review*, 17(1): 3–26.

Dollar, David and Kraay, Aart. 2001. 'Trade, Growth and Poverty, Finance and Development'. *International Monetary Fund*, 38(3), September.

Economic Commission for Latin America and the Caribbean (ECLAC). 2003. *Panorama Social de América Latina 2002–2003*, Social Development Division and Statistics and Projections Division, Santiago, Chile.

Engman, Michael. 2005. 'The Economic Impact of Trade Facilitation'. OECD Trade Policy Working Papers 21, OECD Trade Directorate, Paris.

Fernandes, Ana and Alberto Isgut. 2004. 'Learning-by-Doing, Learning-by-Exporting, and Productivity: Evidence from Colombia'. Working Paper No. 3544, World Bank.

Frankel, Jeffrey A. and Romer, David. 1999. 'Does Trade Growth Cause Growth?' *American Economic Review*, 89(3), June.

Hausmann, Ricardo and Dani Rodrik. 2003. 'Economic Development as Self Discovery'. NBER Working Paper No. 8952, National Bureau of Economic Research, Cambridge, MA.

Heidrich, Pablo. 2006. 'The East Asian Region: From Multilateralism to Bilateralism'. Background paper prepared for the 'LATN—CAF Roundtable Meeting: Could Regionalism Leverage Global Governance?', 28–29 July 2006, Buenos Aires, Argentina.

Hiwatari, Nobuhiro. 2003. 'Embedded Policy Preferences and the Formation of International Arrangements After the Asian Financial Crisis'. *Pacific Review*, 16(3): 331–59.

Inter American Development Bank (IADB). 2001. 'Competitiveness: The Business of Growth'. *Progreso Económico y Social en América Latina*, Washington, DC.

———. 2002. *Mas allá de las fronteras: El Nuevo Regionalismo en América Latina. Progreso Económico y Social en América Latina*, Washington, DC.

International Monetary Fund (IMF). 2002. 'Market Access for Developing Countries'. *Finance and Development*, 39(3), September.

———. 2005. *Direction of Trade Statistics*. Washington, DC: IMF.

Irwin, Douglas and Tervio, Marko. 2000. 'Does Trade Raise Income? Evidence from the Twentieth Century'. NBER Working Papers 7745, National Bureau of Economic Research.

Kearney A.T., 2004. 'FDI Confidence Index'. *The Global Business Policy Council*, October 7.

Kuwayama, M. and J. Durán Lima, 2003. *La calidad de la inserción internacional de América latina y el Caribe en el comercio mundial*, ECLAC, Serie comercio internacional n° 26, Santiago de Chile.

Liu, Jin-Tan, Meng-Wen Tsou and James K. Hammitt. 1999. 'Export Activity and Productivity: Evidence from the Taiwan Electronics Industry'. *Weltwirtschaftliches Archiv*, 135(4): 675–91.

Loayza, Norman, Pablo Fajnzylber and Cesar Calderón. 2002. 'Economic Growth in Latin America and the Caribbean: Stylized Facts, Explanations and Forecasts'. Working Paper No. 265, Central Bank of Chile, Santiago, Chile.

Martínez, Jorge and Villa, Miguel. 2005. *International Migration in Latin America and the Caribbean: A Summary View of Trends and Patterns.* United Nations Expert Group Meeting on International Migration and Development, Population Division. Department of Economic and Social Affairs, United Nations.

McGuire, Greg. 2002. *Trade in Services—Market Access Opportunities and the Benefits of Liberalization for Developing Economies.* Policy Issues in International Trade and Commodities Study Series No. 19, UNCTAD, Geneva.

Rodríguez-Clare, Andrés. 2005. 'Microeconomic Interventions After the Washington Consensus'. Working Paper No. 524, Inter American Development Bank, Washington, D.C.

Rodríguez, Francisco and Rodrik, Dani. 1999. 'Trade Policy and Economic Growth: A Skeptic's Guide to the Cross-National Evidence'. NBER Working Paper No. 7081, National Bureau of Economic Research, Cambridge.

Sala-i-Martin, Xavier. 1997. 'I Just Ran Two Million Regressions'. *American Economic Review*, 87(2): 178–83, American Economic Association.

Smith, Anthony. 2004. 'ASEAN's Ninth Summit: Solidifying Regional Cohesion, Advancing External Linkages'. *Contemporary Southeast Asia*, 26(3): 416–33.

Thee, Kian Wie. 1991. 'The Surge of Asian NIC Investment in Indonesia'. *Bulletin of Indonesian Economic Studies*, 27(3): 55–60.

———. 2003. 'Export-Import Industrialization and FDI in the ASEAN Countries'. In Nissanke, M. (ed.), *Asia and Africa in the World Economy*, Tokyo: United Nations University.

Tybout, James R. 2003. 'Plant- and Firm-Level Evidence on New Trade Theories'. In E. Kwan Choi and James Harrigan (eds), *Handbook of International Trade*, Malden, Massachusetts: Blackwell Publishers.

United Nations (UN). 2005. *UN Commodity Trade Statistics (Comtrade) Database*, New York: Statistics Division, United Nations.

United Nations Conference on Trade and Development (UNCTAD). 2002. Trade and Development Report 2002. Report by the Secretariat of the United Nations Conference on Trade and Development.

World Bank. 1993. 'The East Asian Miracle: Economic Growth and Public Policy'. World Bank Policy Research Report, Oxford University Press, United Kingdom.

————. 2000. *The World Business Environment Survey (WBES)*. Washington, DC: World Bank.

————. 2003. *Realizing the Development Promise of the Doha Agenda*, Global Economic Prospects 2004, Washington, DC.

————. 2005. *World Development Indicators*. Washington, DC: World Bank.

Zignago, Soledad. 2005. 'Increasing Latin America's Trade Presence in the World Economy: Competitiveness and Market Access', Mimeo. Caracas: Corporación Andina de Fomento.

Building Asia's Infrastructure: Issues and Options 9

Haruhiko Kuroda, Rajat Nag and Rita Nangia

Asia's extraordinary transformation

Asia has always recognized the role of infrastructure in creating wealth. Archaeological evidence points to the exchange of goods between Mesopotamia and Indian and Chinese territories between 7500 and 4000 BC. The Silk Route created prosperous clusters of towns and trading posts while connecting Asia and Europe through the Middle East. In more recent history, Asian nations were openly trading with each other long before Europeans arrived in the region. And historians have argued that it is the capabilities developed through this long history of intra-Asian trade which allowed Japan and the newly industrialized economies to emerge as economic success stories in the late 20th century. Also, an interesting fact is that most of this was enabled through private initiative and enterprise.

The private sector has continued to be an engine of Asia's phenomenal growth. Today, Asia hosts four of the world's 10 largest economies—Japan, the People's Republic of China (PRC), India and Korea—accounting for almost 30 per cent of total world GDP. The Asian Development Bank's (ADB) 2006 estimates suggest that developing Asia experienced expansion in 2006 with an average rate of 8.3 per cent despite numerous external challenges and shocks, and that the average growth will continue to be 7.6 per cent in 2007 and 7.7 per cent in 2008.[1] Asia has also achieved rapid poverty reduction: there were 300 million fewer people living in poverty in 2003 compared with 1990 (ADB, 2005).

Strong export growth and high Foreign Direct Investments (FDIs) have been two important drivers of this growth. First the Asian Tigers and then Southeast Asia and PRC have enjoyed a virtuous cycle of regional trade and investment through the medium of production networks. More recently, South Asian countries are also creating their own route to sustained growth and poverty reduction. Over the last 20 years, Asia's exports to the world have grown at the rate of 11 per cent per annum (or from a level of US$ 162 billion in 1980 to US$ 1.9 trillion in 2004). Asia now accounts for a quarter of world exports.

This strong export growth in recent years has been marked by a rapid increase in the absolute and relative significance of intra-regional trade (Table 9.1). Asia as a whole has reported an average growth of nearly 17 per cent per annum for regional exports. Southeast Asia and PRC reported an annual average growth of over 20 per cent during 1980–2004, whereas South Asian exports grew on an average by 10 per cent a year. Data for imports show similar trends. The degree of integration measured through intra-regional trade in East Asia has been rising quickly: from 35 per cent in 1980 to 55 per cent in 2005, if Japan is included, and from 22 to 45 per cent without Japan. This share is similar to the North Atlantic Free Trade Agreement (NAFTA)

Table 9.1 Importance of intra-regional trade in Asia (% of total trade)

Region	1980	1990	2000	2005
East Asia (including Japan)	34.6	43.0	51.9	54.5
Emerging East Asia	22.1	32.8	40.4	44.7
Asian NIEs	6.4	11.9	15.5	13.5
ASEAN	17.9	18.8	24.5	24.0
NAFTA	33.8	37.9	48.8	45.0
European Union-15	60.7	66.2	62.3	60.1

Source: Kawai (2007).

Notes: East Asia = Japan and emerging East Asia; Emerging East Asia = Asian NIEs and ASEAN; Asian NIEs = newly industrialized economies; ASEAN = Association of Southeast Asian Nations; NAFTA = North American Free Trade Agreement.

area, although it remains somewhat lower compared with the European Union (EU).

Much of this is due to rapid trade liberalization in these economies in the 1990s and beyond. Several economies in the region reduced tariff barriers significantly. For example, overall tariff rates were reduced by 50 per cent in the China (PRC), Malaysia, the Philippines and Thailand, whereas South Asian countries, such as Bangladesh and India reduced average import tariffs by two-thirds. In most countries, tariff reductions were also accompanied by removal of non-tariff barriers and simplification of customs rules and regulations (Dollar and Kraay, 2001).

The expansion in trade in Asia has been accompanied by a rapid rise in FDI during this period; though the US and the EU are all important, Japan is the largest investor in Association of Southeast Asian Nations (ASEAN) among the developed countries, with the exception of Singapore. In the case of China (PRC) and Hong Kong (China), China (PRC) is the largest investor. FDI inflows rose more than 28 times in 24 years during 1980–2004. In 2004, the East and Southeast Asian economies accounted for over 59 per cent of all FDI inflows in developing economies (United Nations Conference on Trade and Development [UNCTAD], 2005). Today, one of the most important destinations of FDI remains the PRC: from a level of US$ 57 million in 1980, the PRC was able to attract over US$ 60 billion in FDI in 2004. Most FDIs in Asia were in new, greenfield investments concentrated in manufacturing, but there was also a significant increase in cross-border mergers and acquisitions, largely in the service sectors.

Net private foreign equity flows to emerging Asia have been growing steadily as well in recent years, indicating a resurgence of confidence: from a level of only 8 per cent of net private equity flows at the end of the crisis in 1998, Asia accounted for 39 per cent of such flows in 2005. Most Asian currencies have also appreciated relative to the dollar. The economies are firmly back on the path of sustained growth.

Infrastructure development

The development of infrastructure has facilitated this economic growth by integrating Asia both globally and regionally.

Until the 1997 financial crisis, a large part of domestic savings were channelled towards infrastructure development. In fact, the 1994 World Development Report on *Infrastructure for Development* comparing performance of East Asia with the Sub-Sahara region concluded that Asian growth was due to improvements in infrastructure access. More recently, studies have indicated that infrastructure differences account for about one-third of the difference in output per worker between Latin America and East Asia (Calderón et al., 2003).

Developing Asia has tripled its share of power capacity in the world from 7 per cent in 1980 to almost 22 per cent in 2004 (Table 9.2). Within developing Asia, most of this growth has come about in the East Asia and Pacific Region reporting more than five-fold increase in total power capacity of 108 million Kilowatt (kW) in 1980 to 600 million kW in 2004. During this time, South Asia has quadrupled its capacity from about 35 million kW in 1980 to 140 million kW in 2004. Overall electricity generation has increased from 580 billion kWh in 1980 to over 4,000 billion kWh. Within infrastructure sectors, telephone access has grown the fastest: from a small share of 4 per cent in 1980, developing Asia now accounts for little over one-third of total subscribers in the world. Total number of telephone mainlines and mobile subscribers in developing Asia have increased from about 13 million in 1980 to 1.2 trillion in 2005.

Table 9.2   Increasing share of Asia in the World (%)

	1980	2004
Power Capacity	7.5	21.8
Power Generation	7.3	24.2
Telephones	4.3	34.6

Sources: International Energy Annual 2004 & World Development Indicators CD-Rom 2006.

Not all infrastructure services have seen such phenomenal growth: the transport sector is logging behind when compared to other infrastructure sectors in Asia and also when compared to what is required. Against 10 per cent annual growth in the passenger vehicles and 7.3 per cent growth in commercial vehicles, the road network has grown at an average 3.25 per cent. The network quality is also an important constraint facing many parts of developing Asia as only a small part is paved (Figure 9.1). Railway network growth is much lower than road network at only 1.0 per cent (ADB, 2007a). Finally, the overall performance of water and sanitation is also somewhat mixed: it is estimated that about 81 per cent of population has access to an improved water source; however, it is important to note that access to an improved water source does not necessarily mean access to safe drinking water. Overall performance for sanitation is much lower at less than half the population having improved sanitation.

Overall access to infrastructure services remains uneven across Asia (Table 9.3): while Singapore, Thailand and Malaysia have achieved universal access for most infrastructure services, Cambodia and Lao PDR have much lower access. For example, with less than 15 per cent electrification rate of Cambodia, it means that its per capita power consumption is only 62 kWh compared to over 1,865 kWh in Thailand. Moreover, there is a sharp divide between access rates in rural areas and in cities. In rural areas, access rates to good roads, safe drinking water and sanitation services are very low, not only compared to developed Organisation for Economic Co-operation and Development (OECD) countries, but even compared to urban populations in the same countries. Within individual cities, the poor are particularly vulnerable because they are accommodated largely in informal settlements with much lower access rates for water and sanitation, electricity, telephones and other infrastructure services than the rest of the urban population.

After the Asian financial crisis, there was a slowdown in overall infrastructure investments particularly in some of the East Asian countries. In Indonesia for example, infrastructure investments which accounted for 6 per cent of GDP before 1997, have fallen to 2 per cent in recent years, reflecting a sharp decline in public and private spending on infrastructure, whereas in the Philippines infrastructure investments in 2002 were 2.8 per cent compared to a high of 8 per cent in 1997. Even countries like India, which were largely unaffected by the 1997 financial crisis, saw a deceleration in infrastructure investments to 3.8 per cent

Figure 9.1 Selected infrastructure indicators

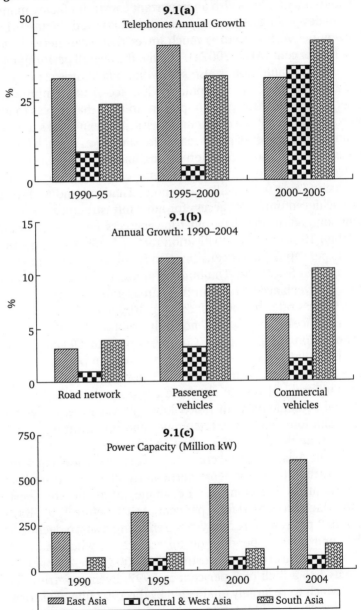

Source: Word Development Indicators 2006.

Table 9.3 Infrastructure indicators—Selected Asian countries

	Telephones per 100 people		Improved water (%)		Improved sanitation (%)		Road network density[a]	Paved road (%)	Power consumption per capita (kWh)	
	1990	2005	1990	2004	1990	2004	2004[b]	2004[b]	1990	2004
Afghanistan	0.2	4.4	4	39	3	36	5	23.7	—	27
Armenia	15.7	26.0	—	92	—	83	27	100	1,958	1,428
Azerbaijan	8.6	39.7	68	77	—	54	68	49.4	2,218	2,437
Georgia	9.9	33.7	80	82	97	94	29	39.4	1,942	1,577
Kazakhstan	8.0	35.4	87	86	72	72	3	93.4	5,354	3,621
Kyrgyzstan	7.2	18.7	78	77	60	59	9	90	1,895	1,421
Pakistan	0.8	11.7	83	91	37	59	34	64.7	277	425
Tajikistan	4.5	4.5	—	59	—	51	20	83	2,982	2,240
Turkmenistan	6.0	7.9	—	72	—	62	5	81	2,006	1,740
Uzbekistan	6.9	8.0	94	82	51	67	19	87	2,122	1,796
Bangladesh	0.2	7.1	72	74	20	39	68	9.5	49	140
India	0.6	12.7	70	86	14	33	114	47.4	275	457
Nepal	0.3	2.6	70	90	11	35	12	30.3	35	69
Sri Lanka	0.7	22.2	68	79	69	91	151	81	154	344
China (PRC)	0.6	56.5	70	77	23	44	20	81	511	1,585
Hong Kong (China)	47.5	177.4	—	—	—	—	186	100	4,178	5,699
Korea, Republic of	30.8	128.6	—	92	—	99	102	86.8	2,373	7,391

(Table 9.3 continued)

(Table 9.3 continued)

	Telephones per 100 people		Improved water (%)		Improved sanitation (%)		Road network density[a]	Paved road (%)	Power consumption per capita (kWh)	
	1990	2005	1990	2004	1990	2004	2004[b]	2004[b]	1990	2004
Mongolia[c]	3.2	27.0	63	62	—	59	3	3.5	1,663	932
Cambodia	0.0	7.8	—	41	—	17	22	6.3	17	62
Indonesia	0.6	26.8	72	77	46	55	20	58	161	478
Lao PDR	0.2	12.0	—	51	—	30	14	14.4	71	160
Malaysia	9.4	92.0	98	99	—	94	30	81.3	1,194	3,166
Myanmar	0.2	1.3	57	78	24	77	4	78	45	104
Philippines	1.0	45.3	87	85	57	72	67	21.6	360	597
Singapore	36.3	143.2	100	100	100	100	463	100	4,860	8,170
Thailand	2.5	34.3	95	99	80	99	11	98.5	98	1,865
Vietnam	0.1	30.2	65	85	36	61	68	19	119	501

Sources: World Bank 2007b, World Development Indicator CD-Rom 2006, CIA World Factbook 2006, International Road Federation Statistics 2004, ADB Key Indicators.

Notes: [a] Kilometres of road per 100 square km of land. [b] Refers to 2004 or the latest available year. — indicates data not available data for power consumption in Central Asian countries pertains to 1992. [c] Data from ADB Key indicators.

PRC = People's Republic of China, kWh = kilowatt hours.

compared to projections of 7.2 per cent of GDP required to sustain economic growth.

Until the onset of the 1997 financial crisis, private investors were playing an important part in meeting the infrastructure challenge in the Asian countries, particularly in Southeast Asia, accounting for nearly about one-third of global private investments in infrastructure. Indonesia and the Philippines welcomed private investors with a set of reforms in legal and regulatory framework for infrastructure sectors (Table 9.4). During 1990–2005, the developing Asia has reported over US$ 300 billion in private investments financing 1,186 projects. Though recent annual investments are not as high as its peak in 1997, there has been a renewed interest in Asia from private investors. Power and telecom sectors seem to dominate these investments. It is interesting to note that after the crisis, there seems to be a shift in the investors: the Asian private sector, both domestic entrepreneurs and multinationals based in Asia rather than global players have returned to infrastructure sectors in Asia. This is an interesting

Table 9.4   Private infrastructure in developing Asia

Year	Investments (US$ billion)	Number of projects
1990	2.1	16
1991	3.7	11
1992	7.2	26
1993	14.2	58
1994	17.6	104
1995	22.9	98
1996	34.5	141
1997	44.7	141
1998	13.1	72
1999	17.0	72
2000	22.3	63
2001	17.8	79
2002	15.9	75
2003	17.8	83
2004	24.8	78
2005	28.0	69
Total	303.8	1186

Source: World Bank (2007b).

phenomenon because the risk perceptions of global infrastructure operators and those based in the region are different[2] and this can have an important impact on infrastructure financing. There is also another reason for this: the lessons from 18th century Britain and 19th century USA indicate that it was the need to mobilize large infrastructure financing that provided the much-needed impetus for the development of domestic capital markets. The private financing could not only help build infrastructure, but also domestic capital markets.

Finally, in the 1990s, the largest source of finance had been commercial banks, either directly or through syndicated loans. Following the 1997 crisis, there has been an increase in the cost of lending: from an average of 160 basis points in 1995–97 to 220 basis points in 2002–03. This increase was largely due to increasing host country risk rather than global infrastructure industry risk (World Bank, 2004). There is some growth in infrastructure financing through bonds, but this is limited to a few countries in Asia.

While emerging infrastructure gaps within Asian countries have not, as yet, affected the overall export performance, there is an increasing concern regarding the upward rise in overall logistic costs. Inadequate transport and communication infrastructure, uncompetitive transport and logistics sectors, and high fuel costs all contribute to relatively high logistics costs in Asia. In PRC, for example, logistics costs represent nearly 18 per cent of GDP, whereas in North America, the ratio is less than 10 per cent. More over, while logistics costs as a percentage of GDP have declined in North America, they have actually increased in Asian countries such as PRC and India (Rodrigues et al., 2005).

A major reason for this is the fast pace of urbanization in Asia resulting in increasing congestion across cities. At the moment, Asia is not as urbanized as some other regions, however, it is expected that Asian cities will need to make space for nearly 1.2 billion new entrants in the next 20 years. Some large cities in the Asian region have begun to reach their capacities and unless large investments in urban transport, roads and efficient linkages to ports are created to connect these cities with the inland areas, Asian exports would face rapidly increasing logistics costs. Major gaps are emerging in the infrastructure services of some of the urban centres in the Asian cities like Manila and Jakarta because the current land-use plans did not envisage such large economic expansions. Retrofitting infrastructure in rapidly growing cities is not only expensive, but may involve large environmental and social risks.

Looking forward, Asia's infrastructure demand is expected to grow rapidly in the next few decades. In the past, demands for power and telephones have risen at a much faster pace than the rise in per capita incomes across countries, whereas the demand for transport has grown at the same rate as income. First, with Asia expecting to grow at 7 per cent per annum, demand for power, water, paved roads or telephones is expected to rise significantly. The second factor driving the high demand is the uneven access rates across countries and even within individual countries. As economies grow, new capacities will need to be created in areas that lack infrastructure services. Third, the overall quality of infrastructure services needs to improve significantly. Power breakdowns, water shortages and road congestion have ceased to be headlines, given the frequency with which these occur across Asia. Finally, with the growing stock of infrastructure assets, the needs for maintenance investments are much greater.

ADB has recently completed an assessment of infrastructure investment needs for its member countries. The study is based on the methodology used in the previous joint ADB–JBIC–World Bank study; *Connecting East Asia: A New Framework for Infrastructure Development* (2005). Using two sets of likely growth scenarios, a top-down macro-model was constructed using panel data for 29 countries, for which reasonable time series data were available for infrastructure stocks. Projected infrastructure stock levels were then valued at best practice costs for new infrastructure at 2006 constant prices. Annual maintenance expenditure was estimated as a fixed percentage of the stock value. Table 9.5 presents total investment requirements for 2006–15 under the two scenarios.

As can be seen, Asia's infrastructure investment requirements are massive; the 29 developing member countries (DMCs) covered in this study would need to invest between US$ 3.7 trillion (low case) and US$ 4.7 trillion (base case) in 2006 dollars during

Table 9.5   Infrastructure investments requirements, 2006–15

	Central and West Asia region		East Asia and Pacific region		South Asia region		Total*	
	Base case	Low case	Base case	Low case	Base case	Low case	Base case	Low case
New investments	166	108	2,020	1,624	882	654	3,068	2,387
Maintenance	96	68	1,022	853	482	407	1,599	1,328
Total*	262	176	3,042	2,477	1,363	1,061	4,667	3,715
As % of GDP	7.8	5.3	6.8	5.5	10.0	7.8	7.5	6.0

Source: ADB (2007b).

Note: * Totals may not match due to rounding off. Regions here represent ADB's country groups except the East Asia and Pacific Region which includes East Asia, Southeast Asia, and the Pacific countries.

the period 2006–15. Out of these, investments in new capacity would total US$ 2.4 trillion under the low case and US$ 3.1 trillion under the base case; the cost of capacity replacement would total US$ 1.3 trillion and US$ 1.6 trillion, respectively. The projected investment requirements are equivalent to 7.5 per cent of GDP under the base case. Due to differences in the relative GDP growth rates and other factors, there are significant differences between the three sub-regions: East Asia and the Pacific account for 6.8 per cent of GDP, South Asia for 10 per cent and Central Asia 7.8 per cent (all under the base case). Within Asia, by far the largest investment needs are in East Asia and the Pacific (US$ 3.0 trillion or two-thirds of the total under the base case), followed by South Asia (US$ 1.4 trillion or 29 per cent, also in the base case), and less than 6 per cent in Central Asia (US$ 262 billion). These estimates reflect the differences in the size and structure of the economies of the three sub-regions as well as the differences in their economic growth rates. China and India dominate these estimates accounting for almost 80 per cent of these requirements. Within infrastructure sectors, power (41 per cent) and roads (24 per cent) will dominate overall requirements. These estimates indicate that with the exception of China, almost all Asian DMCs will have to substantially increase investments in infrastructure. India, for example, will have to double its current investments to ensure that infrastructure bottlenecks do not place constraints on its growth.

Major challenges

Mobilizing large levels of finances for infrastructure is one of the biggest challenges facing most of developing Asia. A number of Asian countries do not have adequate fiscal space to expand investment levels in a short period of time. In today's world, mobilizing financing requires a balanced approach among different stakeholder groups. The governments need to have a strong strategic vision for infrastructure and its role in the economy. Some of the Asian countries, especially the newly industrialized countries, had followed a path of building infrastructure ahead of demand and have been successful in driving strong economic performance. However, the present infrastructure challenge is not the same as it was in the 1980s. With technological innovations having a major impact on the information flows, much more is demanded today. Infrastructure projects have many more stakeholders than before. The role of civil society in any large infrastructure project has changed. The public sector is also under pressure to improve performance and it is not an easy task to simply raise tariffs. A number of reforms would be needed to enhance accountability of all stakeholders and create the right business environment. Infrastructure investments reflect long-term commitment on both sides. Governments want the predictability of knowing that the private sector will remain reliable partners in infrastructure sectors, and private operators need stable and predictable policy regimes and a functioning judicial system. Given that most infrastructure sectors need reforms and restructuring, the most important aspect of creating this environment is to prioritize a series of reforms and prepare an action plan to deliver credible results.

As the *Connecting East Asia* study (ADB et al., 2005) pointed out, there is enough private interest even today to support infrastructure investments; however, this interest is not being transformed into infrastructure investment flows as yet. One of the biggest challenges is to strengthen accountability structures for infrastructure. If the right policy environment and business climate were created, most of the private sector operators would be keen to invest in Asian infrastructure. Most Asian countries have a large continuing agenda of reforms and restructuring for their infrastructure sectors, and it varies depending on the sector (Table 9.A1). The telecommunications sector has been able to adopt competitive market structures that allows for greater accountability for performance. In other sectors, the performance varies. Power sector reforms are at different stages of restructuring depending on the country, size of the markets and the demand growth. A number of countries have been able to appoint regulators for water or power sectors, but these have not as yet translated into better outcomes for the consumers. Some regulators, such as the Indonesian Water Supply Association, have a set of indicators benchmarking its performance and publishing these on the Web, whereas, others, still keep licences and contracts confidential.

A second challenge is human and institutional capacities: Public-Private Partnership (PPP) transactions offer a new way of meeting infrastructure demand. Any expansion in PPP requires considerable political will to achieve a level playing field for both public and private sectors. The role of the public sector in this new mode is still evolving in almost all countries.

In this new environment, despite huge opportunities and large needs, preparing bankable projects has proved to be a major constraint. The crisis has demonstrated that, ultimately, projects must be economically and financially viable: risk mitigation alone cannot offset either poor economics or poor government policies. A viable project requires several crucial elements: an enabling framework of public policy where the private sector has a clear role to play in infrastructure provision; a good, economically relevant project; a responsive government; a reliable private sponsor; credible contracts; and a financing structure that is sustainable. The private sector can play an important role in designing viable projects; however, this is expensive given the complexity of infrastructure projects, long lead time and high mortality rates. The transaction costs for private projects are typically large—between 3–12 per cent of total costs. Infrastructure is capital-intensive; hence, these costs are significant and can become an important deterrent. There is also a long, time-consuming process and for every project that is successful, 10 projects are not.

As financial structuring of PPP projects is new even in developed markets, the already pervasive capacity constraints in developing countries imply that the public sector should find more resources to design projects well in the initial stages. Leaving aside the legal or regulatory impediments affecting private sector participation, it is critical that the contracting agencies or line ministries allocate resources to prepare good quality information memoranda and at least pre-feasibility studies. Recognizing the constraints, ADB is helping some countries in the region through the establishment of Project Development Facilities (PDF). In Indonesia, for instance, discussions are underway to set aside dedicated resources for preparing large-scale national and smaller-scale decentralized projects. By reducing the information gap, a PDF can help both the public and private sectors in achieving greater competition, better quality and lower costs of providing infrastructure services. In particular, detailed assessments done by a PDF can help increase the bankability of a project by feeding good quality information to determine the appropriate type (and level) of risk-sharing. Support will also be provided for transparent bidding and execution of project transactions.

Finally, with its large working-age population, Asia is also a high-savings region. In 2005, almost all Asian countries reported a higher share of GDP going towards savings, compared to 1990. The developing member countries of ADB in 2004 reported a total savings of nearly US$ 1.3 trillion. The biggest challenge is to mobilize a part of these savings through capital market reforms for infrastructure projects. There is a large reform agenda to build capital markets, at the country level, and at the regional level so as to meet the financing requirements for infrastructure.

Asia's infrastructure agenda

Though Asia's infrastructure agenda is complex, there is already a broad consensus on the steps that need to be taken in order for it to be implemented. This is because the Asian countries have always recognized the contribution of infrastructure in overall economic development. Further, the 1997 Asian financial crisis has provided many important lessons and generated the much-needed political will to enhance regional cooperation, not only in regional infrastructure projects, but also in much broader areas of financial and monetary cooperation.

There is a large continuing agenda of reforms and modernization for infrastructure sectors in Asia which varies depending on the size and development stage of the individual country. Country-specific solutions require a country-specific strategy and detailed action plans to deal with binding constraints, that is, creating the necessary fiscal space for infrastructure investments;

improving cost recovery, especially in the lagging sectors; and strengthening accountability structures, either through more competition or through improved regulation. The efforts are ongoing to create an investment climate that would once again make Asian infrastructure an attractive destination for the private sector.

With a severe paucity of bankable projects, national governments and official institutions have an important role to play in supporting development of an infrastructure pipeline that will increase the supply of bankable projects by providing resources and sharing in these preparatory risks.

Although the financing requirements for infrastructure in Asia are huge, there is ample scope for enhancing regional financial cooperation to develop domestic and regional capital markets, harmonize rules and regulations, and allow innovative solutions to meet the huge financial requirements. Asia's savings ratio is much higher than other regions and thus Asia is not only exporting manufacturing goods and services, but is also an exporter of capital. Since the 1997 crisis, Asia's savings have been increasingly intermediated for Asia's investments in foreign currencies through global capital markets. Strengthening regional and domestic bond markets will be one of the first steps in creating a viable source of infrastructure financing to tap these Asian savings. The Asian Bond Market Initiative is one such option that was designed to facilitate access to the market by a wide variety of issuers and to create an environment conducive to developing domestic and regional bond markets. This initiative has significant potential to raise resources for infrastructure. Recent examples include Baht denominated bonds issued for a power plant in Lao PDR and other local currency bonds. Action will need to be taken on several fronts, such as developing municipal finance, supporting utility bonds, the securitization of revenue-earning infrastructure assets and developing appropriate guarantee mechanisms. The domestic markets will not be sustainable unless adequate regulatory reforms are undertaken to ensure appropriate disclosure and capacity-building for investors.

At the global and regional levels, adequate resources to fund Asia's infrastructure exist. There is a need to integrate

Asian capital markets with the global financial system and find innovative solutions. For example, the sheer size of Asian foreign currency reserves opens up a set of opportunities to not only increase the return on these reserves, but also meet an important need of the region. Multilateral institutions and regional governments can come together to discuss potential modalities and possible instruments to channel part of these reserves into creation of infrastructure assets, provided adequate safeguards are put in place. Developing regional and domestic capital markets and instruments would be one way, and some have suggested that there may also be other more direct ways to channel these reserves to infrastructure.

In conclusion, Asia's infrastructure agenda remains large and complex. A set of reforms to improve policy environment and governance are under way across Asia. The action will also have to focus on building human capacities, participative processes and institutions that will strengthen accountability for better infrastructure outcomes. Ultimately, Asia's infrastructure agenda must go beyond simply looking for financial resources because these resources exist, in large part, within the region. What is needed now are bankable projects, continued and intensified sector reforms and the political will to unlock the region's huge domestic savings for adequate long-term infrastructure finance. None of these will come without cost—but to neglect concerted action now will mean we all pay a much higher price later.

Annex

Table 9.A1 Infrastructure reforms indicators as of 2004†

	Bangladesh	*Cambodia*	*India*	*Indonesia*	*China (PRC)*	*Malaysia*	*Mongolia*	*Pakistan*	*Philippines*	*Singapore*	*Uzbekistan*	*Thailand*	*Vietnam*
POWER SECTOR													
Independent Electricity Regulation	Yes	Yes	Yes	No	No	Yes	Yes	Yes	Yes	Yes	No	No	No
Private Power Generation	Yes	Yes	Yes	Yes	Yes	Yes	Public	Yes	Yes	—	*Public*	*Yes*	*Public*
Power Distribution	Public	Mixed	Mixed	Public	Public	Public	Public	Public	Private	*Public*	*Public*	*Public*	*Public*
Water Sector													
Water Sector Ownership	Public	Mixed	Mixed	Mixed	Mixed	Mixed	Public	Public	Mixed	Public	—	Mixed	Mixed
Independent Water Sector Regulation	No	No	No	No	—	No	—	No	Yes	—	—	—	No
TELECOMMUNICATIONS													
Local Phone Monopoly	No	No	No	No	No	No	No	No	No	No	No	No	No
Mobile Phone Monopoly	No	No	No	No	No	No	No	No	No	No	No	No	Yes
Long Distance Monopoly	No	No	No	No	No	No	No	No	No	—	No	No	Yes
Leased Lines Monopoly	Yes	No	—	No	No	No	No	No	No	No	No	No	Yes
Internet Provider Monopoly	No	No	No	No	No	No	No	No	No	No	—	No	No
Independent Regulation	Yes	No	Yes	Yes	Yes	Yes	Yes	Yes	Yes	Yes	No	Yes	No
Private Capital	No	No	Yes	Yes	Yes	Yes	Yes	Yes	Yes	Yes	No	—	No

Notes: † Adapted from Estache and Goicoechea 2005.

— No Information.

Italics indicates that there is now a change in the status.

PRC = People's Republic of China.

Notes

1. Developing Asia includes all of ADB's developing member countries.
2. During the 19th century in the United States, it was found that local participation brought local knowledge, improved information flows and, in the end, became a sustainable source of infrastructure financing.

Bibliography

Asian Development Bank (ADB). 2005. *Key Indicators of Developing Asian and Pacific Countries 2005*, Manila.
———. 2007a. *Asian Development Outlook 2007*, Manila.
———. 2007b. *Assessing Infrastructure Requirements for Developing Asia: 2006–2015*, Manila.
Asian Development Bank (ADB), Japan Bank for International Cooperation (JBIC) and The World Bank. 2005. *Connecting East Asia: A New Framework for Infrastructure Development*, Washington, DC: World Bank.
Calderón, César, William Easterly and Luis Servén. 2003. 'Latin America's Infrastructure in the Era of Macroeconomic Crises'. In William Easterly and Luis Servén (eds), *The Limits of Stabilization: Infrastructure, Public Deficits, and Growth in Latin America*, pp. 21–94. Washington, DC: World Bank.
Dollar, David and Aart Kraay. 2001. Trade, Growth, and Poverty. Paper presented at the 'Asia and Pacific Forum on Poverty: Reforming Policies and Institutions for Poverty Reduction', ADB, Manila.
Estache, Antonio and Ana Goicoechea. 2005. 'A Research Database on Infrastructure Economic Performance'. Policy Research Working Paper No. 3643, World Bank, Washington, DC.
International Road Federation. 2004. International Road Federation Statistics. IRF.
Kawai, Masahiro. 2007. 'East Asian Economic Regionalism: Update'. In Richard Samans, Marc Uzan and Augusto Lopez-Claros (eds), *The International Monetary System, the IMF and the G-20: A Great Transformation in the Making?* pp. 109–39. Houndmills and New York: Palgrave Macmillan.
Rodrigues, Alexandre M., Donald J. Bowersox and Roger J. Calantone. 2005. 'Estimation of Global and National Logistic Expenditures: 2002 Data Update'. *Journal of Business Logistics*, 26(2): 1–16.

United Nations Conference on Trade and Development (UNCTAD). 2005. *World Investment Report 2005: Transnational Corporations and the Internationalization of R&D*, Geneva: UNCTAD.

World Bank. 1994. *World Development Report 1994: Infrastructure for Development*, New York: Oxford University Press.

———. 2004. *Global Development Finance 2004: Harnessing Cyclical Gains for Development*, Washington, DC.

———. 2007a. *PPI Database*. Available at http://ppi.worldbank.org/. Washington, DC: World Bank.

———. 2007b. *World Development Indicators*. Washington, DC: World.

Infrastructure Development and Services in Selected Emerging Market and OECD Countries: Key Indicators

10

HARPAUL ALBERTO KOHLI

Foreword

This chapter presents comparative key indicators of infrastructure development and services in 12 countries between 1980 and 2005. The basic objective is to present a broad and quick comparison across countries of the coverage, efficiency and quality of key infrastructure services during the past 30 years. Such comparative data could be of immense value to policy makers, but is currently not readily available.

The comparisons are presented in a series of tables, charts and graphs based on a comprehensive economic, social, financial and sectoral database developed and maintained by the Centennial Group.

Data sources

The underlying data used in this report comes mostly from the World Bank's *World Development Indicators* 2006 (except where noted), the International Monetary Fund's (IMF), *International Financial Statistics* and *World Economic Outlook* 2007, Asian Development Bank and International Energy Agency. While the international data used in this report is not always complete and in many cases is at variance with the national data, it remains the best (and the only practical) basis for cross-country comparisons.

Coverage

The report covers the following:

- *Countries*: The report covers 12 countries—seven low- or middle-income Emerging Market Countries (EMCs)—Brazil, China, India, Indonesia, Malaysia, Mexico and Turkey—and five high- or upper middle-income countries (Japan, Korea and Singapore in Asia, Chile in LAC, and Germany in Europe). For illustrative purposes, two of the developing countries—India and Brazil—are compared to both sets of countries. First, to the five other EMCs, which are either at a similar stage of development or can be regarded as the major competitors in the global marketplace. And then to the second set of countries, which can be regarded as the current 'best practice' in infrastructure services, to whose level all other EMCs must ultimately rise in order to become truly competitive in the global economy.
- *Sectors*: Five major infrastructure sectors are covered: (*i*) Energy (Energy overall as well as Power); (*ii*) Transport (Roads, Civil Aviation, Ports and Railways); (*iii*) Water and Sanitation; (*iv*) Telephony; and (*v*) other Information and Communications Technology (Internet and Computers).
- *Indicators*: Where possible, four sets of indicators are provided: (*i*) Absolute Quantities (tonnes or kW of energy, km of roads, number of passengers and so on); (*ii*) Per Capita Consumption or Penetration (to see how far apart are the countries in meeting consumer needs); (*iii*) Usage per Unit of GDP (is infrastructure keeping up with economic growth?); and (*iv*) Quality and Efficiency Indicators (are the consumers and the economy being well served by the service providers?).

- *Private Participation*: Finally, the report presents available data on private financing of infrastructure in four specific infrastructure sectors. But, the data is limited and no clear trends can be derived from it, except that private flows are very volatile both at country and sector levels. This data must be used with caution.

It is not the purpose of this report to present any policy conclusions. Instead, it is meant only to present some data comparable across countries to stimulate further analysis and discussion. Accordingly, after this foreword, no further commentary is offered in the report.

Two main messages still stand out even from this limited exercise. First, relative to the 'best practice countries', despite recent progress, most low- and middle-income EMCs still have a long way to go (with the exception of China in some sectors). Yet, the countries must adopt these 'best practice standards' as the long-term goal, at least in areas like transport, power and communications, which are critical to global competitiveness. And second, most countries need not only to invest massively to expand infrastructure capacity, but also very significantly improve the quality and efficiency of the services through much greater emphasis on better management and discipline.

Basic economic data

Figure 10.1 Population (million)

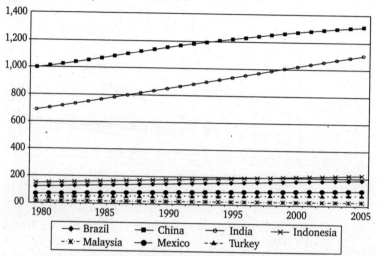

Source: Centennial Group Database, based on IMF's IPS.

Figure 10.2 Population (million)

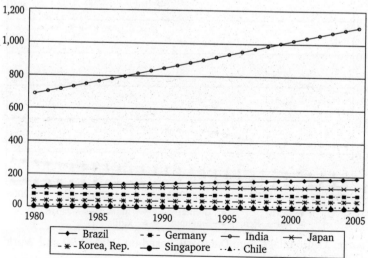

Source: Centennial Group Database, based on IMF's IPS.

Figure 10.3 GDP (US$ trillion constant 2000)

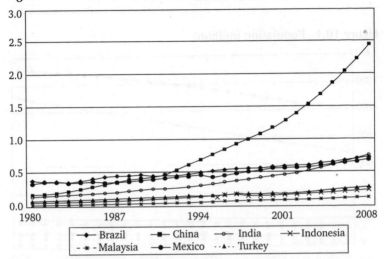

Source: Centennial Group Database, based on IMF's *WEO* and World Bank's *WDI*.

Figure 10.4 GDP (US$ trillion constant 2000)

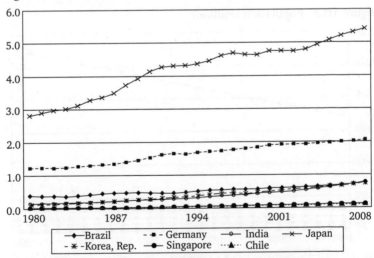

Source: Centennial Group Database, based on IMF's *WEO* and World Bank's *WDI*.

Figure 10.5 GDP PPP (US$ trillion current)

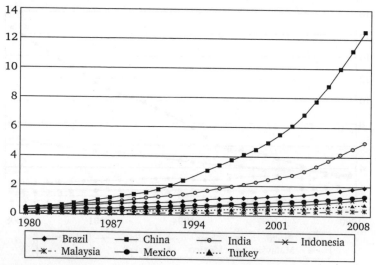

Source: Centennial Group Database, based on IMF's *WEO*.

Figure 10.6 GDP (US$ trillion constant 2000)

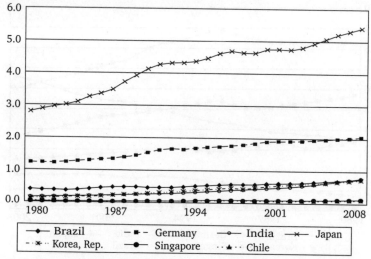

Source: Centennial Group Database, based on IMF's *WEO* and World Bank's *WDI*.

Figure 10.7   GDP PPP share of World total (%)

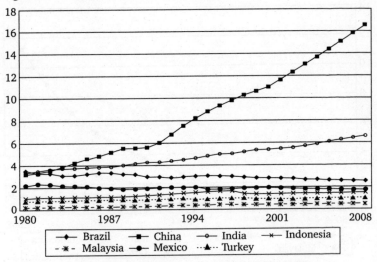

Source: Centennial Group Database, based on IMF's *WEO*.

Figure 10.8   GDP PPP share of World total (%)

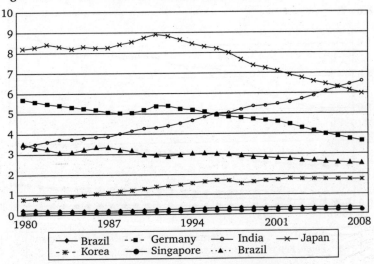

Source: Centennial Group Database, based on IMF's *WEO*.

Figure 10.9   GDP PPP per capita (US$)

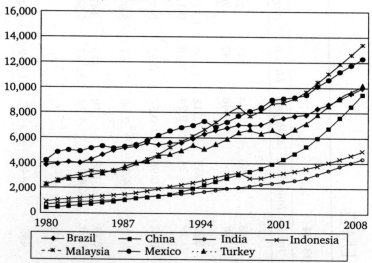

Source: Centennial Group Database, based on IMF's *WEO*.

Figure 10.10   GDP PPP per capita (US$)

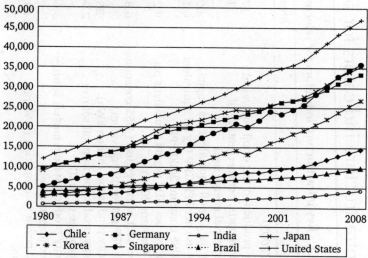

Source: Centennial Group Database, based on IMF's *WEO*.

Key infrastructure indicators for selected EMCs

Table 10.1 Key infrastructure indicators for selected EMCs, 2003–04

2003–04	Brazil	China	India	Indonesia	Malaysia	Mexico	Turkey
ENERGY (2003)							
Energy production (mt of oil equivalent)	171	1,381	453	250	84	243	24
Energy imports, net (percentage of commercial energy use)	11	2	18	−55	−48	−52	70
Energy use (kg oil equivalent per capita)	1,065	1,094	520	753	2,318	1,564	1,117
Energy use per PPP GDP (kg oil equivalent per US$ constant 2000 PPP)	0.14	0.21	0.19	0.24	0.24	0.18	0.17
Energy use per GDP (kg oil equivalent per US$ constant 2000)	0.29	0.94	1.02	0.96	0.54	0.27	0.37
GDP per unit of energy use (US$ constant 2000 PPP per kg oil equivalent)	6.85	4.53	5.25	4.26	3.88	5.61	5.97
Electricity production (billion kWh)	365	1,907	633	113	78	219	141
Electricity production from oil sources (percentage of total)	2.96	3.01	4.59	24.93	4.34	32.37	6.54
Electricity production from nuclear sources (percentage of total)	3.66	2.27	2.80	–	–	4.80	–
Electric power consumption (kWh per capita)	1,883	1,379	435	440	3,061	1,802	1,656

Electric power consumption per GDP (kWh per constant 2000 GDP)	0.55	1.14	0.85	0.50	0.75	0.31	0.56
Electric power transmission and distribution losses (percentage of output)	17.31	7.11	26.21	16.16	5.55	14.56	18.49
Electricity (percentage of managers deeming major constraint)	20.3	29.7	28.9	22.3	14.8	–	17.3
Pump price for super gasoline (US$ per litre)	0.84	0.48	0.87	0.27	0.37	0.59	1.44
TRANSPORT (2004)							
Aircraft departures (thousands)	486	1,216	302	319	171	333	110
Air transport, freight (million tonne/km)	1,500	8,188	689	434	2,599	403	369
Air transport, freight per GDP (tonne/km per US$ thousand constant 2000)	2.3	4.8	1.2	2.2	24.3	0.6	1.6
Air transport, passengers carried (million)	35	120	24	27	19	21	13
Air transport, passengers per GDP (per US$ million constant 2000)	53.8	69.8	40.9	135.8	180.4	34.3	54.6
Roads, total network (thousand km)	1,725	1,810	3,315	368	72	349	354
Roads, paved (percentage of total roads)	5.5	79.48	62.6	58.0	77.9	33.5	41.6
Rail lines (thousand total route-km)	30	61	63	6	2	27	9
Railways, goods hauled (billion tonne/km)	–	1,509	333	4	1	–	7
Railways, goods hauled per GDP (tonne/km per US$ thousand constant 2000)	–	1,097	613	27	11	–	34

(Table 10.1 continued)

(Table 10.1 continued)

2003–04	Brazil	China	India	Indonesia	Malaysia	Mexico	Turkey
Railways, passengers carried (billion passenger-km)	1	551	541	16	2	2	5
Railways, passengers per GDP (passengers-km per US$ thousand constant 2000)	–	321	931	–	18	–	23
Container port traffic (million TEU)	5	75	4	6	11	2	3
Container port traffic per GDP (TEU per US$ million constant 2000)	7.7	43.5	7.3	28.2	105.5	3.1	12.8
Average time to clear customs (days)	13.76	7.88	6.69	5.78	3.65	–	6.4
INFORMATION TECHNOLOGY (2004)							
Fixed line and mobile subscribers (per 1,000 people)	587	499	84.5	184	766	545	751
Fixed line and mobile subscribers per GDP (per US$ million constant 2000)	165	377	157	203	179	91	235
Telephone mainlines (per 1,000 people)	230	241	41	46	179	174	267
Telephone mainlines per GDP (per US$ million constant 2000)	65	182	76	51	42	29	83
Mobile phones (per 1,000 people)	357	258	44	138	587	370	484
Mobile phones per GDP (per US$ million constant 2000)	100	195	81	152	137	62	151
Average cost of local phone call (US$ per 3 min.)	–	0.03	0.02	0.03	0.02	–	0.14

Average cost of phone call to US (US$ per 3 min.)	0.70	2.89	1.19	2.78	0.71	–	2.08
Telephone faults (per 100 mainlines)	1.6	–	126.0	20.0	40.0	1.7	30.4
Personal computers (per 1,000 people)	105	41	12	14	197	108	52
Personal computers per GDP (per US$ million constant 2000)	29.5	30.9	22.4	15.3	45.9	18.1	16.1
Internet users (per 1,000 people)	120	73	32	67	397	135	142
Internet total monthly price (US$ per 20 hours of use)	28.0	10.1	8.7	22.3	8.4	22.6	19.8
WATER AND SANITATION (2002)							
Improved water source (percentage of population w/access)	89	77	86	78	95	91	93
Improved water source, urban (percentage of urban population w/access)	96	92	96	89	96	97	96
Improved water source, rural (percentage of rural population w/access)	58	68	82	69	94	72	87
Improved sanitation facilities (percentage of population w/access)	75	44	30	52	–	77	83
Improved sanitation facilities, urban (percentage of urban pop. w/access)	83	69	58	71	–	90	94
Improved sanitation facilities, rural (percentage of rural population w/access)	35	29	18	38	98	39	62

(*Table 10.1 continued*)

(Table 10.1 continued)

2003–04	Brazil	China	India	Indonesia	Malaysia	Mexico	Turkey
GDP AND POPULATION (2004)							
Population, total (million)	184	1,296	1,080	218	25	104	72
GDP (current US$ billion)	461	1,271	510	173	95	648	184
GDP (US$ billion constant 2000)	655	1,715	581	197	107	619	229
GDP, PPP (US$ billion current international)	1,357	5,829	2,804	673	223	908	445
GDP, PPP (US$ billion constant 2000 international)	1,385	7,024	3,115	722	235	935	511

Source: Centennial Database, based on the World Bank's *World Development Indicators.*

Notes: Energy data are for 2003, except gasoline price, which is 2004, Energy use per GDP and per PPP GDP, which is 2002, and percentage of managers ranking electricity as a constraint data for Turkey (2002) and for Indonesia (2004).

Most transport data are for 2004. However, data is for 2002 for roads total network (save China and Mexico (2003), Malaysia (2001) and Brazil (2000)), paved roads (save Brazil (2000), China (2003), Malaysia (2001) and Mexico 2003), and Brazil and Mexico rail lines. Indonesia rail lines is for 2003.

Also for 2002 are data for China, India and Turkey Rail goods hauled; and China, rail passengers carried. For time to clear customs, Turkey is for 2005, Indonesia is for 2004, and Brazil, China, India and Malaysia are for 2003. For rail passengers, Indonesia is 1998, Mexico is 1996 and Brazil is 1994.

Information Technology data are for 2004, except internet monthly price and cost of local call which are for 2003. For cost of call to US, Brazil's is 2003 and Turkey's is 2002. For telephone faults, Mexico's and Turkey's are 2003, India's and Malaysia's are 2002 and Indonesia's is 2001.

Water and Sanitation data are for 2002.

GDP and Population data are for 2004.

Table 10.2 Key infrastructure indicators for selected EMCs, 1990

1990	Brazil	China	India	Indonesia	Malaysia	Mexico	Turkey
ENERGY							
Energy production (mt of oil equivalent)	98	903	334	161	49	194	26
Energy imports, net (percentage of commercial energy use)	27	–3	9	–70	–117	–57	51
Energy use (kg oil equivalent per capita)	902	775	430	532	1,234	1,491	944
Energy use per PPP GDP (kg oil equivalent per US$ constant 2000 US$)	0.13	0.48	0.25	0.23	0.22	0.19	0.17
Energy use per GDP (kg oil equivalent per US$ constant 2000)	0.27	2.11	1.35	0.94	0.49	0.29	0.36
GDP per unit of energy use (US$ constant 2000 PPP per kg oil equivalent)	7.17	2.05	3.95	4.26	4.46	5.05	5.57
Electricity production (billion kWh)	223	621	289	33	23	123	58
Electricity production from oil sources (percentage of total)	2.51	7.88	4.33	42.71	55.91	57.34	6.85
Electricity production from nuclear sources (percentage of total)	1.00	–	2.12	–	–	2.39	–
Electric power consumption (kWh per capita)	1,425	424	249	152	1,095	1,204	801

(*Table 10.2 continued*)

(Table 10.2 continued)

1990	Brazil	China	India	Indonesia	Malaysia	Mexico	Turkey
Electric power constant per GDP (kWh per constant 2000 GDP)	0.46	1.17	0.79	0.27	0.44	0.24	0.32
Private investment in energy (current US$ million)							68
Private investment in telecoms (current US$ million)	–	–	–	–	870	2,198	–
Private investment in transport (current US$ million)	–	173	02	116	–	4,603	–
Electric power transmission and distribution losses (percentage of output)	14.2	6.9	19.9	13.7	9.0	12.2	11.6
TRANSPORT							
Aircraft departures (thousands)	416	196	126	205	131	177	44
Air transport, freight (million tonne/km)	1,082	818	663	459	574	143	101
Air transport, freight per GDP (tonne/km per US$ thousand constant 2000)	2.3	2.0	2.5	4.6	12.6	0.3	0.7
Air transport, passengers carried (million)	19	17	11	9	10	14	4
Air transport, passengers per GDP (per US$ million constant 2000)	41.5	40.2	40.5	92.8	225.3	34.6	30.9

Roads, total network (thousand km)	1,670	1,181	2,000	289	86	239	367
Roads, paved (percentage of total roads)	9.7	–	–	45.1	70.0	35.1	–
INFORMATION TECHNOLOGY							
Fixed line and mobile subscribers (per 1,000 people)	65.0	5.9	6.0	6.0	94.2	65.6	122.1
Fixed line and mobile subscribers per GDP (per US$ million constant 2000)	20.8	16.3	19.0	10.8	37.7	13.2	48.9
Telephone mainlines (per 1,000 people)	65.0	5.9	6.0	5.9	89.3	64.8	121.5
Telephone mainlines per GDP (per US$ million constant 2000)	20.8	16.3	19.0	10.7	35.7	13.0	48.7
Telephone mainlines, waiting list (thousands)	428	689	1,961	389	82	1,111	1,419
Mobile phones (per 1,000 people)	0.005	0.01	0	0.10	4.87	0.77	0.56
Mobile phones per GDP (per US$ million constant 2000)	0.00	0.03	0	0.18	1.95	0.15	0.22
Average cost of local phone call (US$ per 3 min.)	–	–	0.04	0.05	0.04	0.10	0.06
Telephone faults (per 100 mainlines)	4.7	–	222.0	71.0	76.0	13.5	32.3
Personal computers (per 1,000 people)	3.1	0.4	0.3	1.1	8.4	8.2	5.3
Personal computers per GDP (per US$ million constant 2000)	1.0	1.2	1.0	2.0	3.4	1.7	2.1

(Table 10.2 continued)

(*Table 10.2 continued*)

	Brazil	China	India	Indonesia	Malaysia	Mexico	Turkey
WATER AND SANITATION							
Improved water source (percentage of population w/access)	83	70	68	71	–	80	81
Improved water source, urban (percentage of urban population w/access)	93	100	88	92	96	90	92
Improved water source, rural (percentage of rural population w/access)	55	59	61	62	–	54	65
Improved sanitation facilities (percentage of population w/access)	70	23	12	46	96	66	84
Improved sanitation facilities, urban (percentage of urban population w/access)	82	64	43	66	94	84	96
Improved sanitation facilities, rural (percentage of rural population w/access)	37	7	1	38	98	20	67
GDP AND POPULATION							
Population, total (million)	148	1,135	850	178	18	83	56
GDP (US$ billion constant 2000)	461	413	268	99	45	414	140
GDP, PPP (US$ billion constant 2000 international)	958	1,813	1,445	404	100	627	296

Table 10.3 Key infrastructure indicators for selected EMCs, 1980

1980	Brazil	China	India	Indonesia	Malaysia	Mexico	Turkey
ENERGY							
Energy production (mt of oil equivalent)	63	615	218	125	18	148	17
Energy imports, net (percentage of commercial energy use)	44	–3	10	–123	–50	–52	46
Energy use (kg oil equivalent per capita)	920	610	354	377	884	1,439	708
Energy use per PPP GDP (kg oil equivalent per US$ constant 2000 PPP)	0.13	0.80	0.30	0.25	0.21	0.18	0.17
Energy use per GDP (kg oil equivalent per US$ constant 2000)	0.27	3.52	1.59	1.01	0.46	0.27	0.36
GDP per unit of energy use (US$ constant 2000 PPP per kg oil equivalent)	7.38	1.24	3.33	3.87	4.57	5.39	5.62
Electricity production (billion kWh)	139	301	119	8	10	67	23
Electricity production from oil sources (percentage of total)	4	26	8	72	85	58	25
Electricity production from nuclear sources (percentage of total)	–	–	2.5	–	–	–	–
Electric power consumption (kWh per capita)	975	253	130	42	631	846	439

(Table 10.3 continued)

(Table 10.3 continued)

1980	Brazil	China	India	Indonesia	Malaysia	Mexico	Turkey
Electric power constant per GDP (kWh per constant 2000 GDP)	0.30	1.46	0.59	0.12	0.34	0.17	0.23
Electric power transmission and distribution losses (percentage of output)	11.81	8.07	18.27	18.43	9.00	11.15	12.13
TRANSPORT							
Aircraft departures (thousands)	233	51	100	125	89	177	19
Air transport, freight (million tonne/km)	588	121	366	122	110	132	10
Air transport, freight per GDP (tonne/km per US$ thousand constant 2000)	1.5	0.7	2.4	2.3	4.3	0.4	0.1
Air transport, passengers carried (million)	13	3	7	5	5	13	1
Air transport, passengers per GDP (per US$ million constant 2000)	32.9	15.1	43.3	94.5	177.5	37.2	14.9
INFORMATION TECHNOLOGY							
Fixed line and mobile subscribers (per 1,000 people)	40.8	2.2	3.1	2.5	28.7	40.3	25.7
Fixed line and mobile subscribers per GDP (per US$ million constant 2000)	12.5	12.6	14.1	6.9	15.5	7.9	13.5

Telephone mainlines (per 1,000 people)	40.8	2.2	3.1	2.5	28.7	40.3	25.7
Telephone mainlines per GDP (per US$ million constant 2000)	12.5	12.6	14.1	6.9	15.5	7.9	13.5
Telephone mainlines, waiting list (thousands)	–	164	447	44	144	409	1,627
Mobile phones (per 1,000 people)	0	0	0	0	0	0	0
Mobile phones per GDP (per US$ million constant 2000)	0	0	0	0	0	0	0
GDP AND POPULATION							
Population, total (million)	122	981	687	148	14	68	44
GDP (current US$ billion)	235	188	182	78	25	194	71
GDP (US$ billion constant 2000)	396	170	153	54	25	346	84
GDP, PPP (US$ current international)	446	404	437	117	30	283	96
GDP, PPP (US$ billion constant 2000 international)	827	748	810	217	56	524	177

Key infrastructure indicators for individual EMCs

Figure 10.11   Brazil key infrastructure indicators

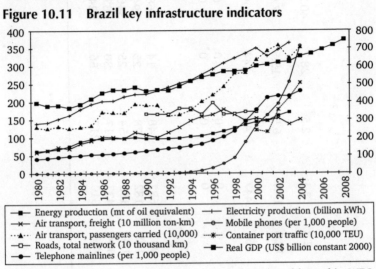

Source: Centennial Group Database, based on World Bank's *WDI*. Projections also use IMF's *WEO*.

Figure 10.12   China (PRC) key infrastructure indicators

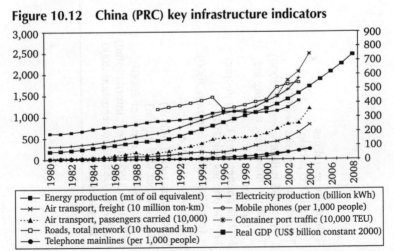

Source: Centennial Group Database, based on World Bank's *WDI*. Projections also use IMF's *WEO*.

Figure 10.13   India key infrastructure indicators

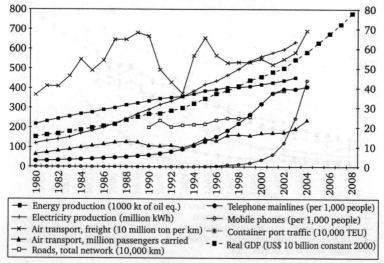

Source: Centennial Group Database, based on World Bank's *WDI*.
Projections also use IMF's *WEO*.

Figure 10.14   Indonesia key infrastructure indicators

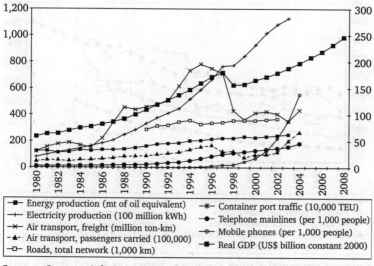

Source: Centennial Group Database, based on World Bank's *WDI*.
Projections also use IMF's *WEO*.

Figure 10.15 Malaysia key infrastructure indicators

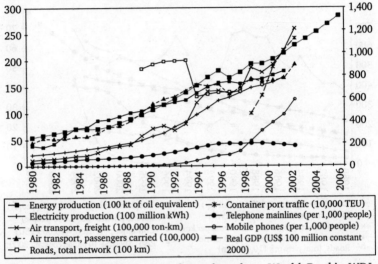

- ■— Energy production (100 kt of oil equivalent)
- ─+─ Electricity production (100 million kWh)
- ─✕─ Air transport, freight (100,000 ton-km)
- ─▲─ Air transport, passengers carried (100,000)
- ─□─ Roads, total network (100 km)
- ─✳─ Container port traffic (10,000 TEU)
- ─●─ Telephone mainlines (per 1,000 people)
- ─○─ Mobile phones (per 1,000 people)
- ─■─ Real GDP (US$ 100 million constant 2000)

Source: Centennial Group Database, based on World Bank's *WDI*.
Projections also use IMF's *WEO*.

Figure 10.16 Mexico key infrastructure indicators

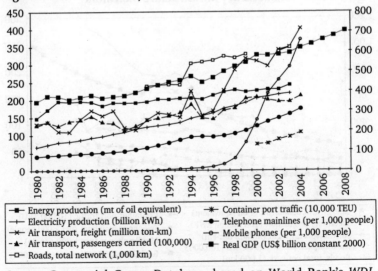

- ─■─ Energy production (mt of oil equivalent)
- ─+─ Electricity production (billion kWh)
- ─✕─ Air transport, freight (million ton-km)
- ─▲─ Air transport, passengers carried (100,000)
- ─□─ Roads, total network (1,000 km)
- ─✳─ Container port traffic (10,000 TEU)
- ─●─ Telephone mainlines (per 1,000 people)
- ─○─ Mobile phones (per 1,000 people)
- ─■─ Real GDP (US$ billion constant 2000)

Source: Centennial Group Database, based on World Bank's *WDI*.
Projections also use IMF's *WEO*.

Figure 10.17 Turkey key infrastructure indicators

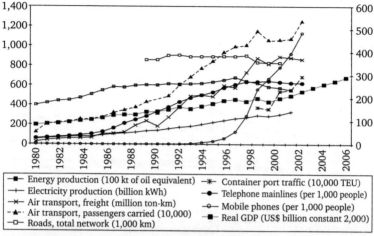

Source: Centennial Group Database, based on World Bank's *WDI*. Projections also use IMF's *WEO*.

Comparison of key indicators for selected EMCs and OECD countries

Energy

Figure 10.18 Energy use (kg of oil equivalent per capita)

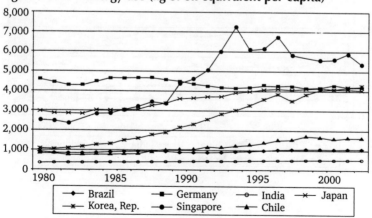

Figure 10.19   Energy use (kg of oil equivalent per capita)

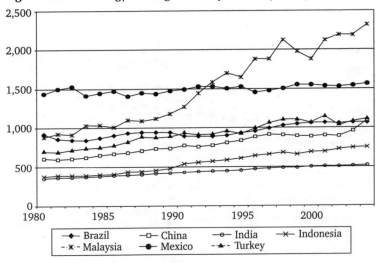

Figure 10.20   Energy use per GDP (kg of oil equivalent per US$ constant 2000)

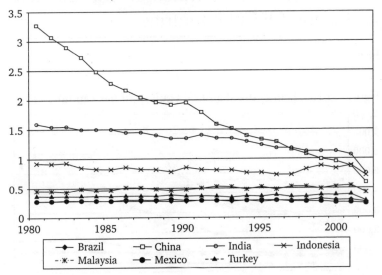

Figure 10.21   Energy use per GDP (kg of oil equivalent per US$ constant 2000)

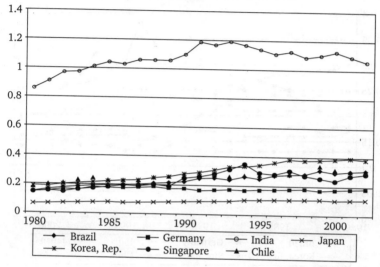

Figure 10.22   Energy use per PPP GDP (kg of oil equivalent per US$ constant 2000 PPP)

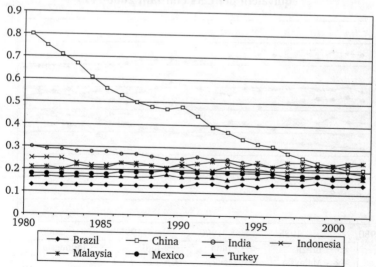

Figure 10.23 Energy use per PPP GDP (kg of oil equivalent per US$ constant 2000 PPP)

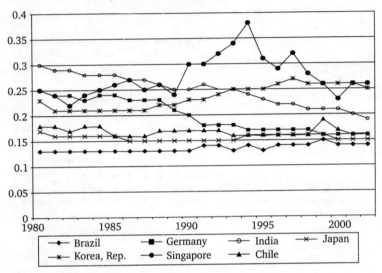

Figure 10.24 GDP PPP per unit of energy use (kg of oil equivalent per US$ constant 2000 PPP)

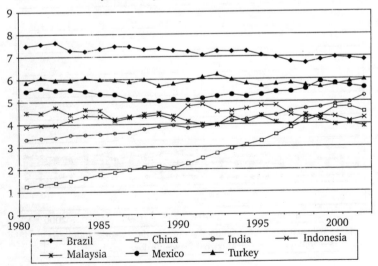

Figure 10.25 **Energy use per PPP GDP (kg of oil equivalent per US$ constant 2000 PPP)**

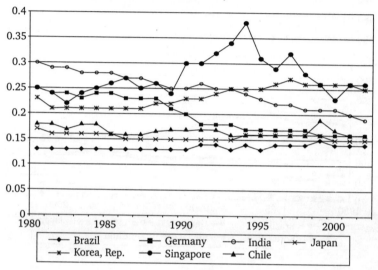

Figure 10.26 **Energy production (thousand kT of oil equivalent)**

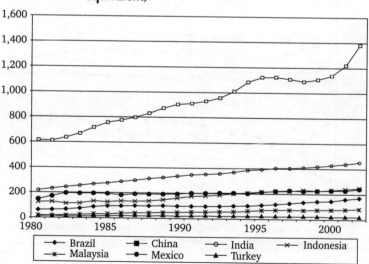

Figure 10.27 Energy production (thousand kT of oil equivalent)

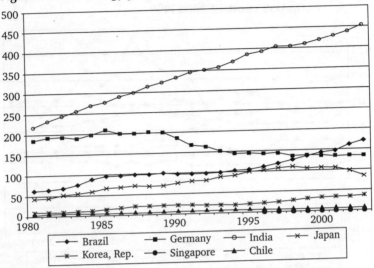

Figure 10.28 Energy imports, net (% of commercial energy use)

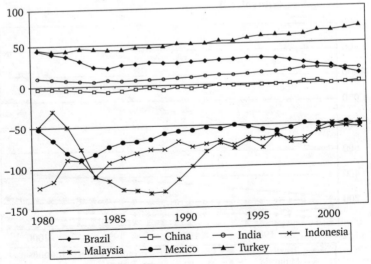

Figure 10.29   Energy imports, net (% of commercial energy use)

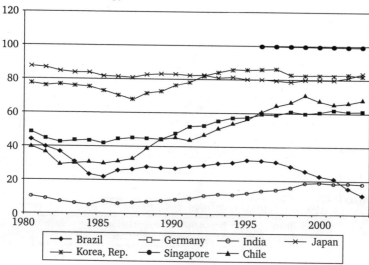

Figure 10.30   Pump price for super gasoline per liter (US$)

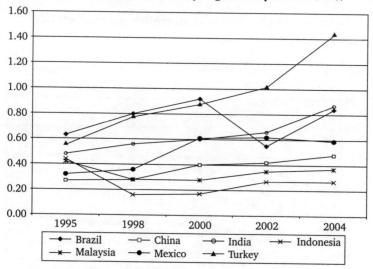

Figure 10.31   Pump price for super gasoline per liter (US$)

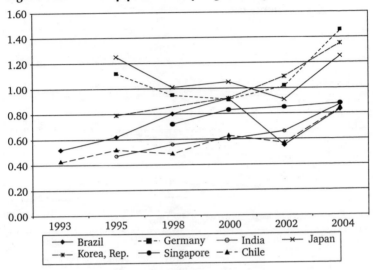

Power

Figure 10.32   Electric power consumption per capita (kWh)

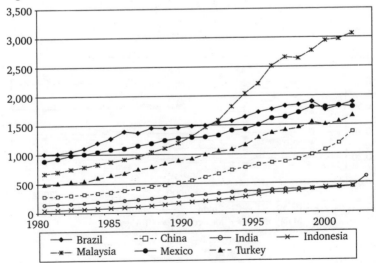

Figure 10.33 Electric power consumption per capita (kWh)

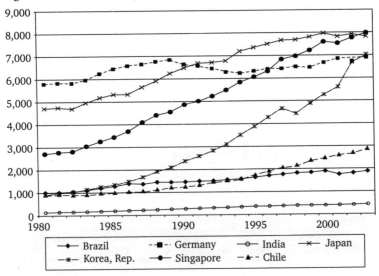

Figure 10.34 Electric power consumption per GDP (kWh per constant 2000 GDP)

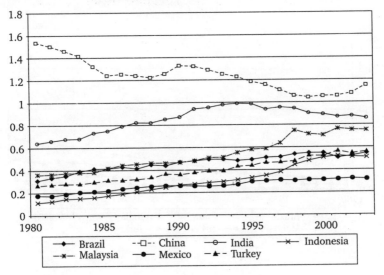

Figure 10.35 Electric power consumption per GDP (kWh)

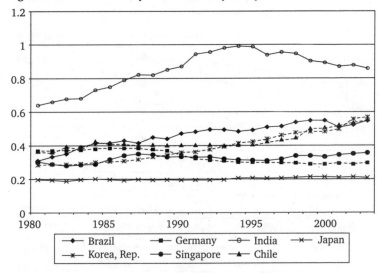

Figure 10.36 Electricity production (kWh)

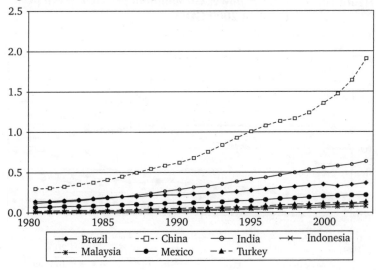

Figure 10.37   Electricity production (kWh trillion)

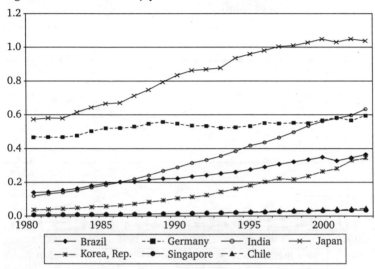

Figure 10.38   Electricity production from oil sources (% of total)

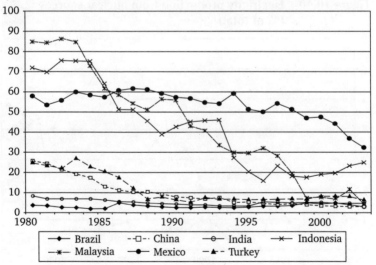

Figure 10.39   Electricity production from oil sources (% of total)

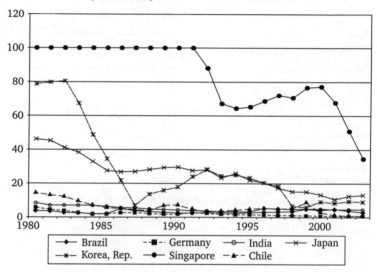

Figure 10.40   Electricity production from nuclear sources (% of total)

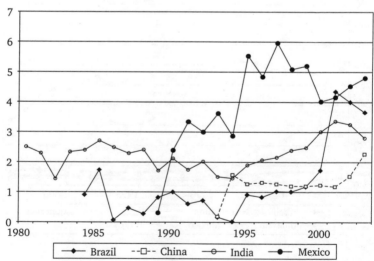

Figure 10.41   Electricity production from nuclear sources (% of total)

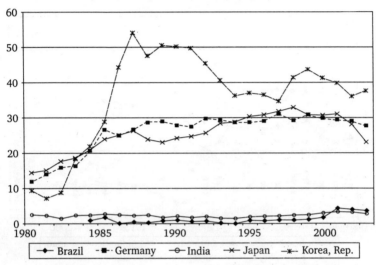

Figure 10.42   Electric power transmission and distribution losses (% of output)

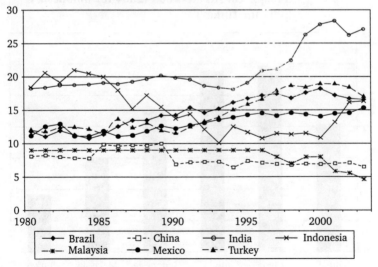

Figure 10.43   Electric power transmission and distribution losses (% of output)

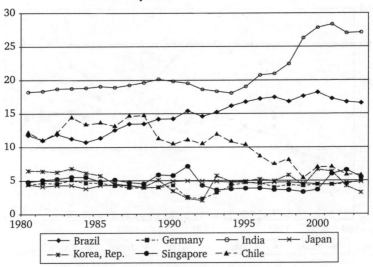

Figure 10.44   Electricity (% managers surveyed ranking this as a major constraint) 2003 (2004 for Indonesia & 2005 for Turkey)

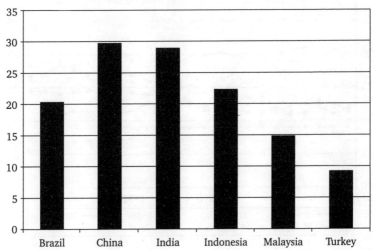

Figure 10.45   Electricity (% managers surveyed ranking this as a major constraint) 2005 (Brazil & India are 2003)

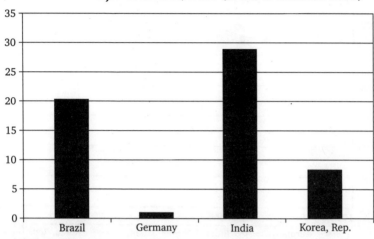

Roads

Figure 10.46   Roads, goods transported (billion ton/km)

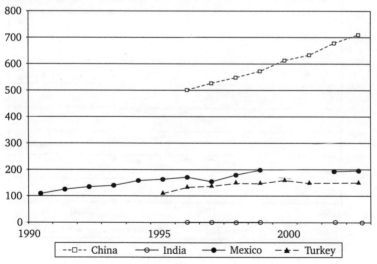

Figure 10.47   Roads, goods transported (billion ton/km)

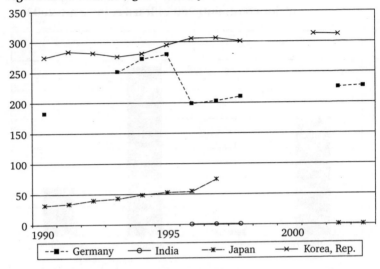

Figure 10.48   Roads, goods transported per GDP (ton/km per US$ thousand constant 2000)

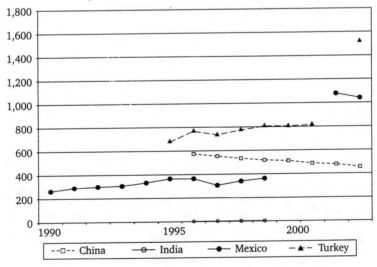

Figure 10.49   Roads, goods transported per GDP (ton/km per US$ thousand constant 2000)

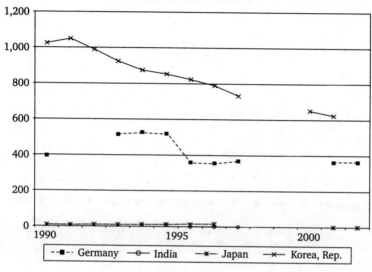

Figure 10.50   Roads, total network (km million)

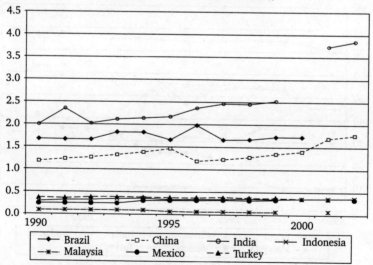

Figure 10.51   Roads, total network (km million)

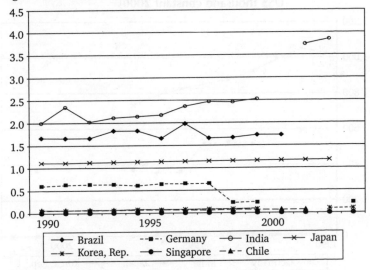

Figure 10.52   Roads, paved (% of total roads)

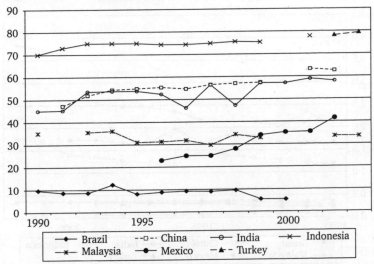

Figure 10.53   Roads, paved (% of total roads)

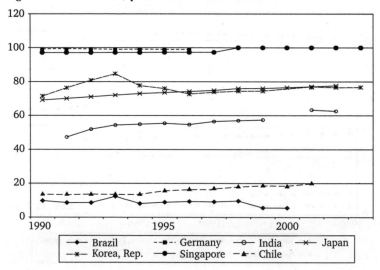

Railways

Figure 10.54   Rail lines (thousand route/km)

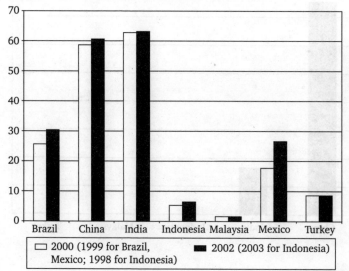

Figure 10.55   Rail lines (thousand route/km)

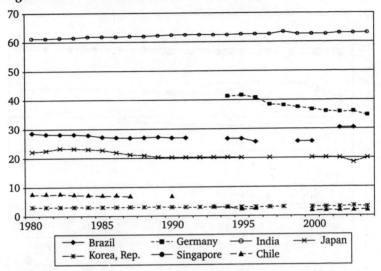

**Figure 10.56   Railways, goods hauled (trillion ton/km) 2002
(2003 for Indonesia, Malaysia)**

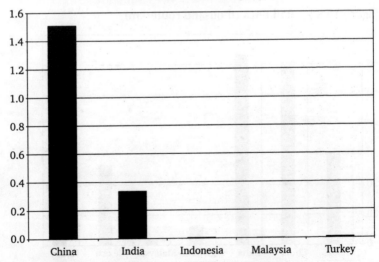

Figure 10.57 Railways, goods hauled (ton/km) 2002 (Chile 2003)

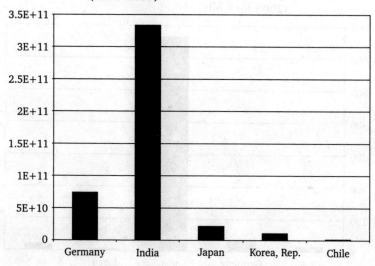

Figure 10.58 Railways, goods hauled per GDP (ton/km per US$ thousand constant 2000) 2002 (2003 for Indonesia, Malaysia)

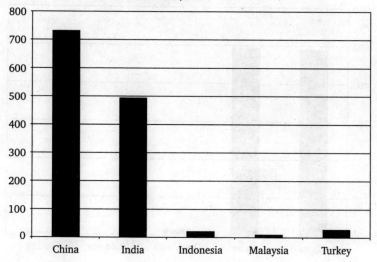

Figure 10.59 **Railways, goods hauled per GDP (ton/km per US$ thousand constant 2000) 2002 (2003 for Chile)**

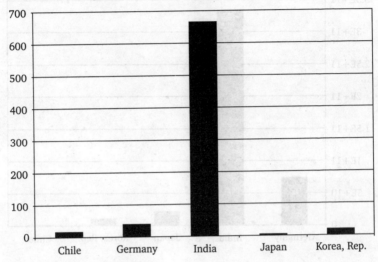

Figure 10.60 **Railways, passengers carried (billion passenger/km) 2002 (2003 for Indonesia)**

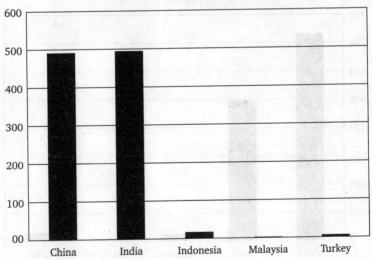

Figure 10.61 Railways, passengers carried (billion passengers/km)

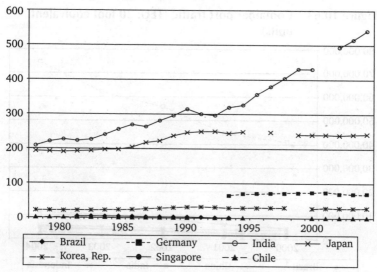

Figure 10.62 Railways, passengers carried per GDP (passengers/km per US$ thousand constant 2000) 2002 (2003 for Indonesia)

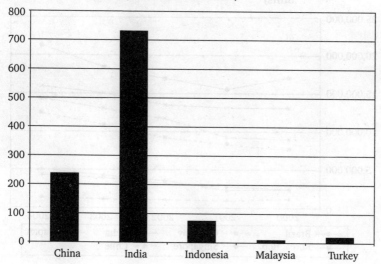

Ports

Figure 10.63 Container port traffic (TEU: 20 foot equivalent units)

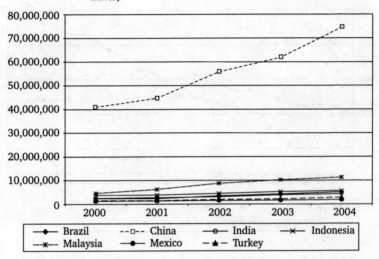

Figure 10.64 Container port traffic (TEU: 20 foot equivalent units)

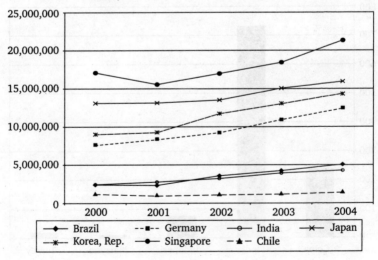

Figure 10.65   Container port traffic per GDP (TEU per US$ million constant 2000)

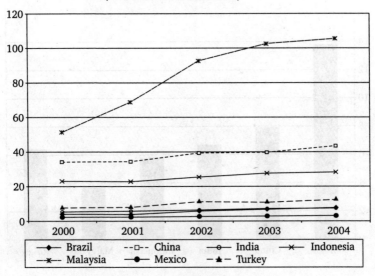

Figure 10.66   Container port traffic per GDP (TEU per US$ million constant 2000)

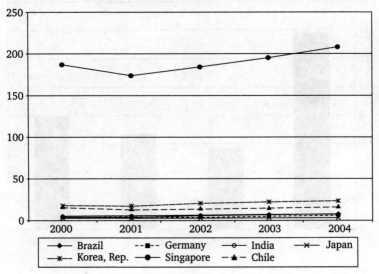

Figure 10.67 Average time to clear customs (days) 2003 (Turkey 2005; Indonesia 2004)

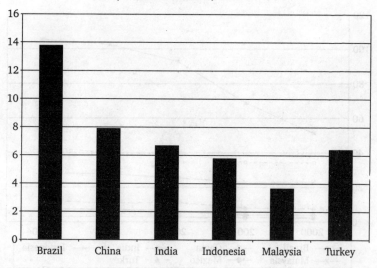

Figure 10.68 Average time to clear customs (days) 2005 (Brazil & India are 2003)

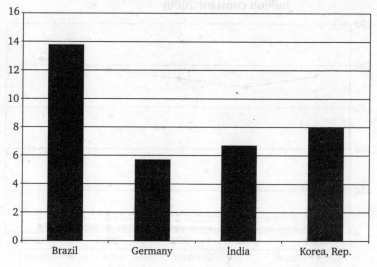

Air transport

Figure 10.69   Air transport, million passengers carried

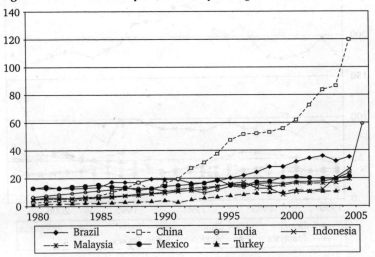

Figure 10.70   Air transport, million passengers carried

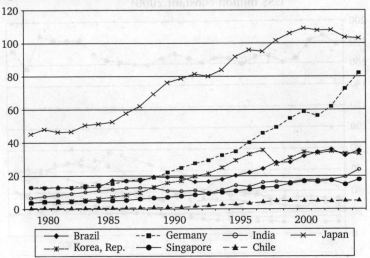

Figure 10.71   **Air transport, passengers carried per GDP (per US$ million constant 2000)**

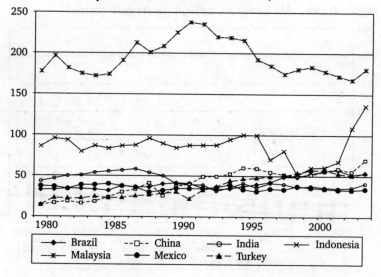

Figure 10.72   **Air transport, passengers carried per GDP (per US$ million constant 2000)**

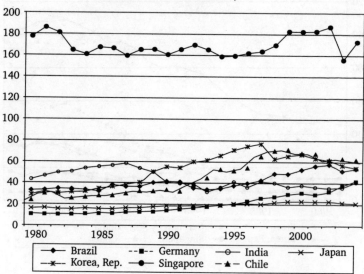

Figure 10.73   Aircraft departures

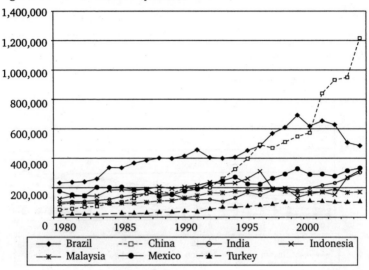

Figure 10.74   Aircraft departures

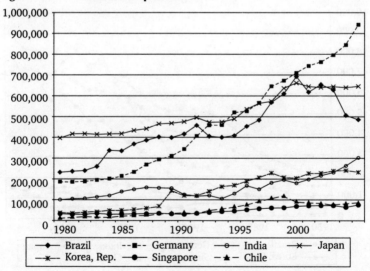

Figure 10.75   Air transport, freight (million ton/km)

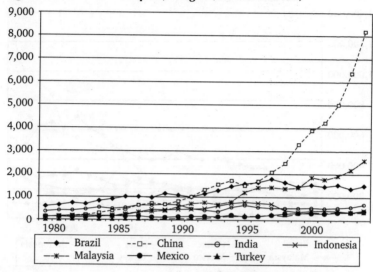

Figure 10.76   Air transport, freight (million ton/km)

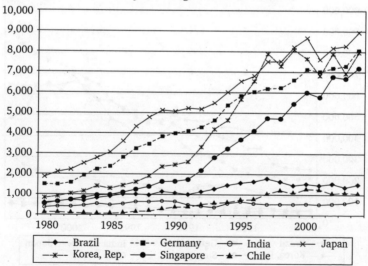

Figure 10.77   Air transport, freight per GDP (million ton/km per US$ constant 2000)

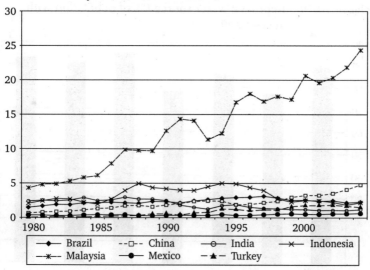

Figure 10.78   Air transport, freight per GDP (ton/km per US$ thousand constant 2000)

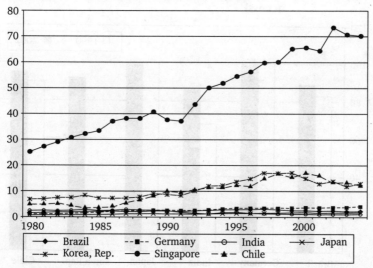

Water and sanitation

Figure 10.79   Improved water source (% of population with access) 2002

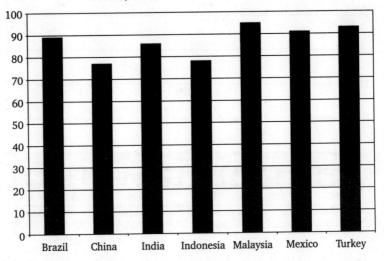

Figure 10.80   Improved water source (% of population with access)

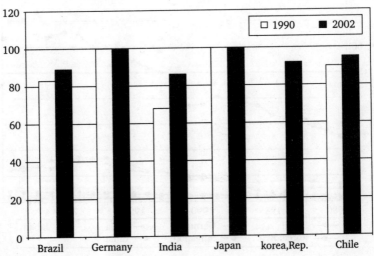

Figure 10.81   Improved water source, rural (% of rural population with access) 2002

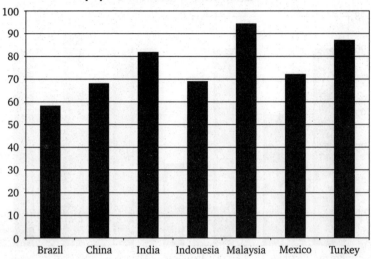

Figure 10.82   Improved water source, rural (% of rural population with access)

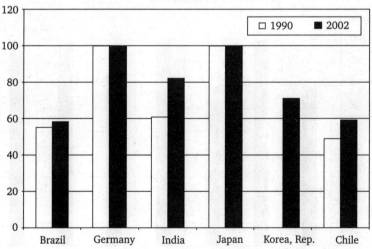

Figure 10.83   Improved water source, urban (% of urban population with access) 2002

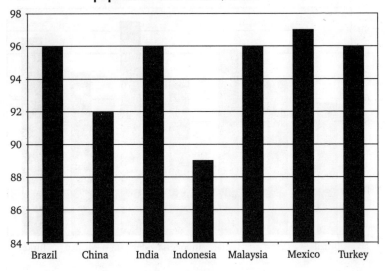

Figure 10.84   Improved water source, urban (% of urban population with access)

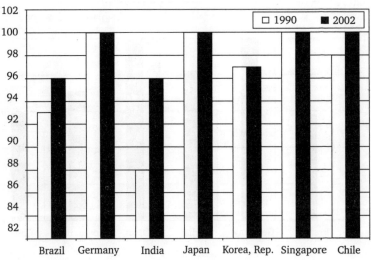

Figure 10.85   **Improved sanitation facilities (% of population with access) 2002**

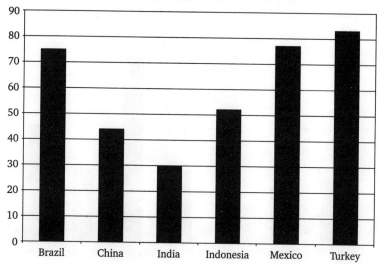

Figure 10.86   **Improved sanitation facilities (% of population with access)**

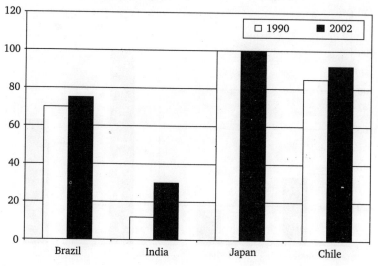

Figure 10.87   Improved sanitation facilities, rural (% of rural population with access) 2002

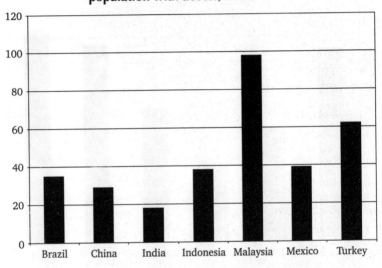

Figure 10.88   Improved sanitation facilities, rural (% of rural population with access)

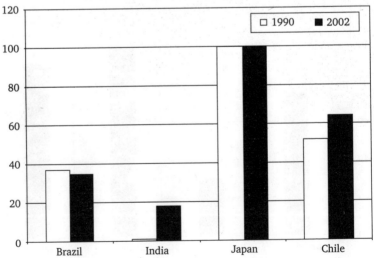

Figure 10.89   Improved sanitation facilities, urban (% of urban population with access) 2002

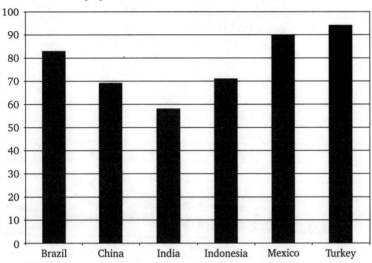

Figure 10.90   Improved sanitation facilities, urban (% of urban population with access)

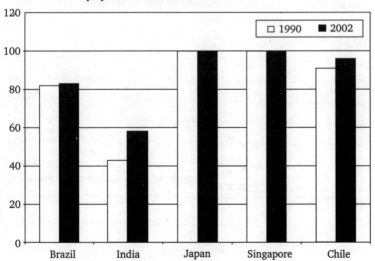

Telephony

Figure 10.91   Telephone mainlines per GDP (per US$ million constant 2000)

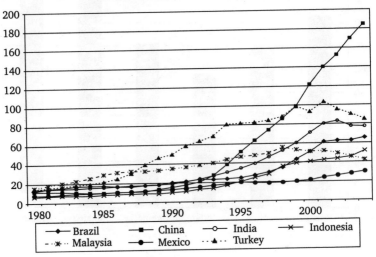

Figure 10.92   Telephone mainlines per GDP (per US$ million constant 2000)

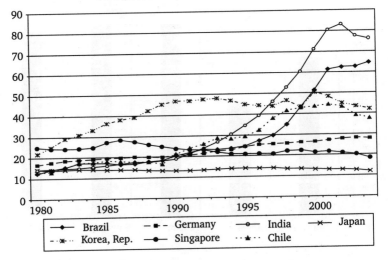

Figure 10.93   Fixed line and mobile phone subscribers per GDP (per US$ million constant 2000)

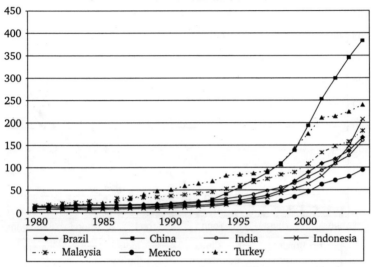

Figure 10.94   Fixed line and mobile phone subscribers per GDP (per US$ million constant 2000)

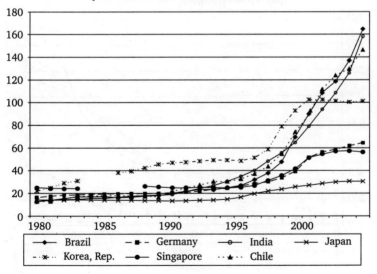

Figure 10.95   Fixed line and mobile phone subscribers (per 1,000 people) 2005

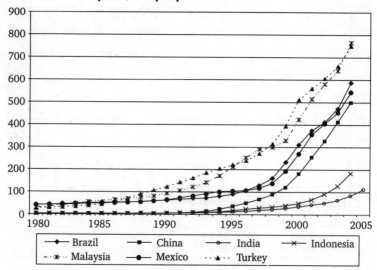

Figure 10.96   Fixed line and mobile phone subscribers (per 1,000 people)

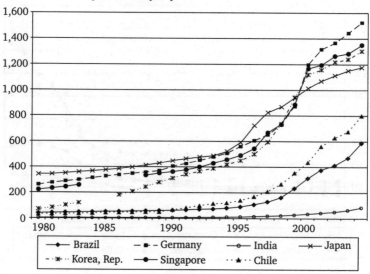

Figure 10.97   Telephone mainlines (per 1,000 people) 2005

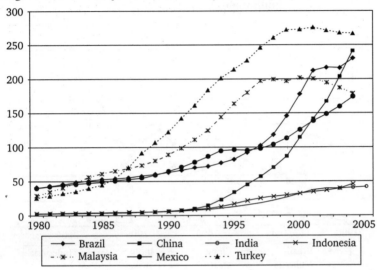

Figure 10.98   Telephone mainlines (per 1,000 people)

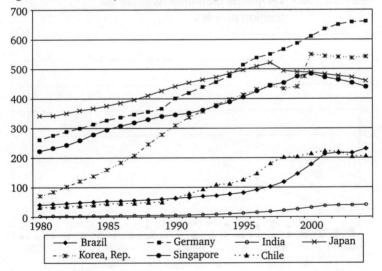

Figure 10.99 Telephone mainlines, waiting list (million people)

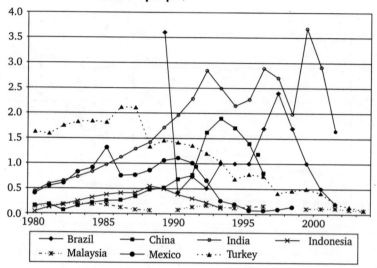

Figure 10.100 Telephone mainlines, waiting list (million people)

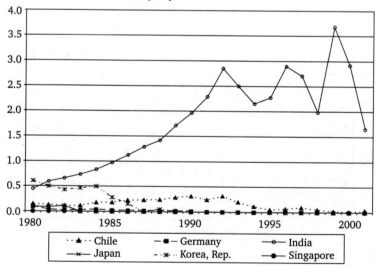

Figure 10.101   Telephone faults (per 100 mainlines)

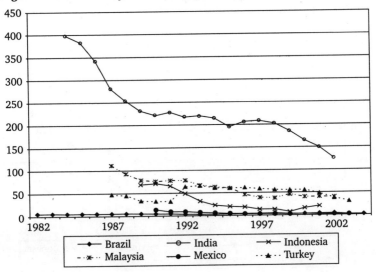

Figure 10.102   Telephone faults (per 100 mainlines)

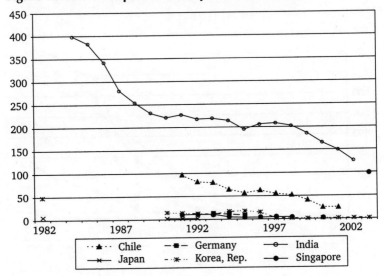

Figure 10.103 Mobile phones (per 1,000 people) 2005

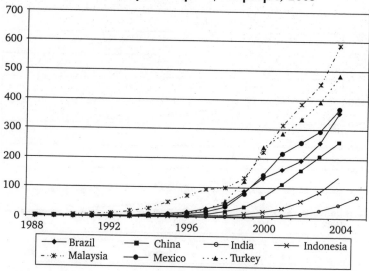

Figure 10.104 Mobile phones (per 1,000 people)

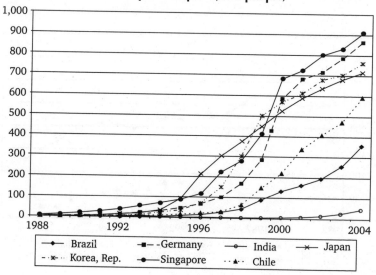

Figure 10.105   Mobile phones per GDP (per US$ million constant 2000)

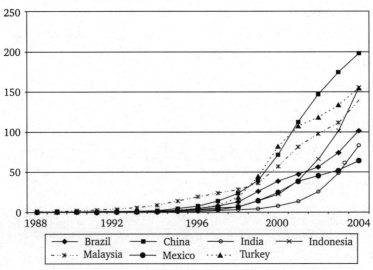

Figure 10.106   Mobile phones per GDP (per US$ million constant 2000)

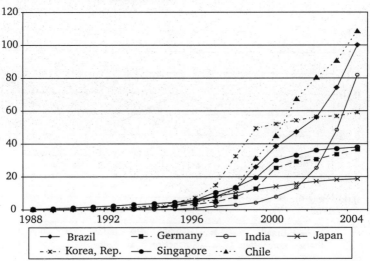

Figure 10.107 Telephone average cost of local call
(US$ per three minutes)

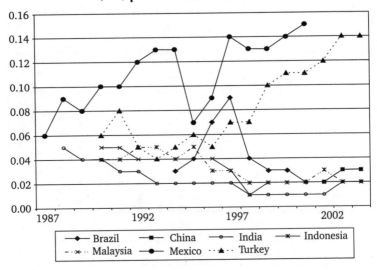

Figure 10.108 Telephone average cost of local call
(US$ per three minutes)

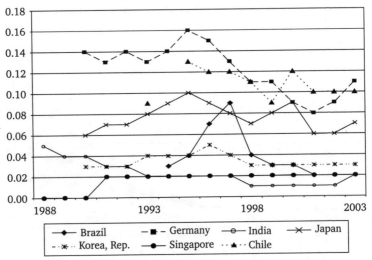

Figure 10.109 Telephone average cost of call to US (US$ per three minutes)

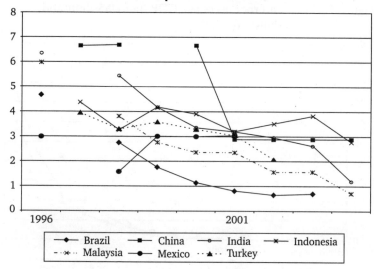

Figure 10.110 Telephone average cost of call to US (US$ per three minutes)

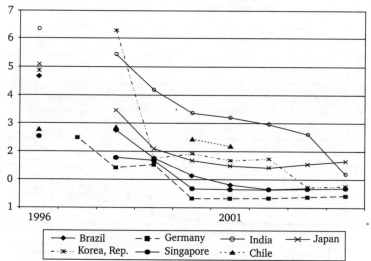

Information technology

Figure 10.111 Internet users per GDP (per US$ thousand constant 2000)

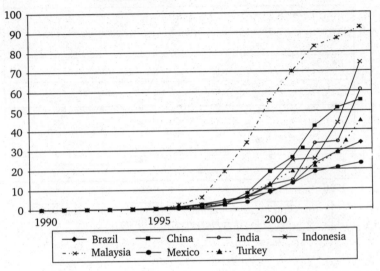

Figure 10.112 Internet users per GDP (per US$ thousand constant 2000)

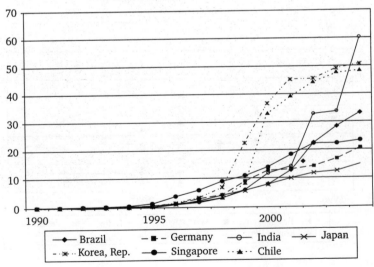

Figure 10.113   Personal computers (per 1,000 people)

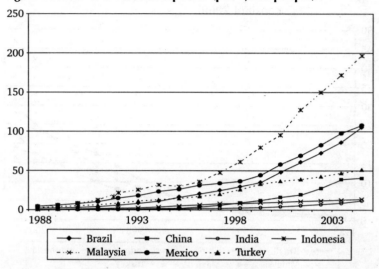

Figure 10.114   Personal computers (per 1,000 people)

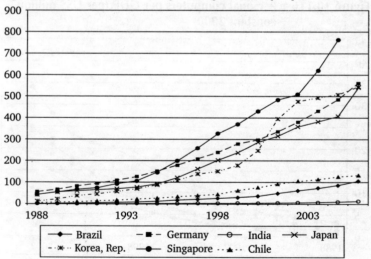

Figure 10.115 Personal computers per GDP (per US$ million constant 2000)

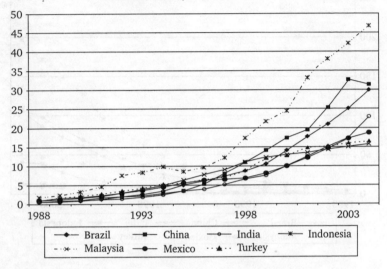

Figure 10.116 Personal computers per GDP (per US$ million constant 2000)

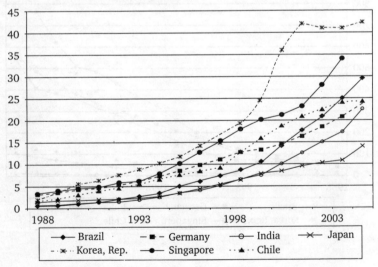

Figure 10.117   Internet total monthly price (US$ per 20 hours of use) 2003

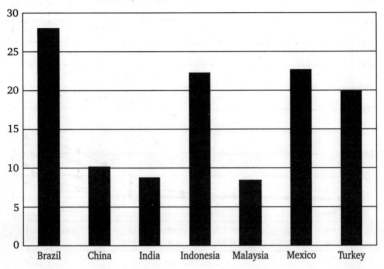

Figure 10.118   Internet total monthly price (US$ per 20 hours of use) 2003

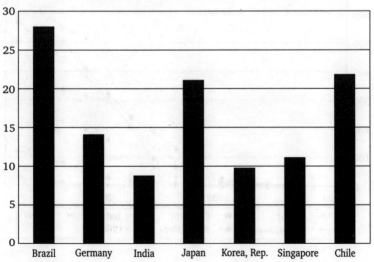

Figure 10.119   Internet users (per 1,000 people)

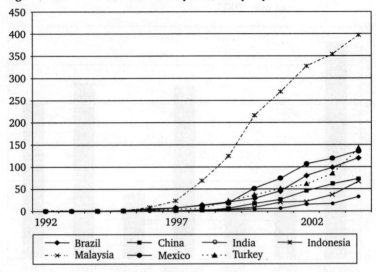

Figure 10.120   Internet users (per 1,000 people)

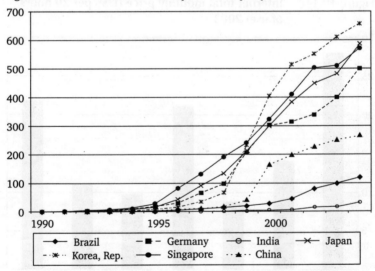

Private investment in infrastructure

Figure 10.121   **Private investment in energy (US$ billion current rate)**

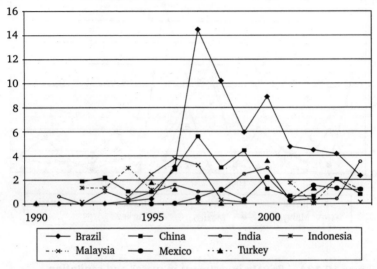

Figure 10.122   **Private investment in telecoms (US$ billion current rate)**

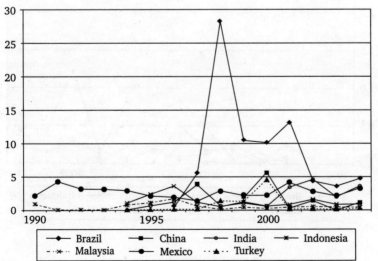

Figure 10.123   Private investment in transport (US$ billion current rate)

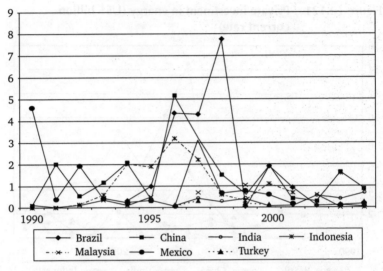

Figure 10.124   Private investment in water and sanitation (US$ billion current rate)

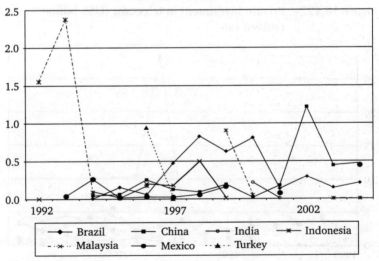

About the Editor and Contributors

Editor

Harinder S. Kohli is President and CEO of the Centennial Group. He is also the Chief Executive of the Emerging Markets Forum and is on the Advisory Board of the Asian Institute of Technology.

Prior to starting the Centennial Group, Kohli spent 26 years with the World Bank in a series of senior positions. He has led World Bank teams that participated in the Multilateral Working Groups of the Middle East Peace Process and developed a conceptual programme for Economic Development in the Middle East. This work became the foundation for the international development assistance to West Bank and Gaza after the peace accord.

He is the principal author of the report of an Eminent Persons Group entitled *Towards a New Asian Development Bank in a New Asia* and of World Bank's report *Infrastructure Development in East Asia and Pacific: Towards a New Public Private Partnership*. In addition he has written articles and delivered speeches on Asian Economics, Private Capital Flows, Regional Economic Cooperation, Industrial Development, Enterprise Development and Privatization, Energy, Information Technology and the Middle East Economic Development issues.

Prior to joining the World Bank, Kohli worked with the Union Carbide in India and the Pechiney Group in France. He has a Masters in Business Administration from the Harvard Business School (elected Backer Scholar with High Distinction) and a Bachelor of Science in Mechanical Engineering from Punjab University, India (First Class Honors). He is married to Paulina Ledergerber Crespo, an anthropologist at the Smithsonian Institute's Museum of Natural History.

Contributors

Jack Boorman is the Former Counselor and Director of Policy Development and Review Department, International Monetary Fund (IMF). Prior to working with the IMF he was a Financial Economist for the Federal Deposit Insurance Corporation. He also served as an Assistant Professor at the University of Maryland.

He received his Bachelors of Science in Mathematics from LeMoyne College in Syracuse, New York and his Ph.D. in Economics from the University of Southern California. Boorman is a member of the Advisory Board of the Emerging Markets Forum.

Luis Miguel Castilla is Chief Economist and Vice President of *Corporacion Andina de Fomento* (CAF). From 2006, he led the department of Public Policy and Competitiveness, which is in charge of the research agenda of CAF, the economic and sector analysis of the member countries and some strategic programmes such as the one on competitiveness.

He holds a Master's degree and a Ph.D. in Economics from the John Hopkins University.

Heinz Hauser is the head of Swiss Institute of International Economics and Applied Economic Research, and Professor of Economics at St. Gallen University, Switzerland. He is a leading authority on international economic and business management issues and has published widely on these subjects. He studied Economics and Business Administration at the University of St. Gallen and got a Ph.D. in 1971, with a thesis in Public Finance. Hauser is a member of the Advisory Board of the Emerging Markets Forum.

Rakesh Jha is a Senior General Manager at ICICI Bank Limited, India. He has a bachelor's degree in engineering from the Indian Institute of Technology (IIT), Delhi and a Masters in Business Administration from the Indian Institute of Management (IIM), Lucknow.

Harpaul Alberto Kohli is Manager, Information Technology at the Centennial Group. He is also a Microsoft Certified Technology Specialist. He earned a degree with honours in Mathematics and Philosophy from Harvard University, where he served as President of both the Society of Physics Students and of the Math Club.

Kohli is currently pursuing his MBA part-time at Georgetown University. He developed and manages the extensive database of the Emerging Markets Forum.

Haruhiko Kuroda is President of the Asian Development Bank (ADB), Chairman of ADB's Board of Directors and Co-Chairman of the Emerging Markets Forum. Before joining the ADB, Kuroda was the Special Advisor to the Cabinet of Japanese Prime Minister Junichiro Koizumi and a professor at the graduate school of economics at Hitotsubashi University in Tokyo. Prior to that, he had a distinguished career at the Ministry of Finance of Japan, rising to the position of Vice Minister.

He holds a BA in Law from the University of Tokyo and a Master of Philosophy in Economics from the University of Oxford.

Claudio M. Loser is President of Centennial Group Latin America and is a Senior Fellow of Latin America Dialog. He has an extensive background in economic issues in Latin America. Loser was also the Director of the Western Hemisphere Department at the IMF, which covers 34 member countries from North, Central and South America, and the Caribbean.

He graduated from the University of Cuyo in Argentina and received his Masters of Arts and Ph.D. from the University of Chicago in 1967 and 1971, respectively.

Rajat Nag is Managing Director General, Asian Development Bank (ADB). Before taking his current office, he was the Director General of ADB's Southeast Asia Department, as well as concurrently Special Advisor to the President on Regional Economic Cooperation and Integration.

Nag has degrees in Engineering from IIT, Delhi, and University of Saskatchewan, Canada. Later he studied Business Administration at University of Saskatchewan, Canada and Economics at London School of Economics (LSE).

Rita Nangia is Director of Special Operations, Southeast Asia Department at the ADB. Before taking up her current position, she was the Director of Infrastructure and Finance Department.

She has written extensively on infrastructure development issues in Asia. Earlier in her career she worked in various policy making positions in India, including as an economist in the Prime Minister's Office (PMO).

Andrew Sheng is the holder of the Tun Ismail Ali Chair in Monetary and Financial Economics, Faculty of Economies and Administration, University of Malaya and Adjunct Professor at Graduate School of Economic Management, Tsinghua University. He has been a former head of Hong Kong Securities and Exchange Commission. Sheng is also a member of the Advisory Board of the Emerging Markets Forum.

V. Sundararajan is Director and Head of Financial Practice of the Centennial Group. He is widely regarded as one of the leading financial economists in the world, with global experience in advising central banks, supervisory agencies and governments on financial sector policy and operations as well as macroeconomic policy issues. Sundararajan was formerly the Deputy Director of the Monetary and Financial Systems Department at the IMF.

Index